TURN AROUND

TURN AROUND

REACH OUT,
GIVE BACK,
AND GET MOVING

Leigh Anne Tuohy

with Miriam Drennan

life
Bible Study

Published by **Life Bible Study, LLC**

Published by **Life Bible Study, LLC**
*A Christian Publisher serving churches and Christian communities in order
to advance the Gospel of Jesus Christ, making disciples as we go.*

Life Bible Study, LLC
1400 Meadowbrook Road
Suite 100
Jackson, Mississippi 39211
www.lifebiblestudy.com
1-888-811-9934

© 2015 by Leigh Anne Tuohy

....

ISBN-13: 978-1-63204-013-8

Portions of this text written and revised by Miriam Drennan.

Cover and page design by Ellen Parker Bibb.

Scripture taken from the New Kings James Version®.
Copyright ©1982 by Thomas Nelson, Inc. Used by permission.

Library of Congress Control Number: 2014952276

1 2 3 4 5 6 7 8 / 19 18 17 16 15 14

This one is for you Mom

C⟲NTENTS

TABLE OF CONTENTS

TABLE OF CONTENTS

FOREWORD

Let me share a few of the comments that I often hear when traveling the country:

"How can I make a difference?
"I can't make a difference."
"I want to make a difference!"

Guess what? You *can* be the difference-maker in someone's life! For me and my family, it was one simple random act of kindness . . . we turned our car around. That's it—and almost everyone has the ability to do that.

God continues to use that one simple act to move the needle and affect people from all walks of life. There is never going to be the perfect time or conditions for you to get involved. If you are waiting for someone to follow—*don't.* This is about you looking in a mirror and realizing this is about *you helping one person.*

So after much thought and prayer—and the Lord knows I'm bossy—I decided that if I provided a roadmap or instructions for people to follow (as opposed to screaming, yelling, and harassing, which is my normal approach), maybe I could share with you my convictions and confrontations.

Turn Around is a weekly devotional book that I hope will encourage you to realize that all people have value and that you can be that person to make someone realize that they do matter! You do not have to be famous to make an impact; you are very significant and special in God's plan, and you have the ability everyday to make someone smile and more. This is not a book that you will do everything it says to do everyday (if you do, please track me down and let me kiss you on the lips!). This is a compilation of ideas and suggestions—simple suggestions and long-term plans—something for everyone.

I hope during your quiet time that you will read something on a page that gives you pause to say, "I can do that!" If one person completes one "Difference-maker" found at the end of each entry—one act of kindness, one person, one day at a time—then in my eyes this will be considered a success . . . because that will be what causes your friend, your relative, or the person whom you don't even know to look up and ask, "What's going on?"

Here's a universal truth: Everything ends, including life. When your final days are closing in on you and your time here is coming to an end, it will not be your fancy car, nice watch, or big diamond ring that will comfort you; it will be those whom you encountered along the way. The ones that you lifted up, encouraged, loved, provided for, and fretted over . . . the ones for whom you turned around.

Everything in your life is a reflection of a choice you made. My prayer is that this book will provide you with wonderful choices that will not only define you as a person, but will provide you with results that provide others with hope, love, and opportunity. I am challenging you to be a one-person team. I am asking you to realize that every single thing you do makes a difference—it's up to you as what kind of a difference it is!

WEEK
ONE

Embracing the Power of Giving

So let each one *give* as he purposes in his heart, not

grudgingly or of necessity; for God loves a cheerful giver.

—2 Corinthians 9:7

was raised in a family where giving back was not an option; it was expected. A cheerful heart was also required because without that, you might as well be doing nothing at all. Throughout the years, Sean and I have been asked to donate to this, be involved here, help this person or that organization, and we have always gone back to the same question, "Will this have a direct impact on someone's life?" If the answer was *yes* and we could swing it, we would volunteer not only our money, but also our time.

You see, time is a valuable commodity and it can change someone's life. Those early small steps of volunteerism and social awareness led us down the path of adopting Michael, who later became a four-year starter for Ole Miss and a first-round NFL draft pick in 2009. One random act of kindness changed our lives forever.

Sometimes, we may think we don't have much to offer; we're too young, too old, financially strapped, have too many commitments already . . . the list goes on. Over the next fifty-two weeks, we're going to discover how to plug in and truly make a difference in someone's life. Whatever your season in life, you have walked a path that has made you wiser than you were yesterday. Or a month ago. Or certainly, a year ago. Right now, you are primed to give something—so ask yourself, "What have I done for someone else today?" If you're drawing a blank, then ask yourself "What *can* I do for someone else today?"

Time is something we all have, and we have it to share. We're not just gonna read it, think about it . . . no, we're gonna *do* it. Hands-on and with cheerful hearts. If you really want to change the world, then change a person's life. Are you ready? Then hang on!

....

DAILY DIFFERENCE-MAKER

Call someone you know who is either hurting or lonely; make a point to say, "I care about you." Do not text, email, or use social media—go old-school and actually pick up the phone!

....Notes..

Making It Happen

I know that You can do everything,

and that no purpose *of Yours* can be withheld from You.

. . . Therefore I have uttered what I did not understand,

things too wonderful for me, which I did not know.

—Job 42:2–3

After Sean and I had been married a few years, we hocked everything, borrowed from everyone we knew, and even raked leaves and trimmed bushes to scrape together enough money for our dream: to have a business of our own. We filled out stacks of papers, signed things that we didn't even know what they meant, and waited for what seemed like an eternity.

Then one afternoon, Sean walked into the house, and I knew from the look on his face that it was bad news. He just looked at me and said, "We didn't get approved." We did everything right, we played by the rules, and this was not fair! We could not have imagined anything being any worse. Guess what? We were so very wrong.

There is no instruction manual or outline on how to fix the life-altering misfortunes that many of us encounter. They often leave us feeling inadequate, fearful, angry, and many times desperate. *Why?*

becomes our mantra: *Why* is this happening to me? *Why* isn't life going according to our plan?

There's one big 'Tuohy Rule' for those times when things don't go our way, and that rule is *persevere*. These can be growth opportunities if we give the struggles and suffering permission to build character and awareness instead of anger and bitterness . . . if we continue to serve, regardless of our own troubles. Remember, we see great things from the valleys and only small things from the peaks.

Today, I'm really thankful our plan was altered. For some reason, the worst of times can make us more grateful, hopeful, and stronger. The Holy Spirit has a way of turning things that way. When we allow God to build our character, and continue to serve in the midst of our sufferings, we can trust Him to put things in perspective. Our world is groaning in pain; as believers, we trust that our sufferings are temporary and in the meantime, there are ample opportunities to put your God-given talents to His use. It's truly amazing how helping others can eliminate so much suffering, even our own! What are you waiting for?

....

DAILY DIFFERENCE-MAKER

Buy someone a meal. Doesn't matter if it's from the ninety-nine-cent menu, or whether you even know the person. Feed someone today!

....Notes...

Hope for the Suffering

For I consider that the sufferings of this present time
are not worthy *to be compared* with the glory
which shall be revealed in us.

–Romans 8:18

It's hard to look suffering in the face. There is nothing pretty, nice, or pleasant about it. In a world that tells us image is everything, we try and make life appear as picturesque as possible, yet the realities are unavoidable. Poverty, sex trafficking, crisis pregnancy, physical abuse, homelessness, unemployment, malnutrition, mental illness, physical illness . . . with each passing day things seem to spiral more out of control. On one channel, we're threatened with Ebola and it's ISIS on another; how do you look into the face of all this suffering and say, "there is hope"?

Well, for some reason, the worst of times seem to make Christians more grateful, hopeful, and stronger. Christians know that the unknown, the uncharted territory, the suffering and rejections will one day be a memory, and the sufferer will once again unearth the treasures life has to offer, to find true happiness and fulfillment. But as we study Jesus's earthly ministry, and His interaction with unbelievers, we find that very often he met physical needs before he addressed the spiritual; and not everyone who received His healing also received His message of eternal hope. So if we address the physical needs of those who are suffering, we must also be prepared for rejection if we address their spiritual needs further down the road. Do not lose hope if that happens—you planted a seed, and it will be up to God and that individual as to whether it grows. And you continue to love on that person, because your Savior loves them, too. We know any suffering in this world is temporary—but this does not mean we ignore it. We endure it, we endure others', and we make every effort to provide the same peace and comfort that our Savior did two thousand years ago.

....

DAILY DIFFERENCE-MAKER

Do the legwork and coordinate with your local hospital or an organization that houses orphans to provide a birthday cake and presents for any child who will be celebrating a birthday during his/her admission. Be willing to meet whatever safety measures are in place—obtaining the proper permission, passing a background check, whatever it takes—respect the policies so that you can bring joy to a child who would otherwise have a fairly dismal birthday!

.... Notes ....

A New Season

Therefore, if anyone *is* in Christ, *he is* a new creation;
old things have passed away; behold, all things
have become new.

–2 Corinthians 5:17

Hope is a powerful thing. It gives way to a new beginning, a tomorrow, another chance, a do-over. Hope can chase away the darkest of days, despair, and evil. Hope will illuminate a path that had previously seemed impossible to pass.

I think that's why I like springtime so much—it paints a picture of rebirth, new life, new beginnings that remind us that hope is a gift that God gives us time and time again, unconditionally. Think about it: The dismal landscape becomes brilliant with trees budding and flowers rising out of the cold, hard ground; caterpillars forming their cocoons while beautiful butterflies emerging from theirs; large bears awakening from their long winter slumber; etc. If spring is a celebration for all of God's creatures—shouldn't we celebrate, too?

We can celebrate that springtime can occur anytime in our hearts . . . celebrate that we worship a God so powerful, He can transform us into entirely new creatures. A God so into the details, He counts every strand of hair on our heads. A God so loving, He never leaves us even when we are fickle. A God so compassionate, He sacrificed His own Son so that we could restore what was lost in The Fall.

So much of God's glory is visible in nature, and hopefully, it draws you closer to His hand—it's the same hand that created you. Even if you're reading this while there's snow on the ground or scorching summer temperatures, usher in a season of spring in your heart today and celebrate new beginnings, renewed hope, and a promising tomorrow.

....

DAILY DIFFERENCE-MAKER

Whether you pick them from your yard, buy them at a grocery store, or order them from a florist, deliver some colorful flowers to a nursing home today.

.... Notes ....

To the Least of These

Assuredly, I say to you, inasmuch as you did *it* to one of

the least of these My brethren, you did *it* to Me.

—Matthew 25:40

People ask me daily, "What can I do? I can't make a difference in someone's life. I'm just one person in this big world. Nothing I do will really make a difference."

Well, ladies and gentlemen, here's a newsflash: You may be the whole world to someone, so get ready to dig deep and get dirty enough to leave a mark that says, "I've been here, and I've made a difference."

When we passed Michael on that November day, we had a choice: Keep driving or turn the car around. No one had briefed me on Michael's talent and capabilities; I had not sat down with Sean and budgeted a way to adopt a teenage boy; in fact, I wasn't sure what my next steps were, except that we needed to turn around. There were no foregone conclusions . . . only a choice to be made.

Our simple act of kindness was to turn the car around. Yours may be to smile at the person who cuts you off in traffic, or do a solid for your coworker who is way behind in his responsibilities. Maybe it's simply to ask someone, "Everything okay?" and truly listen to their response.

There is an old Quaker saying that goes something like this: "What shall I do? I expect to pass through this world but once. Therefore, any good work, kindness, or service I can render to any person or animal, let me do it now. Let me not neglect or delay to do it, for I will not pass this way again." Don't miss your moment to make a difference—you might not get another chance. Whatever it is, do it for Him, do it as though it *is* Him, and be prepared for this crazy joy that will overwhelm your heart—trust me, it feels great!

....

DAILY DIFFERENCE-MAKER

Find a playground in a neighborhood that might have hungry children and deliver some treats—candy, cheese sticks, bananas, doesn't have to be fancy. If you're a budding baker, bring some home-baked goodies; if you're a someone-else's-home-baked goodies type of person (like me), pick something up at the store. Bring some fruit for children who might not eat sweets or for them to eat later.

.... Notes ....

WEEK
TWO

We Have Conquered

Who shall separate us from the love of Christ? *Shall*

tribulation, or distress, or persecution, or famine, or

nakedness, or peril, or sword? . . . Yet in all these things

we are more than conquerors through Him who loved us.

–Romans 8:35, 37

Interestingly enough, when our lives are rocking and rolling along we have no questions, but when our lives take a turn for the worse and things seem to spiral out of control, we then have no answers: When innocent kids get killed for wearing the wrong thing; when someone gets bullied because they are a certain faith; when we lose family and friends over a mistake we've made.

Sin is in our world, and with it comes decay and death; pain and suffering; hurt and misunderstanding. Beyond apologizing for our own transgressions and making wise choices, so much of what's rotten in the world is beyond our control. We cannot control what others say, do, or think.

So what is within our control? We can love each other, forgive each other, and offer hope to each other. We can remember those who stood by us during our time of need, and be ready to stand by them. We can receive encouragement when we are discouraged, reminding ourselves and others daily that nothing—no-thing—can separate us from Christ's love. No rotten, stinking person, situation, or entity can separate us—we have conquered it because He has conquered it.

So ladies and gentlemen, let His hope flood into your world, warming your soul with an opportunity for love and forgiveness. Consider what God has given you as opposed to what the Enemy has convinced you he's taken from you. God's love will rescue you from the cold, the pain, and the despair.

....

DAILY DIFFERENCE-MAKER

Are you the go-to for most people, and now find yourself in despair? Set aside your pride, and ask a trusted friend or family member for help, even if it's just to talk. God rarely does things one-sided; don't deny another person the opportunity to participate in God's work, nor deny yourself the same opportunity. Ask. For. Help.

Notes

7

Within Reach

His mother said to Him, "Son, why have You done this to us?
Look, Your father and I have sought You anxiously."
And He said to them, "Why did you seek Me? Did you
not know that I must be about My Father's business?" . . .
they did not understand the statement which He spoke to
them. . . . but His mother kept all these things in her heart.

—Luke 2:48–51

Okay, in my personal experience with this sort of thing, I have to confess that I wasn't exactly treasuring anything in my heart; but neither did Mary, at the time.

S.J. was probably three or four years old, and I had a mile-long "to-do" list. While in a department store, S.J. vanished. I panicked! Suddenly, nothing on the list mattered except finding S.J. I screamed his name, I didn't care what anyone thought (no surprise), and all that mattered was finding my son.

In typical S.J. fashion, he popped out from under a coat rack and said, "What are you screaming about?" I didn't know whether to spank him or kiss him until he couldn't breathe.

When Mary and Joseph realized their eldest was missing, they were frantic. Now keep in mind, there were thousands who traveled to the Feast of the Passover, and Jesus was old enough to not require constant supervision. More than likely, Mary and Joseph thought he was with friends or other family members. And I'm certainly not comparing S.J. to Jesus, but I do know a mother's heart. Mary's 'treasuring' occurred *after the fact*—after her frantic search for her son. Admittedly, I am comforted in knowing it can happen to any mother, even the mother of God, and her reaction wasn't all that different from my own.

In moments like that, the to-do lists are not so important; the outside obligations don't seem like such a priority. Now before you beat yourself up over not being a perfect parent, just remember to use your time wisely—guilt and shame are not productive uses, by the way. Remember, there is only so much sand in the hourglass—who gets yours?

....

DAILY DIFFERENCE-MAKER

Arrange one-on-one dates with each of your children—for cocoa, for ice cream, anything that engages deeper dialogue (not a movie, sports event, or class). Learn how they feel, what they dream, what they fear. In the blink of an eye, eight-year-old issues will become eighteen-year-old issues; know how and when to embrace these moments fully, and it will be time well-spent.

.... Notes ....

Small, but Mighty Gestures

Above all things have fervent love for one another,

for "love will cover a multitude of sins."

−1 Peter 4:8

D o I take my own medicine while I'm dispensing it to others? Let me tell you something, I make my share of mistakes (did I just say that?). As the Tuohy family has grown and matured, we have also grown as givers. But throwing money at something doesn't always fix things, either; in fact, it rarely does. Yes, money can buy sports equipment, food, clothing, shelter, cars . . . but money must also be managed. And sometimes, the problem isn't money at all—the problem is neglect. How can you know how to help someone if you're ignoring them? Sure, I can donate a bicycle— but that's a silly way to help if the child in need is an infant.

As you reflect on your own ways of giving, you might arrive at the point Sean and I did and realize your approach is too formal. Giving doesn't always have a formula to it, nor does it always require a pledge or tax-exempt status; if that's what we're waiting for, then we're failing at the simplest ways to give. We're overlooking every day kindnesses that we can extend—some may not even require spending a dime.

We can all do small things with great love—each one of us has the capacity. If we can do that, we may watch those small opportunities grow beyond anything we can imagine. So if you are giving a little . . . give a little more!

....

DAILY DIFFERENCE-MAKER

At some point, you will be standing in line—at a movie theater, restaurant, checkout, the DMV . . . let someone go in front of you.

························· Notes ·························

Turn Around

If a brother or sister is naked and destitute of daily food,

and one of you says to them, "Depart in peace, be

warmed and filled," but you do not give them the things

which are needed for the body, what *does it* profit?

—James 2:15–16

There he was . . . a large figure, wearing shorts and an oversized t-shirt in the cold weather, walking toward the school. In our neighborhood. We'd seen this kid, on the fringe of our world, because he was easy to spot: He was enormous, and was always wearing the same clothes. We'd seen him, yes—but today, at that moment, I actually *saw* him. Something wasn't right.

"Turn the car around," I directed Sean.

"What?"

"You heard me. Turn around."

The figure, of course, was Michael Oher, a young man who had spent most of his sixteen years either homeless or in foster homes. If you've heard of me, then you've heard how this story unfolds: We gave Michael a home, legally adopted him, and equipped him to take his talents and skills beyond what any of us could dream for him. You may know Michael as a pro football player, but he is also a scholar, a philanthropist, and for me personally, an eye-opener. God used Michael as a catalyst; he forced me to turn around and take a good look.

Sometimes, God speaks to you and you don't even know why. I look at people differently now; I pull up to the red light and see someone holding a sign or encounter them on the street, I no longer pass by. I turn around, I take a look, and I have a conversation.

Adopting a six-and-a-half-foot, 350-pound African-American teenager isn't for everyone; but each one of us has the capacity to make a difference. Don't out-daunt yourself into thinking you can't. There are Michael Ohers in every city, every state in our country; don't fool yourself and think they're not out there. If someone as talented as my son almost fell through the cracks, can you imagine how many out there actually do?

Turn around—what's behind you needs attention. What's behind you could change your life forever; don't miss it.

....

DAILY DIFFERENCE-MAKER
Do you know a family who is shunned because of their child? Maybe he has special needs, or has behavior problems. Invite the whole family to dinner; make a point to show that child love.

.... Notes ....

Wisdom in Action

Now give me wisdom and knowledge,

that I may go out and come in before this people;

for who can judge this great people of Yours?

−2 Chronicles 1:10

Solomon could have asked the Lord for anything—and because he asked only for wisdom, God gave him everything! While his life didn't end as well as it began, Solomon's wisdom is renowned; his prayer reminds us of what is truly the most valuable possession to obtain. God entrusted untold wealth and power to Solomon because his priority was wisdom and knowledge—not riches. During his reign, Solomon's wisdom moved mountains.

Our country was founded by people determined to make a change. They also relied on wisdom, not wealth and security, to put change into motion; and because of this, attributes like bravery, leadership, and confidence were by-products of this wisdom, enabling their success.

We need to be mindful of the same when we put change in motion for those children still needing forever homes. Or to stop animal abuse. Or to end elderly neglect, homelessness, human trafficking, disease, and hunger. Or some other cause that needs addressing—we have too much pain in this country, given the amount of wealth, wisdom, and resources available.

Now adoption is a wonderful thing, and I highly recommend it, but it is not for everyone (and sometimes, it takes maturity to admit that). So even if you don't adopt, there is something you can do in the life of a child to improve his or her lot in life. Maybe you can't take in every stray that you find wandering, but you can do something to help rescued animals. Or the homeless, or those in crisis. But first, you need to "get wise" . . . and then, take action.

Use all the skills you have been blessed with to create a lifetime of tomorrows for your community and, ultimately, your country. You may be changing the course for someone just enough that they are inspired to make good choices, too.

We can't do it all, but we can all do something. Work hard for your cause, seek wisdom in your choices, and exercise courage in carrying out your course of action.

DAILY DIFFERENCE-MAKER

Engage in a dialogue with someone who may have the counterpoint to your point, with regard to your cause. Truly listen, ask questions, and most importantly, reassure them they have been heard. Healthy debate and discussion must also be respectful.

Notes

WEEK
THREE

Punctuating Moments

For what profit is it to a man if he gains the whole world,

and loses his own soul? Or what will a man give

in exchange for his soul?

—Matthew 16:26

Do you remember reciting your wedding vows? Or how your child sounded when he uttered his first word? Do you remember hearing birds chirping on a sunny day, the wondrous smells of family picnics, leaving milk and cookies out for Santa Claus, making up after an argument with your spouse, or teaching your youngest to ride a bike? How did you feel when you learned your loved ones were safe after a car accident or finding a way to pay your bills during a particularly tight month? Do you have a moment of gratitude when you breathe in fresh air or drink clean water? These are the moments that punctuate your life—memory-triggers that unfold a special time and place that edified, enriched, or even changed your life.

On the other hand, if your life story is filled with nothing but big job promotions, pursuing the next best thing, 'attaboys, and self-congratulating, I have to ask—what have you been doing in your life that's worthwhile?

There's an old cliché about stopping to smell the roses . . . and I'll add that when you do, turn around. That's where the good stuff, the worthwhile stuff, resides; we often miss it if we're racing forward all the time. When you turn around and take in what is going on just behind you, you'll have a different perspective; you've stopped and slowed down enough to catch what you would have missed otherwise.

Today has so much to offer. And right now is all we are guaranteed. What are you doing with it? Add some punctuation to your life story!

....

DAILY DIFFERENCE-MAKER

It won't be long before you're at the gas station and see someone putting only a few dollars in—go hand them a twenty. In fact, clean their windshield!

.... *Notes* ....

The How-to of Happiness

Do not forget to do good and to share,

for with such sacrifices God is well pleased.

—Hebrews 13:16

Nearly every week, I speak to a charitable organization, and I'm often asked, "How has all this impacted your life?" It's a whopper of a question, but my answer is that we have learned that giving has made us happier than we ever imagined.

Choosing to spend money on others versus yourself *will* change your life. Choosing to give your time to make a difference in someone's life, or volunteer with a worthy organization, *will* change your life. You are making an impact, yes—but what's unexpected is the joy and fulfillment that reflects right back on you.

Where do we find joy *and* happiness? Here are a few pointers:

- Spend more time with your loved ones
- Smile on a regular basis
- Attend church
- Engage in more social activities, even if it is going to the movie or walking a neighbor's dog
- Volunteer at the local library one day a week

The "sacrifices" of giving and sharing, to use Paul's word, are minimal compared to the overflowing blessing you will receive. No, more than likely the blessing will not come in the form of a new car, financial bonus at work, or luxury vacation—it's the expression of a face who has been fed for the first time that day; it's the hug from an impoverished child who just received the first new pair of shoes he has ever owned; it's the shriek of a teenager who has never owned anything new and is handed a shirt with a sales tag still on it; it's the hand-squeeze of an elderly relative who is grateful you stopped by to watch college football for a few hours; it's overhearing someone say, "That person changed my life," and they're talking about *you*.

We all make choices each day. Think about how your choices will affect other people. Will your choice bring happiness or peace of mind to someone? Will it bring joy and fulfillment to you? When you realize it's not about you—you're a part of it, but it's not *all* about you—God releases so much blessing and opportunity!

DAILY DIFFERENCE-MAKER

Do you have a handyman who stops by regularly to work on your house? Casually make conversation about tools to see if he needs any repaired or replaced. Look at the tires on his vehicle. Surprise him with either a gift card to have something repaired or replaced, or even new tires!

Notes

To Whom It Is Due

Do not withhold good from those to whom it is due,

When it is in the power of your hand to do *so*.

–Proverbs 3:27

D o me a favor—take a pair of scissors and cut out today's verse. Or, if you want to print it out in some fancy font, knock yourself out. But get this verse etched in your mind, heart, and post it everywhere you can to remind you of the power that's been entrusted to you by God.

You have no guarantee that you'll awaken tomorrow. But today, you have the power to do good. When you invest time in people, you change their lives and hopefully, they will change yours.

One interesting phrase I'd like to highlight: "to whom it is due." Sometimes, this is obvious but really, sometimes we just need to hope for the best and not linger too much on the 'deserve' part; after all, we certainly don't deserve eternal life, but Jesus provided a way for us to have it. Some needs simply don't have time for you to waffle through a screening process . . . to borrow a phrase from a particular athletic-wear company, sometimes you gotta "just do it," no questions asked, and let God take care of the rest.

Let's train our minds to try and see the good in everything. We should be kind to everyone, extend kindness where we can, and prayerfully consider if we can do more. Do not withhold your kindness—exercise your power to do good.

....

DAILY DIFFERENCE-MAKER

Release your inner Robin Hood: Take as many coins as you can find—in your furniture, in your pocket or purse, or just go get a roll of them—and put money in all the expired parking meters you encounter. If you want, leave a note on the windshield that says, "I came, I cared, and I coughed up more coins for you. Signed, Robin Hood." It will be a wonderful surprise for the owners of the vehicles parked in those spaces.

.... Notes ....

Standing Firm

But Daniel purposed in his heart that he would

not defile himself with the portion of the king's delicacies,

nor with the wine which he drank.

–Daniel 1:8

One of my favorite sayings is, "Just because you *are in* the environment doesn't mean you have to *be of* the environment." If we're representing Christ in some less-than desirable places, then we've got to be clear about who we are (or is that "Whose?").

Daniel and his friends had been taken into captivity, along with many young men from Judah deemed "the best of the best" by eunuchs who served Nebuchadnezzar, the king of Babylon. Ironically enough, however, the young prisoners were fed rich foods and wine, with the idea that after three years of training they would serve him—not God. Daniel and three of his friends refused the tempting food and insisted they would be healthier than their peers if they would be allowed only vegetables and water. After ten days, Daniel was proven to be right!

While the four men were promoted at that point, this would not be the last time they had to remain steadfast with the Lord and in opposition to Nebuchadnezzar.

Daniel, Shadrach, Meshach, and Abed-Nego had no choice but to live in the environment they were in; we have a choice! When you help those who are less fortunate, you will encounter some situations that are ungodly (and believe me, I'm exercising restraint here and using a nice word!). These are not Sunday go-to-meeting environments. With that said, however tempting these situations may be to bring us into sin, we need to stay above it. We cannot fulfill The Great Commission sitting tight in our pews at church, but we are not representing our Christ very well if we engage in activities, language, or outbursts that are not from God.

It took a while, but Nebuchadnezzar finally dropped to his knees, praising God—ultimately in part to the courage displayed by these four men. What sort of courage are you displaying when you navigate ungodly situations?

DAILY DIFFERENCE-MAKER

Who in your 'roster' has blatantly stated they do not believe in God, or do not believe in salvation through Jesus? Find that person today—help them with something, anything, but do not preach to them. Do not treat them as though you have an agenda, just *be* Jesus instead of *speaking about* Him today.

Notes

Be a Trailblazer

Do not give what is holy to the dogs;

nor cast your pearls before swine,

lest they trample them under their feet,

and turn and tear you in pieces.

–Matthew 7:6

There was a time when I had my Internet privileges taken away. It was near 'bout the time we also formally adopted Michael. And yes, the two are related.

Now I would love to say the "make-it-official" moment was calculated and there was swelling, dramatic music playing in the background that climaxed the split second after Michael agreed to be legally adopted; but the truth is, we were just sitting around the dinner table, like any other night. I simply mentioned the possibility of making this official—since Michael had been added to our wills, trusts, insurance, etc., it was kind of a natural next step.

Michael said, "I already thought I was a part of this family." And of course, he was. So he agreed to make it legal. What happened next simply floored me.

When word got around, people had the nerve to ask me, "How do you handle it?" Why do people think they're being sly and subtle when they're not? The implication was clear: Michael couldn't possibly control his libido around my teenage daughter, right? Some of these nasty remarks were posted online, and I decided I wanted to hunt every single one of them down. So yes, I was in Internet time-out until I cooled off.

Since I didn't have the opportunity to do it back then, I'll just say it here: We *all* have a bit of housekeeping to do, including those who criticize our decisions because it doesn't "look right," or whatever their so-called reasoning is. If you stay caught up in their web, you won't ever break free long enough to accomplish anything that makes an impact. And those who make criticism a full-time job are probably not paying enough attention to their own kids—and trust me, that neglect will come back in spades.

If someone approaches you with a half-smirk/half-smile and thinks they're subtly giving you a dose of "reason," simply tell them to mind their own business, and you will take care to mind yours. There is no singular methodology for helping someone in need. No one on this planet owns the map on how to make an impact, so everyone has the capacity to be a trailblazer.

....

DAILY DIFFERENCE-MAKER

There are a lot of angel-tree opportunities around Christmas—create one in March, July, or whenever, when clothing and other needs are different.

.... Notes ....

WEEK
FOUR

Kindness 101: A Primer

For if these things are yours and abound,

you will be neither barren nor unfruitful

in the knowledge of our Lord Jesus Christ.

−2 Peter 1:8

Welcome to Kindness 101! Today, you will be asked to complete the following pop quiz:

1. Say thank-you. If you were loaned a pencil, given a place in line, complimented, or you happen to recall a nicety from last week, make a point to say thank-you. Depending on the situation, you may deliver this thank-you immediately and verbally, or write a nice note. It's a guaranteed boost for the recipient.

2. Smile. This is mutually beneficial for all parties involved. Let it spread all over your face—your eyes, your cheeks, your nose are all a part of that smile, your mouth should not bear the sole burden (besides, that's creepy. You know what I'm talking about . . . people who only smile below the nose. Eeek!)

3. Now you're ready to work your way up to opening a door for someone. Bonus if you smile while doing so.

4. Okay, final challenge . . . give a dollar to the person holding the sign at the red light, the one who needs assistance. Do not worry how they will spend it—that's not your worry. Kindness 101 is concerned about whether or not you're willing to give that dollar. (Yes, yes, of course there are bonus points if you can do so with a smile, but it *cannot be one of those mouth-only smiles.*)

Now I'm being tongue-in-cheek here, but there are just some days we don't want to help. We get out of bed grouchy, see someone in need, and want to take the day off from helping. That is your choice, and sometimes we need to be reminded that we are measured by the choices we make in life. And there are just some days we have to return to the 'pop quizzes' of kindness in order to make better bigger choices. Dial it back to the thank-yous and smiles, hold a few doors, give a few dollars, and that desire to help will be renewed.

All of your choices—good, bad, little, big—make you the person you are. Saying you can't make good choices is basically saying you don't *care* to make good choices—don't be that person. What if, instead, we acted like every choice we made would make a difference?

. . . .

DAILY DIFFERENCE-MAKER

Have you ever left a server a one-hundred percent tip? Let today be that day.

. . . . Notes . . . .

See It Through

And whatever you do, do it heartily,

as to the Lord and not to men.

−Colossians 3:23

As an interior designer, I've had my share of days where I've wanted to pull my hair out: A client changes his mind, or can't make up her mind; maybe the job began as one thing, and turned out to be another. But as a business owner and Christian, I am determined to see it through as though I was designing the interior of the White House. I can't leave a commitment simply because I am tired, frustrated, or would rather be on a beach somewhere.

Some of us are meant to help for a season while others of us must commit to a lifetime. Regardless, don't be fickle and inconsistent about this. Too often, we get that "church-camp high" where we're so fired up about something, we expend all our energy before the job is done. We lose interest, feel frustrated, or something else catches our eye; if a child's future hangs in the balance of this, you're creating more chaos than you've prevented.

When we make a commitment, we need to honor it. See it through. Finish it out. Complete the job as promised. When the commitment directly affects another person, such as a homeless person or a foster child, they are not a needlepoint project we never finished or a instrument we stopped practicing, something to put away in the back of a closet to collect dust; they are human beings who are counting on you.

So when you decide to get involved, be very clear in your heart and in your mind about what you are committing to; don't overextend so that you can't honor it well or honor it at all.

....

DAILY DIFFERENCE-MAKER

Reconsider what you are involved in, whether it's an organization or less-fortunate individual's life. Get a progress report by simply asking, "What can I do for you, or what can I do better?"

.... Notes ....

Protect Your Reputation

A good name *is* better than precious ointment.

—Ecclesiastes 7:1

Now I just want to state right off the top: Reputation is what other people know about you. Honor is what you know about yourself. But today, I do want to focus on our reputations, because I have heels that are higher than some people's standards! (Oh, and how I love a good pair of heels . . . sorry, I think *heels* and drift . . . am back now.)

We've been on a slippery slope for a long time, doing things halfway and doing things that we think won't circle back around to bite us. Going back to my first statement, if your intentions aren't honorable, your reputation will eventually crumble.

Social media, email, cell phones, and ever-present cameras have taken this to a whole new level. We've raised an entire generation, now young adults, who have very little regard for privacy, yet fail to consider the long-term effects of their posts, snapshots, and actions. Every moment of your life does not have to be captured or captioned; and if you choose to do so, proceed as though your grandmother, your boss, and Jesus Christ is watching . . . because, in effect, they are.

People have lost jobs, spouses, and credibility because of what they've posted out there in cyberworld; don't flirt with the idea of being the next casualty. The next time someone shouts, "Wait, let me get a picture," take that under advisement—wait. The next time an old flame from the past posts, "How have you been?" on your wall, think before you reply. Consider the consequences. Consider the message you're putting out there. Consider that most who see it will make a judgment call—and you won't have the opportunity to elaborate or explain. Spend a little more time living your life versus posting about it. Stay honorable on the inside so your reputation won't tarnish on the outside.

....

DAILY DIFFERENCE-MAKER
Put the cell phone down. Bow out of inappropriate photo-ops. Make sure your posts are positive and inspiring.

.... Notes ....

Our Most Vulnerable Spots

You are the light of the world. A city that is set on a hill

cannot be hidden. Nor do they light a lamp

and put it under a basket, but on a lampstand,

and it gives light to all *who are* in the house.

—Matthew 5:14–15

What is the "blind side"? The title comes from the very valuable left-tackle position that Michael played on the field in high school, college, and many times in the NFL.

As left tackle, Michael protected the quarterback's most vulnerable spot, known as his "blind side." Using this metaphor, we have to protect each other better, paying particular attention to our most vulnerable spots—our "blindsides"—in our communities, in our neighborhoods, and with individuals. Protecting blind sides isn't about a title, or a flow chart, or a PowerPoint® presentation. Nor do we have to always think big; in fact, when we take things down to the individual level, we can initiate a domino effect that creates real change, permanent change, the sort of organic, grassroots change that grows . . . in reach *and* in depth.

If we are to be "the light of the world," then it stands to reason we must first see what others don't, including these blind sides. We need to be light, share light, and shed light, no longer content to ignore and overlook the injustices that are in this world. Whether it's taking up for the guy who's being picked on in school or busting thugs in your neighborhood, you cannot make a difference with indifference; taking a stand against injustice is a bold, but sometimes scary move—but it's always the right thing to do. It's time we found our backbones.

Remember, if you are the light, then that means the path isn't clear just yet, and it may just be up to you to do the clearing. You have to identify the blind side in order to protect it.

....

DAILY DIFFERENCE-MAKER

Enlist some friends and 'adopt-a-bundle' at a local laundromat. Be the odd folks hanging around, handing out quarters, detergent, dryer sheets, etc. Be sure at least one person has a delicate detergent handy for baby clothes. Make a point to learn about the people you're helping, see if you can meet up for another laundry date!

....Notes...

20

Be a Difference-maker

Create in me a clean heart, O God,

and renew a steadfast spirit within me.

—Psalm 51:10

One summer day, my son S.J. needed someone to "shag" base-balls with him. I'm not sure what that means, but Sean hap-pily agreed to go along on this outing. That evening Sean exclaimed with great pride it felt good to get out there and toss the ball around with S.J.

However, the next morning, the story was a little different. After taking several Tylenol® and stretching a good bit, Sean still couldn't identify which body part was in the most pain. This got me thinking about pain. Sometimes being in pain has nothing at all to do with dis-ease or overextending our muscles; sometimes, the pain is emotional. Pain from the decisions we make or the relationships we are in, or the things that we wish we had done or didn't do. Learning to balance many of these complex issues is what makes us the individuals we are.

We are all in this together, and so many times it becomes so much more bearable when we have someone who will just hold our hand and tell us it's going to be okay. It doesn't matter if you are old or young, your race, what your socioeconomic status is, or what your traditions or faiths are, we all have instances in this life that pain us and many times we need a caring community to be there for us and hold our hand. This tender act is meant to be shared; when we give or receive care, we often receive healing for pain we had numbed to, pain we'd just be living with.

Someone in your community is hurting—someone needs your hand. Don't assume that because a person gets a clean bill of health that they don't have issues in their lives. They need reassurance that it will be okay. They need action, even in baby steps, to guide them toward 'okay.' Will you answer that call?

....

DAILY DIFFERENCE-MAKER

Find someone—a neighbor, a total stranger in a coffee shop, a child who is picked on at school—whose expression may indicate pain. Introduce yourself, shake their hand, and don't let go—ask them if they're okay. Listen to what they say—but more importantly, listen for what they're *not* saying. Don't worry about your next words—listen, ask questions, gently squeeze their hand, and reassure them you want to help with next steps. Just be there!

.... Notes ....

WEEK
FIVE

Be a Rule-breaker

We should serve in the newness of the Spirit

and not *in* the oldness of the letter.

−Romans 7:6

You probably already know that I believe that sometimes, you have to push the envelope. Instead of meeting someone half-way, go the other half as well and be more aware of the other person's needs. We have so many customs and formalities about how to do this or that—too many, when you consider the victims of this form of legalism.

Now it's a pretty comfortable path to take, because we don't have to look at those people who are actually carrying our true riches—and we won't discover those true riches without investing in them. People with talent, people who might have had dreams . . . people who fall through the cracks because we're told it's inappropriate, unfit, too risky, breach of social protocol, or simply, "it's just not done that way."

I'm glad Jesus didn't see it that way. He was often accused of breaking the Sabbath, touching lepers, and respecting women. (He was also responsible for the Saul/Paul transformation, by the way.)

The spirit of serving goes beyond protocol. It's bold, and not afraid of the unknown. Be seen, be heard, be sympathetic, and please get out of your comfort zone! Now of course use caution and good judgment . . . but I have looked behind the curtain, and there is something truly amazing about being a part of something that is larger than you.

People are so much more important than achievements, possessions, or customs. So take some time away from the daily routine and discover how fulfilling it is to break a few rules and serve in compassion and generosity; trust me, it's a game-changer. Those we serve hold our true riches—don't settle for cheap imitations. Be the very best version of yourself you can be, and last but not least, *be brave!*

....

DAILY DIFFERENCE-MAKER

Go load up on some after-4:00 p.m. specials fast-food places often advertise—forty-nine-cent burgers or the ninety-nine-cent menu at Taco Bell, for example. Find an after-school program, inner-city playground, or some other hangout where hungry children might be and distribute the food. The children may be reluctant at first—and, quite frankly, they should be cautious with strangers—but if you do this often enough you will no longer be a stranger. Be steadfast—this may be the only meal they will have all day.

.... *Notes* ....

Someday Is Today

But if anyone does not provide for his own,

and especially for those of his household,

he has denied the faith and is worse than an unbeliever.

–1 Timothy 5:8

Wow, that verse packs a wallop! Unpack it with me, and remain transparent in the process.

Sometimes we cannot see the forest for the trees in our everyday lives. I know that sometimes, I become so obsessed with what's going on in the outside world that I ignore what is right under my nose. No matter how much "good" we're trying to bring into our communities, if we're neglecting our homes then we're missing a very valuable point. While it's true no one has seen me and Wonder Woman in the same room at the same time, none of us are action figures—we are humans, mere mortals! So say it with me: "I am not superhuman."

So yes, set aside that to-do list (I make them every day!) and let's think about the areas we've neglected and how we'll move forward. Think about how we'll make the time to be a spouse, a parent, a relative, or a good friend. Make a conscious effort to remind yourself of why you wanted to marry your spouse, why you made a decision to have children, why your cousin has been such a presence in your life, or what makes that friend of yours so special. And to be clear, fellow list-maker—we're not doing this to mark it off another list; this has intent and purpose.

No matter our circumstances, time is a gift from God, and our first responsibility is to our immediate circle. When that is in working order, we can move beyond that—but we can no longer take them for granted. Our kids grow up and move out, lukewarm friendships fade away, and so many marriages end in failure.

"Someday" is today. Don't let the opportunity to reach out to those within your immediate circle slip through your fingers. Yes, we all need to be a force for the homeless, the hungry, the abused, and the neglected, but we won't be effective if we aren't first a force for our nearest and dearest!

....

DAILY DIFFERENCE-MAKER
Hug each and every member of your inner circle today. Maybe that's your family, your best friend, your roommate, heck, even your dog. Tell them why they matter to you, and commit to do so on a regular basis; do not expect them to know or remember that they are your priority.

.... Notes ....

He Empowers Us

I have filled him with the Spirit of God,

in wisdom, in understanding, in knowledge,

and in all *manner of* workmanship.

—Exodus 31:3

Author Victor Hugo said, "Winter is on my head, but eternal spring is in my heart." And Victor was right—age does bring some limitations with it, but it's not a prison sentence. No matter what our age, we have some skill sets and life experience that can benefit another person. Whether you're just starting a career or retired, continue or even get started to use this God-given power for good.

You will always have critics; in fact, you can count on it. Someone to tell you you're too young, you're too old, or that's "just not done." Don't let these moments to reach out and change a life slip past your fingers just because of society's rules. Find a way to make more time and have the freedom to step up and put your name on that volunteer list. This may mean getting up out of your armchair, spending less time on social media, or foregoing something else that doesn't bring fulfillment to anyone, but you can find the time. And now is just as good a time as any to realize that giving back will enhance not only your life but also someone else's. What you do or don't do—right now—could make a life-changing impact on that someone!

God equipped you, and continues to equip you, with whatever skills, knowledge, and wisdom necessary to do His work. So set aside those fruitless fears—trust that He has equipped you. Of course, we should remember the obvious: use balance, moderation, and good judgment . . . but don't let age stop you from continuing to live a life that inspires a spirit of charity and community service. One day each one of us will be a memory to someone—be sure you are a good one!

....

DAILY DIFFERENCE-MAKER

Find a way to compliment someone today, someone whose personality you might not care for. Smile and be sincere, whether you're complimenting their shoes or how they handled a particular situation. Come on . . . you can do it!

.... Notes ....

Trust His Provision

And my God shall supply all your need

according to His riches in glory by Christ Jesus.

—Philippians 4:19

We can't fight every battle, but we can try to make a difference when an opportunity comes our way. And we can trust the Lord will supply whatever we need, as we need it, in accordance with His will.

Let me be clear: His provision is His—we didn't do it ourselves. Oh, it may appear that way to others, but be very careful to assign credit to the One who provided. And that doesn't mean that His provision doesn't require hard work on our part—when we join the Lord in His plans, we will be working, I can assure you!

We must also trust Him when our role is small. Maybe you have great ideas, maybe you're great at trouble-shooting or planning—but right now, your battle position isn't as high-profile as you'd hoped. Stay patient. Stay faithful. Stay diligent. And also ask His spirit for a dose of humility—just because you're not in a leadership role does not mean your role is insignificant. God doesn't do insignificant! Serve with joy and embrace the support roles with as much fervor as the leadership roles.

Take, for example, Hugh Freeze and Gus Malzahn, head football coaches for Ole Miss and Auburn, respectively. Not many years ago these men coached high-school football and God put them on a path that included many support roles to prepare them for the roles they occupy today. So don't discount a role of seemingly lesser importance.

When your opportunity arises, I hope and pray you will step up, cross the battlefield, and fight. In all roles, remember that you are inspiring self-worth in others and adding value to your community. Be ready!

....

DAILY DIFFERENCE-MAKER

Enlist some friends and shop for cosmetics, hair color, magazines, and gift boxes (if you really want to amp it up, use purses instead of gift boxes). Make care packages for residents in a battered women's shelter; give them manicures, and spend time just being women together!

.... Notes ....

A Better Block

That the generation to come might know *them*,

the children *who* would be born,

that they may arise and declare *them* to their children,

that they may set their hope in God,

and not forget the works of God, but keep His commandments.

—Psalm 78:6–7

think I have finally grasped what "the rest of your life" means. We've all heard the phrase time and again, but for me, it didn't really register until recently, when the reality of the phrase sunk in. And when it did, I received a keen awareness of what is truly important in life, and what is not.

Aging is a process over which we have no control, but we can control how we spend the rest of our lives. So if our legacy we're currently leaving consists of only turning the television up a little louder and sinking down in the recliner, we need to rethink our exit strategies.

For starters, drive around your town paying particular attention to the less desirable areas of your neighborhood. What makes them less desirable? Are the houses dilapidated? Is there a lot of crime? Is the area too congested or over-developed, with a lack of green space

or play areas for children? I'm not talking about developing an afflu-
ent neighborhood, or one that will incur taxes so high long-term
residents are forced out of their homes; I'm talking about turning the
entire neighborhood around, block-by-block, making it safer, cleaner,
greener for its current residents. Research an abandoned lot to see
if it could be your starting point. Abandoned lots can be cleaned
and sodded—abandoned lots can become playgrounds, community
gardens, dog parks, or courtyards. Abandoned lots can become com-
munity-gathering spots.

None of this happens overnight, and one person can't do it all—
but it will never happen without someone decidedly taking that first
step. Don't leave it for the next generation to figure out—step up,
step out, and move forward!

DAILY DIFFERENCE-MAKER

Help plan a block party for a low-income neighborhood to encourage community and give residents a glimpse of what could be. Buy
some washable paint and paint crosswalks and bike lanes (if city
officials try to make an issue, hose it off!). Benches, tables, even
garden beds can be made from recycled materials (if they haven't
been chemically treated). The possibilities are endless, and as long
as the items are portable, they can be set up anywhere the community wants to gather.

Notes

WEEK
SIX

Shine Your Light

Let your light so shine before men, that they may see your
good works and glorify your Father in heaven.

—Matthew 5:16

Why do you think you're better than I am, or think I'm
better than the guy down the street? As you might imagine, I am not the type of person who likes to choose
between either/or; I don't like to cut the herd because when that's
done, there's no real *why* behind the selection process. I want everyone to have opportunity; it gets my juices flowing to know that every
day I am going to cross paths with a person who can be a successful
contributing member of society if only given a chance.

There are so many great examples of this in the Bible: Elijah
and Elisha (2 Kings); Eli and Samuel (1 Samuel); Paul and Timothy
(1 Timothy); Ruth and Naomi (Book of Ruth); Mary and Martha
(Luke 10); Jesus and just about everyone He encountered during His
earthly ministry!

The power of choice is great, and if you're alive today you have
another opportunity to make the choice—we can impact others'
lives or we can pursue things that will die right along with us—our
portfolio, our fame, our selfishness. My hope and prayer is that you

make a choice that allows you to see yourself in a whole new light; and that, in turn, will change another's for the better. And hopefully, when others see that light of yours reflecting so positively in others, then they too will be inspired for their light to shine as well.

Run toward whatever it is that inspires you, run with passion and desire to leave the world a better place than when you entered it. I hope you will do this with no other motivation than knowing the more you give, the more you will get. Find out what it is that inspires you, and use it to change the world!

....

DAILY DIFFERENCE-MAKER

Here are three tasks that come in handy in life: knowing how to fix a flat tire, knowing how to roast a chicken, and knowing how look up a word in the dictionary. Believe it or not, someone out there does not know how to do one of these—find that person, and teach them what you know. In turn they might just teach you something as well!

.... Notes ....

Serve Those Who Serve

You shall surely give to him, and your heart

should not be grieved when you give to him,

because for this thing the LORD your God will bless you

in all your works and in all to which you put your hand.

–Deuteronomy 15:10

Who delivers your mail? Do you know the birthday of your favorite babysitter? Does the server at your favorite restaurant or hangout call you by name? What are the names of your child's teachers at school and at church? Who handles the landscaping at your office, or mows your lawn?

It takes a village for all us to function in life. At least once a year—birthdays or Christmas are good possibilities—acknowledge those who provide you with services during the year. They are often overlooked, perhaps invisible, to so many until they are not there and something's left undone. Make sure you show your genuine gratitude with a token of appreciation to these people who keep your life in gear by fulfilling some of their genuine needs. Your options are endless, and these gifts will be actually used and most likely not re-gifted—like gift cards for oil changes, salon services, dry cleaning, lawn services, gym memberships, even a one-time house cleaning . . . you get the idea.

Look at what the verse says. When we give, don't let our hearts "be grieved," because the Lord will continue to bless us. All of us want to know we matter and that someone takes notice of us; I realize service providers are "just doing their jobs," but these jobs are not easy, and they're often thankless. They bless us each day by caring for us, our children, and community—let them know that someone has taken notice.

....

DAILY DIFFERENCE-MAKER

Give your favorite babysitter a gift card for a free manicure/pedicure that has already included the tip, or the person who cleans your office a restaurant gift certificate (fast food is fine—that way, they can feed their entire family!).

.... Notes ....

Not for a Reason, Not for a Season

Love suffers long *and* is kind . . . bears all things,

believes all things, hopes all things, endures all things.

—1 Corinthians 13:4, 7

Sometime during Michael's senior year, a teammate suffered an injury—and Michael's mind started whirring. What if he was injured? Would this change anyone's feelings toward him? Most of the country knows Michael plays football . . . but in high school, he was also on the basketball and track teams, so the concern was reasonable, as far as the likelihood of an injury. A friend of Sean's set him straight.

"Michael, you'll always have a home with Sean and Leigh Anne," she explained. "I know from personal experience that when they love you, it's not for a day, not for a reason, and not for a season. They will love you to eternity." That was two-hundred percent accurate times ten.

When we started interacting with Michael, we intended to help him—I didn't count on falling in love with him, which took all of about a nanosecond from the moment we truly engaged. The connection between us is so powerful, I'm pretty sure I gave birth to him. But to pinpoint *why Michael? Why not some of the others we've helped?* That's a great question! The best answer I can come up with is because the Holy Spirit chose this time and this person.

Think about the people in your life whom you "love." Have you ever considered why? Is it because they can advance you socially, economically, or professionally? Is it because they're attractive? Or is it something much deeper, something you know, but cannot adequately explain?

If we want authentic love, we must also be willing to love authentically. Each one of us should be loved because we are God's creation, made in His image, and therefore, we have value; and in return, we need to love the way God loves each one of us. All the other ways—*they're cute, they're smart, they're athletic, they have money, they can advance me in some way*—are cheap imitations.

Today, you will interact with someone who needs to be loved this way . . . "not for a reason, not for a season." How will you respond?

DAILY DIFFERENCE-MAKER

Clean up your block, pick up trash, pull up weeds. Rake and bag leaves in an elderly or sick person's yard. (Oh for heaven's sake, *of course* you can use your fancy leaf-blower!)

Notes

Father, May I?

A man's heart plans his way, but the LORD directs his steps.

–Proverbs 16:9

ree will has always been a curious concept for me; God is omniscient, yet God allows us room for choices. Yes, we are free to make our own plans; but for those of us who have chosen to worship and obey the Lord Almighty—and again, He allows this to be our choice—we should want Him to direct our steps. Which means sometimes, the plans that we've concocted are not going to take root; He should be asked on the front end of our plans, not when we're drowning in missteps. He wrote our stories with the intention that He would direct them, knowing that our human nature would occasionally take us off-script. For some of us, these are rare detours but others spend many years living off-script.

You see, your life story is played out by one person and only one person, and that person is *you*. We carry each and every page of our unique life story; each moment becomes part of our own personal blueprint. You can decide whether you are going to be a hero, a bully, a best friend, a good spouse . . . but whatever the title, the adjective, the noun, or role, we must also decide whether we will be a faithful follower of the Lord and His precepts. He may have something different planned.

Each new day, God's grace provides us the opportunity to start fresh, shed the negative build-up, and wipe the slate clean—and reclaim our role in the story that will be recounted again and again to future generations. Hopefully, your story will be a treasure to your grandchildren, your nieces, nephews, and ones you will never have the pleasure to know. It only makes sense, then, that we would be good stewards of each and every moment that is available to us. I mean, He knows all past, present, and future—we don't. Wouldn't you want the One who *knows* to determine your path?

....

DAILY DIFFERENCE-MAKER

When's the last time you consulted the Father on your decisions? I'm not talking about just the major decisions, or even just asking Him to bless the plans you already have in motion. When's the last time you've asked, "Father, may I?" If you can't remember, it's time to drop to your knees in prayer.

....Notes..

Risky Business

Create in me a clean heart, O God,

and renew a steadfast spirit within me.

—Psalm 51:10

When's the last time you did a spring cleaning on your own life? I'm talking sweep the front porch of our minds, knock the cobwebs out of the brain, sharpen and polish our thoughts . . . reevaluate whether we are on the right path, reconnect with the Lord if we've strayed. We were made with soft, compassionate hearts and sometimes that requires ripping off the layers of buildup caused by stress, hurt, pain, and rejection.

Admittedly, the layers seem safe; as they build up and enclose us, we get a false sense of security that no one or nothing can reach us. But you know what the problem is? No one and nothing can reach us.

The reality is, those same layers disconnect us from the good stuff, too—our compassion, our ability to love, our conviction, each other, even our Lord. The world becomes dull and less beautiful.

It's risky business, cleaning out your head and your heart to make it supple again, but think about all the room that will be left—room that once occupied hardened bitterness, regret, shame, and drama can now be filled with fluid hope, care, compassion, and His Spirit—a

Spirit that can sustain us so that the next time He cleans, it won't be quite as much undertaking.

Ask for His help and start chipping away.

....

DAILY DIFFERENCE-MAKER

Study up on some native plants and trees in your area and take some inner-city children on a nature hike. See if you can identify any of the plants and trees in their natural habitat. It will clear your mind and be a fun outing for them!

.... Notes ....

WEEK
SEVEN

One Battle At a Time

Defend the poor and fatherless;

do justice to the afflicted and needy.

Deliver the poor and needy;

free *them* from the hand of the wicked.

—Psalm 82:3–4

During these rough patches we call "life," we are still called to step it up! If we all take it up one notch, give an inch, do just a little more . . . wow! Can you imagine the results? *But what can I do?* you ask. *I have bills, I have responsibilities, I cannot tackle another thing right now!*

Look, no one is asking you to break your piggy bank and give away all your life savings; money is the means by which we navigate this world. No one is suggesting you hand off your first-born, cheat on your taxes, take out a second mortgage, or go without . . . I'm talking about taking one extra step. It's not painful—but it might be new and slightly uncomfortable at first, much like a brand-new pair of leather shoes or blue jeans.

Look at today's verse—we are to seek justice for those who cannot seek it themselves, including orphans. We need to help those who are ill or poor get back on their feet, we need to help those who need our strength. We have it; we have an extra ounce of strength to offer someone.

Even if you live in the most tranquil community, the truth of the matter is we are really at war every single day. The Enemy preys on our health, our safety, social media, our children, our decisions about aging parents, work-related issues, finances, education, household responsibilities, and anything else he can use to turn us from our Lord and our purpose in glorifying Him. Yet by doing the simple task of taking one extra step, we can get closer to winning the battle.

Right now is the perfect time. The war will rage on, but one battle at a time is doable. We all need to up our game.

....

DAILY DIFFERENCE-MAKER

Are you a numbers person? Volunteer to help with bookkeeping and accounting for an organization that provides this service to adults with special needs, the elderly, or business start-ups.

.... *Notes* ....

Following Instructions

If you love Me, keep My commandments.

—John 14:15

Polls suggest that nearly all Americans who have left the Christian church still believe in God; most try to be kind to their neighbors and trust me, if a propeller fell off the plane that they were riding, one-hundred percent would resort to prayer.

If you fall into this category, are you ever moved by your belief in God? When you're kind to your neighbors, is it because you are motivated by the Holy Spirit, or Christ's example? The Bible commands Christians to, among other things, welcome strangers. Matthew 25 says when you have done it to the least of these you have done it to Him. In Romans 12 and Hebrews 13 it says as Christians, we are to extend hospitality to strangers. John Wesley, founder of the Methodist religion, once admonished his followers to do as much as they can for as many as they can for as long as they can. We would all be better served if we lived by those words.

Whatever it takes to inspire you, your neighbors, or your best friend to get involved, I hope it happens sooner than later . . . Don't wait for someone else to ask you to join—take the initiative to find a need, and start fulfilling it! You will not have to look far, I can assure you.

In the career world, we're fired for not following instructions. I'm sure God has wanted to fire me so many times for not following His that it's not even funny. With that being said, it doesn't mean I'm going to stop trying and I hope you won't, either. No one is perfect, but because Christ died on a cross for us, we still have another chance.

God's directives are neither options, nor mere suggestions . . . so the next time you have an opportunity to make a difference or a chance to change a life, remember His instructions. They're pretty clear and straightforward—and you will be the one who is rewarded far more than the one who receives your care.

....

DAILY DIFFERENCE-MAKER

Where will you be waiting today? Doctor's office? Pick-up line at school? Grocery store? Post office? Job interview? Restaurant? Start a conversation with a stranger who is waiting with you. Depending on the setting, ask questions about the food, the weather, their day . . . and however you leave things, make sure you smile and tell them to have a nice day.

.... Notes ....

Take Delight

Trust in the LORD, and do good; dwell in the land,
and feed on His faithfulness. Delight yourself also in the LORD,
and He shall give you the desires of your heart. Commit your
way to the LORD, trust also in Him, and He shall bring *it* to pass.

—Psalm 37:3–5

I love this verse, because of the straightforwardness of the imperatives. We are simply to enjoy God above everything else—and
everything else will come our way (Now, if you have to look up
the word *imperative* in the dictionary, I apologize, but I just felt compelled to use a big-girl word in this).

So take another look at some of them. Before we delight in
Him, the Scripture says, we must develop our trust in Him, do good
things in His name, and feed on His word and faithfulness. We may
discover that our previous desires aren't beneficial to us or in His
greater plan.

You see, when we put Him first, above all else, our desires will
align with His and His blessings will be beyond anything you or I
could have cooked up on our own. We will seek Him, find Him, see
Him, experience Him in ways we never would have if we stayed our
own course.

And when we take delight, according to this passage, we will subsequently commit to His ways. We will know Him and trust Him on a much more intimate level, and want to handle life the way Jesus did, in ways that please the Father.

Where are you on this list of imperatives today? They're not a linear progression, of course, but they are distinct ways we grow in Christ. Maybe you're still learning to trust Him, or maybe you are motivated by His Spirit to "do good." Perhaps you're taking time each day to feed on His word, examining His faithfulness in the past and in your present. My hope and prayer is that your desires are in transition to align with His; this may mean having to loosen your grip on a relationship, a work problem, or even where you're currently located. Remain committed, no matter what the world tells you; trust Him to take you deeper, broader, and to a level of wealth that no amount of money can touch.

DAILY DIFFERENCE-MAKER

Where are the closest farming communities in your area? Look into launching a food hub to help them reach a broader audience and get healthier food to the food deserts in your city.

Notes

Take a Pajama Day

Unless the LORD builds the house, they labor in vain who build it

. . . *It is* vain for you to rise up early, to sit up late,

to eat the bread of sorrows; *for* so He gives His beloved sleep.

—Psalm 127:1–2

There are just those times we're worn out and going through the motions. And it seems like the harder we try, the worse we make things. We need to check out and take a pajama day. Yes, you read right: Wear pajamas all day. Unplug from Internet, email, and cell. Read a magazine or a book. Watch an old western on television. Meditate. Simply rest. Revive your brain and renew your senses.

If God took a day of rest, He intends that we do, too. This side of heaven, we are finite beings and our physical bodies have limits, as do our minds. And we have a breaking point in our productivity, even on a daily basis; most of us have 'peak hours' where we're at our best each day.

God wants to be a part of every nanosecond of our day, to help us and sustain us—if He has to reach us through a point of exhaustion, then that's what He'll do to get our attention. When the deadline looks impossible, the reports look grim, the relationship is falling apart, grades are failing—the answer isn't always 'work harder,' it may be to take a break. Pull the covers up over your head and take a personal day. Replenish and refresh.

When we forget the Lord, we are usually preoccupied and need His wake-up call. If you are running in vain, working day and night, or wallowing in grief—it's time to slip back into those pajamas and just take a day.

DAILY DIFFERENCE-MAKER

You know, you won't be productive if you're going, going, going non-stop. So make today different—unplug from everything. Stay off social media and your cell phone. Today is about rest and replenishment. Maybe take a walk or a yoga class . . . meditate on today's verse.

Notes

Do Love "Now."

The manifestation of the Spirit

is given to each one for the profit *of all*.

—1 Corinthians 12:7

L ooking back on Michael's progression and ultimate success, we believe God gave us the opportunity to join Him in His work because we stayed open and alert to His presence. I'll admit, that's scary stuff—God could have directed us to go live in a hut somewhere—but He didn't. I think He placed us exactly where we needed to be physically, mentally, and spiritually, that cold November day. We'd seen Michael a few times before then, yet that night, that moment, the Holy Spirit said, *"now."*

God had plans for Michael's life, and He entrusted us to simply facilitate Michael's success—but let's be clear, God's plan was for Michael to succeed, regardless. We could have said *no* and then, perhaps years later, applauded this kid we knew back when he was in high school, a kid who succeeded at some sort of endeavor. But we don't want to be on the Lord's sidelines—we want to be in the game.

As Christians, each one of us has the Holy Spirit dwelling in us. When we ignore the Spirit's "now," we are passing up on some life-changing good stuff—not just for others, but for ourselves! The "now" is the Spirit's way of saying, "You're ready. I trust you to handle it. And you can trust Me to equip you. *Go.*" Don't carry a lifetime of *nos* around in your heart—open it up so the Lord can make use of you. Live each and every day with purpose and passion—for His glory, and for "the profit of all"!

....

DAILY DIFFERENCE-MAKER

Write some favorite, uplifting messages on some self-adhesive notes. Pick random spots around town to place them—the locker room at your gym, grocery store aisles, bus stops, inside a school, even on doors at the office. If you know someone personally, the message can be something you admire about them specifically, but do it anonymously.

.... Notes ....

WEEK
EIGHT

Love, Like, and Dislike

Love your enemies, bless those who curse you, do good to

those who hate you, and pray for those who spitefully use you

and persecute you . . . for He makes His sun rise on the evil and

on the good, and sends rain on the just and on the unjust.

For if you love those who love you, what reward have you?

Do not even the tax collectors do the same? And if you greet

your brethren only, what do you do more *than others*?

—Matthew 5:44–47

We simply aren't going to like everyone we encounter—yet we are commanded to love everyone. So is 'like' the same as 'love'? Not necessarily.

When we dislike, we also tend to disrespect, degrade, and humiliate. There is no room for that kind of behavior when we love. When we like someone, and they like us, love comes much easier; when we dislike someone (or someone's behavior) but find a way to love them, the Lord puts a peace in our hearts that lets us know He is pleased. We have shown distinction in His name by loving our enemies (or those who simply aren't our favorite people to be around).

Be a standout for your Savior—treat everyone with respect. Do not degrade them when their backs are turned, nor humiliate them to gain someone's approval. Always, always be a little kinder than necessary, even if it isn't reciprocated; for "Hatred stirs up strife, but love covers all sins" (Proverbs 10:12).

DAILY DIFFERENCE-MAKER

Give someone you dislike a sincere compliment today. Smile a full-face smile when you do so! Really try to figure out what it is you don't like about them and why.

Notes

The Popcorn Theory

Bear one another's burdens, and so fulfill the law of Christ.

—Galatians 6:2

Day in, day out, Sean and I aren't the fancy type. Now, we have our moments where we like to clean up, dress up, and show out, but that's not the norm. Black sneakers versus multicolored sneakers are about as fancy as I can get Sean to go on most days!

Our lifestyle is about as formal as a sandbox, and we live according to what Sean coined as the Popcorn Theory. Popcorn kernels pop by way of heating the water inside the kernel, building pressure; those that are hottest will pop first. So Sean's Popcorn Theory is, basically, that you can't help everyone, but you can offer to help the hot ones that pop right up in front of you.

Living by the Popcorn Theory means that you have to notice others, and recognize them as brothers and sisters no matter what they look like. It's about looking past the outer shell to see the beauty and value in that person. Doesn't matter what they're wearing or what color their skin or hair might be; the need may be great or small, and they may decline your offer, but we believe there is a reason these individuals pop up in our paths.

When making popcorn, one cannot predict which kernels will pop; the same holds true for people who need help. You'll see them with emergency blinkers on, standing on street corners, walking home from school, in the grocery-store parking lot. They're everywhere. Open your eyes—I mean, really open them. Look and listen for the kernels popping. And reach out and grab one.

....

DAILY DIFFERENCE-MAKER

Help five 'kernels' that pop in front of you today. No one's talking about moving mountains—it may be simply returning an elderly person's grocery cart, or helping a child cross the street—it could be something that seems insignificant to you, but may mean the world to a person in need.

.... Notes ....

Casting Out Demons

And they cast out many demons, and anointed with oil

many who were sick, and healed *them*.

—Mark 6:13

Sometimes, we give and have no idea of the impact our gift makes. It may be a relationship that lasts for a particular season, or a check we write to an organization. I don't want to downplay that sort of giving, because it is important; but I do want to talk about those times when we collide head-on with a need that requires more than getting acquainted or cutting a check.

One summer, Collins traveled to Guatemala on a mission trip; among the tasks included daily trips to the city dump, where she would hand out sandwiches to those who lived within its perimeter. Yes, *within* the dump's boundaries, not just around it or nearby. Every day, Collins saw thousands of adults and children, some young enough to still be in diapers, scrounging for anything that could be used or sold. Amid the makeshift homes of metal scraps and cardboard were crucifixes and pictures of Christ—glimmers of hope and faithfulness amid the filth. Collins was moved.

We need to be more observant, in order to be more sensitive to the unmet needs around us. When we match a face with a need, it becomes personal. It becomes a responsibility that cannot be fixed with just a check—it requires giving of ourselves. We have to look at the need, squarely, in order to meet it. You can be comfortable or courageous, but you can't be both—the choice is yours.

What have you overlooked? What have you ignored or denied? It's time to face it and fix it.

....

DAILY DIFFERENCE-MAKER

Visit a place who needs volunteers, one that takes you out of your comfort zone: a home for special-needs children or adults; a hospital; an animal shelter; an underfunded after-school program; a crisis pregnancy center. Look the director squarely in the eye and ask, "What do you need? What can I do to help?"

.... Notes ....

All Is Never Lost

For if there is first a willing mind, it is accepted according to what

one has, and not according to what he does not have.

—2 Corinthians 8:12

f you survive a crisis, that can be a healthy thing. Sean and I had that opportunity in 2001, when Sean's company nearly went bankrupt. We'd been living paycheck to paycheck, and it was a nice paycheck . . . but the company was carrying a lot of debt. The economy was tanking, competition was fierce, and things looked almost Chapter-11-bleak. So we gave ourselves a reality check. We reminded ourselves that this was not a surprise to God and we had an opportunity to reduce, simplify, and for goodness sake, get off the pity pot! Someone out there still had it worse than us, and we intended to give to them, whomever or wherever they were.

You see, when a blow like that occurs, you have to discern what is most important, which means you start casting off what is expendable. And whether you recover or rebound exponentially, it won't matter because you already have what truly matters.

For us, we realized we weren't scared. We had healthy kids and a strong marriage. Things changed for a while, but we never suffered because we already had what we needed—and that was everything to us. We still had much to give, even if it wasn't in the same style or to the same extent. We had to make some adjustments, but we kept on going.

If you're facing some sort of crisis today, here's a story to ponder: Following a storm, a man and young boy were walking along the beach when they discovered a bunch of starfish that had been washed to shore. The boy frantically started picking them up and throwing them back into the ocean. "You can't save all of them," the man called. "So stop trying."

The boy picked up another one, tossed it into the ocean, and said, "Well, I just saved that one."

Never underestimate the power of one; it's more important than you think.

··

DAILY DIFFERENCE-MAKER

Hold the elevator door for someone today. It seems like such a small thing, but you may be helping someone in pain, someone running late, or someone who is just having a bad day.

·································· Notes ··································

Don't Be Color Blind, Be Color Brave

"So which of these three do you think
was neighbor to him who fell among the thieves?"
And he said, "He who showed mercy on him."
Then Jesus said to him, "Go and do likewise."

–Luke 10:36–37

When Michael joined our family, he'd certainly not had much love and opportunities up to that point. Plenty of black families had helped him, and plenty of whites had failed him (and vice-versa). And we were aware of a legitimate debate about race in adoption, with some adoption advocates still not in favor of "trans-racial placement," to use the official government phrase. The primary argument was that such placements could "rob" a child of their cultural identity. Give me a break!

Did we rob Michael of this? Like I said, we just knew how to love fiercely. To be honest, his race was seldom thought about because we were so busy trying to parent him. And years later, Michael said it shouldn't matter—if you're getting a child off the streets, whether you're black, white, polka-dot, or plaid, race shouldn't be an issue. We only have our personal observations and experiences to guide us.

What does it mean to "neighbor" someone, as today's scripture says? To show mercy. To care for physically, emotionally, and spiritually. As Jesus tells the story of The Good Samaritan, he doesn't say the Samaritan went out to look for someone to help—he literally stumbled upon him. If you read the entire story, Jesus says that the Samaritan—a cultural enemy of the Jews—"had compassion" when he saw this man (v. 33). Compassion looks beyond the differences to see another person's sufferings and need; *compassion* doesn't hesitate offering assistance. And ironically, compassionate people usually discover their own needs are met by meeting those of others.

We are a family who loves the Lord and loves our neighbor—but He delighted us with something unexpected. We'd helped others before him, would help others after him—but the Holy Spirit moved me that day I told Sean to turn around. Why him? Why this time? I'm not sure—I wasn't looking, or even hoping, for a third child. When we hand our lives over to Christ, sometimes we get what we haven't asked for—and realize it's exactly what we needed.

....

DAILY DIFFERENCE-MAKER

Attend a church where you would be considered a minority. Be open and willing to make new friends while you're there, and 'neighbor' someone—they just might 'neighbor' you right back!

.... Notes ....

WEEK
NINE

Our Problem Children

The LORD is near to those who have a broken heart,

and saves such as have a contrite spirit.

–Psalm 34:18

Sean and I are more interested in grassroots giving. We don't want to just help the smartest kids, or the ones who demonstrate the most promise; now I don't want to take anything away from those who do help based on this criteria, certainly, but there are so many more whose futures are uncertain. In fact, we simply don't know their talents and abilities because they remain unseen and fading into the backdrop. These are the kids we want to help—the marginal ones.

Look guys, they are out there—in schools, clubs, organizations, clinics, soup kitchens, and definitely on the streets. They cannot focus on school, athletics, or even friendships, because all they have time to focus on is survival. They are breaking—and all most of them need is a chance. One opportunity, one moment . . . a second glance.

They may come from abusive homes, or very loving homes where parents are in survival mode, too. They may be sleeping in cars, eating from garbage cans, or drawing bills from a hat to see which one might get paid that month. Regardless, they have to trade their childhoods for hands-on adulthood; none of them requested this, prayed for it, or put it on a wish list.

These are not problem children—they are *our* problem children. They're not hiding—we're just not seeing them. The Lord loves them, and you may be the comfort they desperately need. You may be the one to help their crushed spirits; just because they are unknown or uncertain doesn't mean they are not valuable. Doesn't mean they don't count. They matter—to our world, and to God. Someone needs to show them just how much; is that someone you?

....

DAILY DIFFERENCE-MAKER
Volunteer to chaperone a class trip. Request that you supervise a group consisting of 'problem children.' Find moments throughout the day to speak to each one individually, treat them respectfully, even if they are boisterous. In the course of the day, you will no doubt learn ways to help them in the future.

.... Notes ....

Connect the Dots

Now the city shall be doomed by the LORD to destruction,

it and all who *are* in it. Only Rahab the harlot shall live,

she and all who *are* with her in the house,

because she hid the messengers that we sent.

—Joshua 6:17

Yes, I realize the Tuohy family has been blessed with financial resources—among many other, much more valuable blessings. But quite often, I still get the remark made to me, "Well, I can't do anything that great like your family did." My reply is always the same: "If you can't do something great, do something small greatly."

Rahab gave some guys a place to hide. She wasn't a pure, blameless, Jewish woman; she was the exact opposite. When Israel overtook Jericho, however, her life was spared—as were those of her family. All because she had given them a place to hide. She did a small thing, greatly.

There are two scenes in *The Blind Side* that I find particularly poignant. At one point, Michael's character approaches two little girls on a swing-set and at first, the little girls were afraid and ran off. Later in the next scene, the same little girls were now squealing with delight as "Michael" pushes them higher and higher, while he chuckles and plays along. It's a small gesture—pushing a child in a swing—that spoke volumes about the progress made and the lives that were ultimately enriched because somewhere, somehow, a connection had been made and trust emerged where fear had been.

And that's really the point. Michael didn't fall in love with us as quickly as we did him—he'd had nothing permanent, nothing he could count on (except more upheaval) when we met him. But eventually, we connected on a deeper level that went beyond buying him a meal or a shirt, and went beyond any sort of conditional arrangement; finally, Michael could love freely. He could trust us to be there, no matter what. Now that's the 'big-great' that came out of a lot of doing small things greatly—it's priceless, it's precious, and it's permanent.

Don't look for a 'big-great'—what small things can you do greatly? Connect the dots—don't worry about painting the whole picture.

....

DAILY DIFFERENCE-MAKER
Depending on the season, take a group of children to a blueberry patch or orchard to pick fruit, pumpkins, or even flowers from your garden.

.... Notes ....

Go Team Go

Let Your priests be clothed with righteousness,

and let Your saints shout for joy.

–Psalm 132:9

My daughter Collins is definitely the entire family's go-to girl, and will always be our cheerleader. She is our vacation planner and fashion consultant; she's always charming, and her conversation skills are wonderful. She has dared to go where her own mother won't—she actually cooks (see? Miracles *do* happen!), and is now the co-owner of Whimsy Cookie Company, a boutique bakery. But most importantly, she sees value in every individual. She believes with every fiber in her being that every individual should be treated with dignity and respect. Over the last ten-plus years, Collins has seen it all, heard it all, and has been judged by all—and she continues to live her life, regardless of the previously mentioned.

She realizes that there's value in action. Among other projects, she mentors inner-city kids; spending time with those who haven't had some of the fortunate breaks she has experienced has caused her to realize that some are happy with much less than what many of us have. But she does caution them by saying, "This is not a dress rehearsal, so be your best every day and give one hundred and ten percent in all you do."

But you know what? This is advice not just for the have-nots, but for each one of us. We all have that, and no one can do it for us—just as Collins continues to find her way using her skills and blessings to bless others, each one of those kids has the same one hundred and ten percent of themselves to offer someone else. And so do we.

Tragically, so many people build their lives on a foundation that is pursuing so many of the wrong things; we're so backwards to think more, bigger, and all are the keys to lasting happiness. Let's take a lesson from Collins and emulate her example of demonstrative love, infinite compassion, and consistent sharing with others. Let's be loud and proud cheerleaders and value others, help them reach their individual potentials, and finally, slow to a crawl our judgment on those less fortunate.

....

DAILY DIFFERENCE-MAKER

Go buy some athletic socks, all sizes. Donate them to an athletic program or physical education program at an inner-city public school. Ask the school administrator what else they might need—and find a way to fulfill it by engaging friends, family, church, and any other group you're involved in—your organizational skills alone will make a big impact.

.... Notes ....

Push the Pause Button

Nevertheless, brethren, I have written more boldly
to you on *some* points, as reminding you,
because of the grace given to me by God.

—Romans 15:15

As S.J. entered his senior year of high school, all I could think about was how time flies by and then they are gone. Just when I thought I was almost getting a handle on this parenting thing, he grows up. I know it's hard to realize he's not that little freckled face kid in the movie anymore. I just wanted to be right back in the frying pan of confusion!

Cherish the time. All those sleepless nights when they are sick. All those times they missed curfew. The bloody noses, the mountains of homework, the glued-macaroni pictures, the half-dead wildflower bouquets, the will-I-ever-get-this-muddy-stain-out laundry, the stitches, and the multitude of grubby hugs and peanut-butter kisses . . . cherish each one for what it is: A moment that will never be again. So stop long enough to inhale the scene and all of its smells and sounds, etching them into your memory.

All those times you longed for peace and quiet . . . when you glanced at your spouse with that "remind me why we wanted them?"

look, wondered if you'd ever catch up, maybe even move ahead . . . that time is coming. They will leave home. Your house will grow three times its size and the quiet, believe it or not, is deafening. So enjoy those moments that you label immediately as life-ending disasters! Trust me, they never, ever are. Since there are no do-overs, embrace the life and the moments you are given.

. . . .

DAILY DIFFERENCE-MAKER
If you are not in the habit of writing letters to your children, get into it. If they are young, tuck each one away until a special occasion, like an 18th birthday or college graduation. Leave notes in suitcases or dorm-room dresser drawers if they're in college (I do that for S.J. myself!). If they are adults, write them to remind them how valuable they are, recount funny memories of them as children, etc., and mail them—it will be such a welcome sight amid all the bills and junk mail they receive.

. . . . Notes . . . .

Agelessness

Beloved, I pray that you may prosper in all things
and be in health, just as your soul prospers.

—3 John 1:2

'Age is just a number.' You've heard that a million times. And just like a lot of other clichés, this one is true.

At any and all ages we should be looking for new opportunities, meeting new friends, visiting old friends, smelling the flowers, finding out how something works, and trying not to take ourselves too seriously! So each year when your birthday rolls around, don't let that new number build a wall between you and something you want to achieve. You are never too old to do something new.

Don't let society impose restrictions on you, either. When was society allowed to determine a cut-off date for achievements? At age eighty-nine, Frank Lloyd Wright completed the Guggenheim Museum and at age ninety-nine, golfer Otto Bucher carded a hole-in-one on the 130-yard, twelfth hole at Spain's La Manga golf course.

Today is the only today there will be. This is your life and it's up to you how you spend each one you're given. Just because you've hit a certain age doesn't mean you stop making an effort having parade-worthy moments. There are kids who want a forever family and trust me when I tell you that your age does not matter to them!

···

DAILY DIFFERENCE-MAKER

Whether you need to go to the supermarket today or not, visit one today for however many minutes you can spare. Go around the parking lot and retrieve the random carts that everyone else fails to return properly. Either return them directly into the store or in the appropriate cart return rack. If someone is struggling with bags and children, if someone is struggling, offer to return their cart for them. *Any* age is a useful age!

··· Notes ···

WEEK
TEN

Your Leave-behind

Let nothing *be done* through selfish ambition or conceit,

but in lowliness of mind let each esteem others

better than himself. Let each of you look out not only

for his own interests, but also for the interests of others.

–Philippians 2:3–4

Sometimes I think people live in fear about the rest of their lives, almost counting down the days. Don't live in fear of the future. When we do that, we rob ourselves of being vital contributors to the present. We didn't have a thing to do with when we arrived here, and we aren't going to have a thing to say about the day we leave—but you certainly can have an impact between the two.

Success is not so much about what you accomplish in your own life; it's more about what you inspire in others. What is the one thing you wish you could impart on today's youth? What would be your 'leave-behind'? Instill a love of reading? Learn where food really comes from (it's true, my daughter did not know that pickles came from a cucumber!)? That the mean girls and arrogant boys at their high school do not have to affect them now, and will not matter within four years? That failing a test or class doesn't mean they will fail in the future?

What do you wish for the younger generations? And why would you risk them never knowing because you decided someone else should handle it? Newsflash: There's no guarantee that there *is* anyone else who will; you may be the only opportunity someone ever has.

I understand the 'slow-down'—some of us just don't have the bodies we had thirty years ago! We've come a long way in this journey, and we can definitely leave the heavy lifting to someone else, but let's continue to persevere. The highs and lows we have all experienced gave us wisdom to share and give; this is our time to be fabulous, be passionate, be seen, be heard, and most of all, be available. You are never too old to inspire, so do not fear the future—educate it.

. . . .

DAILY DIFFERENCE-MAKER

Have any books lying around? Install a few book exchange boxes near low-performance schools or low-income neighborhoods. You would be shocked at how many schools desperately need more books!

. . . . Notes . . . .

Deny No One

God sent forth His Son, born of a woman, born under the law,

to redeem those who were under the law, that we might

receive the adoption as sons. And because you are sons,

God has sent forth the Spirit of His Son into your hearts,

crying out, "Abba, Father!" Therefore you are no longer a slave

but a son, and if a son, then an heir of God through Christ.

—Galatians 4:4–7

You'll often hear the Tuohys say that the heroes of this world are our military, police officers, fireman, teachers, and people who adopt children, in part because unpredictability is so . . . well, *predictable* each day of their lives. Steve Jobs, for example, was the adopted son of a working-class family, and his parents would have had no way of knowing what he would become when they chose him—they just knew he needed a home, and they had the room. And he's just one of many thousands of famous and not-so famous individuals who were adopted and made a lasting contribution to our world.

Recently, I heard a very sad story on the news about an individual who had "aged-out" of the childcare system, lived on the streets, and had an unhappy ending. The person being interviewed made the statement, "He obviously proved to be 'unadoptable' and his life took a tragic turn and as a result, had this ending."

Listen to me, hear me loud and clear: *No one is unadoptable.* God knows this firsthand, making His adoption available to everyone through His Son. No one is denied, condemned, or suddenly dropped; no one is told they're too old, belong to the wrong race, or that it just 'doesn't suit'—we all have the opportunity to join His family.

Oh, if only the world would follow this example on this side of heaven! Truly amazing things can happen when you invest in someone's life. We can make this world a better place through adoption. Be an advocate, be a foster parent, or actually go for it and find the child who's been searching for you—love is replenishing, so we always have the capacity!

....

DAILY DIFFERENCE-MAKER
Did you know that November 19th is National Adoption Day? Contact an overloaded agency in your area—trust me, they're all overloaded—and ask what you can do to help them connect children with forever families. Maybe plan an event for Adoption Day, or spend time with the orphans who need to be loved in the meantime.

·· Notes ··

Trimming the Fat

"They have grown fat, they are sleek;

yes, they surpass the deeds of the wicked;

they do not plead the cause, the cause of the fatherless;

yet they prosper, and the right of the needy they do not defend.

Shall I not punish *them* for these *things*?" says the LORD.

"Shall I not avenge Myself on such a nation as this?"

—Jeremiah 5:28–29

Whew! Those are some tough words to read, but very convicting. Here is a nation that not only lacks compassion, but also does not come to the defense of the poor and orphaned. Instead, they are polished, well-fed to the point of obesity, and really good at manipulation and coercion, among other "deeds of wickedness." Does this nation sound familiar to you? This warning wasn't intended just for Judah—we need to sit up and pay attention.

Listen, giving is so much more important than the gift itself. We really can live without the big-screen televisions and trips to Hawaii, when we consider that maybe only a couple of neighborhoods over, there is a child who wishes for a family. A woman whose power has been turned off. A man who hasn't eaten in a few days. A baby being abandoned by a scared teenager who hid her pregnancy.

We can do something more exciting with our cash, like give gifts that actually impact and change lives! We should be giving wings to a child who doesn't know life beyond the walls of a housing project by taking her to museums, libraries, and shows; we should fill the tummy of an elderly man, so he never again must decide between food or medicine; we should encourage an incarcerated teenager to gain entry into college by supplying him with an e-reader and library card. Our gifts can be ones that will touch the lives of others, provide meaningful aid to those in need, and most importantly, give dreams to those who've never dared to have them.

It's time to trim the fat in our own lives to fortify others.

....

DAILY DIFFERENCE-MAKER
Grab some friends and turn a shopping or camping excursion into a day or two of showing kindness to your community.

.... Notes ....

"Cute Little Blonde" Syndrome

Be diligent to present yourself approved to God,

a worker who does not need to be ashamed,

rightly dividing the word of truth.

—2 Timothy 2:15

A few years ago, I wrote some blog entries for a well-known organization. A man wrote in, criticizing the "cute little blonde" responsible for the blog when important things like Social Security and Medicare were in jeopardy.

Other than wanting to hug this man's neck for the offhanded compliment, I did appreciate where he was coming from; but the Lord gave me a platform and I intend to make ample use of it to His glory. There is an audience out there who may be willing to listen to a "cute little blonde" instead of an analyst, economist, or political talking head about what's going on in our communities.

As Americans, we are free to express our opinions, but as Christians, we also need to take responsibility for them, too. If someone's not going about something the right way, then what are you doing about it yourself? If you can back up your statements, that person may want to listen and learn. In fact, they're probably more apt to hear what you have to say if you have something beneficial to say—instead of criticizing either what they've done, or who you think they are based on superficial assumption.

This goes double for all those e-mail forwards and social media posts that either slant or flat-out lie about various issues. When you find out they're false, do you send another email or post an apology? Again—we are free to speak our opinions in this country, but as Christ-followers, we should take responsibility for our freedom.

Let's respect that we all are passionate about different things, and that is good. Don't let the noise from others' passions and opinions drown out your own; but as you speak loud and proud, speak the truth, speak it in love, and practice what you're preaching. The "cute little blonde" has spoken!

....

DAILY DIFFERENCE-MAKER

At some point today, you will think or say something critical. *Can* you do better than the one you're criticizing? *Are* you doing a better job than the one you're criticizing? If the answer is no to either question, re-think how—or if—you want to express your personal opinion about this person.

....· Notes ·...

Shorten the Distance

Command those who are rich in this present age not to
be haughty, nor to trust in uncertain riches but in the living God,
who gives us richly all things to enjoy. *Let them* do good,
that they be rich in good works, ready to give, willing to share.

—Timothy 6:17–18

When Michael arrived in our home, it would seem to everyone who knows us that there would be some disruption to our household—at the very least, his size-15 sneakers would have collided with my carefully organized interiors—but oddly, there was never any real conflict. He just *fit perfectly*, sneakers and all.

Now what was interesting is that Michael always figured our upscale neighborhood was about thirty minutes away from the boarded-up and broken-window urban housing project that he grew up in. And metaphorically speaking, he was right; the economic distance between our genteel subdivision and his housing project was vast. But in reality, it was a short drive from our front door.

In fact, none of us has to travel halfway across the world to see poverty, abuse, hunger, neglect. Maybe the poorest of neighborhoods is several miles away and you assume the government has programs in place to "take care of these situations." Well, open your eyes: they're not taken care of, or these issues might be resolved. No government program guarantees a happy childhood, a stable marriage, or a job; you might be someone's only economic development program.

And what about those who don't qualify for any sort of assistance? These are the folks who cannot make ends meet, even though they work hard at two, possibly three jobs. The people who fall through the cracks and, without help, inadvertently take their children with them. We still have a high-school dropout rate of about seven percent; of that percentage, nearly one-fifth of those are minorities*. Whether they are dropping out to help their families, join a gang, because they're pregnant, or for some other reason, they are not seeking alternatives like a GED or trade-school certificate. What happens to them? Where do they go? Get in your car, drive five or ten minutes, and find out.

....

DAILY DIFFERENCE-MAKER

Talk to a social worker or law enforcement who can point you to some cases or neighborhoods where children and families are falling through the cracks; most social workers have caseloads that are bursting at the seams. Sometimes, the people involved are not looking for a hand-out, they just need a helping hand.

.... Notes ....

*Source: U.S. Department of Education, National Center for Education Statistics

WEEK
ELEVEN

Swarming Pestilence

You shall not be afraid of the terror by night,

nor of the arrow *that* flies by day,

nor of the pestilence *that* walks in darkness . . .

Only with your eyes shall you look, and see the

reward of the wicked. Because you have made the LORD,

who is my refuge, *even* the Most High, your dwelling place.

–Psalm 91:5–6, 8–9

We were scheduled to speak at an event in Oshkosh, Wisconsin; prior to our departure, our host notified us that the lake flies had arrived several weeks early due to the warm weather, and we needed a raincoat over our clothes for protection. Since we had no idea what she was talking about, we pretty much shrugged it off.

As we pulled up to this beautifully restored building right on Lake Winnebago, it was like something out of an Alfred Hitchcock movie! The bugs were so thick, they made a wall. Cars were covered; columns on the building were black due to these insects all over them. We sat there, stunned. All I could think of as we sprinted to the front door was that it was either them, or us; I was not going to let them win.

There are just those times when we will be swarmed by sin and evil. At every turn, it seems there is no relief, only more, covering us, trying to eat away at our hearts, our minds, our character. We are bombarded with lusts, temptations, and outbursts while, ironically enough, being repulsed at the notion. Life will drag you down (with difficulties) but embrace the idea that your faith needs to be stronger than your fear!

Tough times don't last, but faithful people do. Though it may look bleak and convincing, the wicked cannot touch those who make the Lord their refuge. The arrows may look sharper and the pestilence more sinister, but listen, you are safe and you are free when you claim God's promise. You'll no longer feel the need to swat and swing; you realize, just like the lake fly, their wrath is short-lived; when you know there is nothing they can do to you, you can clean up someone else's mess, not lose your temper . . . in fact, you are free to shift your focus to more important things, like volunteering more, going back to school, running an errand for a friend . . . leaving the gnat swarm to its own self-destruction.

··

DAILY DIFFERENCE-MAKER
Offer to baby-sit for a neighbor who needs some me-time.

····································· Notes ··

The Surprise Gift of Giving

Whoever has this world's goods, and sees his brother in need,

and shuts up his heart from him,

how does the love of God abide in him?

—1 John 3:17

I once read about an experiment where people were given twenty dollars and told to either use it for themselves or give it away. At the end of the day, the people who gave it away tested happier than the ones who kept the money.

Charitable giving, or any giving in my opinion, is a good feeling probably because it will always surprise you. Even when we've done it enough, anticipate the joy it brings, we're still surprised by it. It gives you a sense of a life worth living.

When we reach out to others in need, we lead to a much more caring and connected life. God wired us to lean on each other, and there are enough lessons for all of us to learn from one another. We live in a selfish world, a world that resents and is full of negative folks. This is heartbreaking, because if we'd invest in others, a lot of our cynicism would melt away! As Christians, we need to be distinct; we need to be light in the darkness. We strive to be happy, just like we strive for everything else—but happiness is fleeting. If you are not experiencing life in a way that brings joy and happiness to others on a daily basis, then you are missing out!

Be thankful to God for what He has given to you, but remember He has purpose for doing so. We need to use our resources wisely, not to impress people, but to provide peace, comfort, joy, and hope to those less fortunate—I promise it will reflect on you in surprising ways. Don't let someone dim your light because it's shining in their eyes; Christ meant for us to be radiant. Shine on!

....

DAILY DIFFERENCE-MAKER

Why don't you try that little experiment I mentioned on yourself this week? Start small, with five bucks; designate it for someone with a need, give more money if you can swing it. The next day, spend the same amount on yourself. I would be willing to bet at the end of day just reliving the memory of your gifting the money to someone else will in itself bring you much greater satisfaction.

.... Notes ....

53

Hidden Children

Do not provoke your children to wrath,

but bring them up in the training and admonition of the Lord.

—Ephesians 6:4

Of the roughly 215,000 inmates currently in our federal prison system, nearly half of them are there for drug offenses. Most of them are incarcerated between five to fifteen years, but over ten percent are there for more than twenty*. Nationally speaking, over seven million children have at least one parent in jail or prison, and about seventy percent of them will follow suit.†

Frederick Douglass said, "It is easier to build strong children than to repair broken men." Given the above statistics, how do we break the cycle and start building strong children?

First of all, we must find them; some are hidden in plain view. We drive by them, or look at them suspiciously, or fear their influence will "rub off" on our own children. There may be no one at home to hug them, or worse, someone is home, ready to punch or abuse them in other ways. Some haven't eaten in days; others have no running water at home, or electricity. They sit next to your child in school; they attend local ball games, or even play sports. Don't think they're not in your town just because you haven't 'seen' them.

We must find them and show them a better way. Show them that they have a choice to make, and help them work through that process with support and encouragement. Introduce them to new things; all kinds of music; feed them a hot meal; show them places where life-saving scientific advancements are being made. Take them to church or to the movie. Urge them to stay in school. Yes, petition your church, your friends, and anyone else who is willing to listen and get on board—but you and I can't look away any longer. Our world will not change for the better unless we get better about finding these precious ones that desperately need our help.

You'll often hear me say that the cure for cancer, the solution to world hunger, even the next great technology gadget may exist in the minds of one of these hidden children. We won't know unless we find them. I'll close with something I want you to think about: When it comes to God, schools have some limitations on how He can be presented; yet our prisons have all sorts of programs and opportunities to learn more about Him. That's skipping a lot of years, and while I respect the First Amendment and the U.S. Constitution, I believe there is a direct connection between the two. What are you doing to fill that gap?

DAILY DIFFERENCE-MAKER
If there isn't an organization in your town that works with children of incarcerated parents, start one.

Notes

Sources:
*Federal Bureau of Prisons, September 2014 (bop.gov)
†Texas Department of Criminal Justice (tdcj.state.tx.us/gokids)

Haters

By covetousness they will exploit you with deceptive words.

—2 Peter 2:3

Most of the time my motto is, "in order for you to insult me, I must first value your opinion." I think some of you out there may simply say, "Haters gonna hate."

I get a lot of criticism, some of the harshest from those I've never met. Total strangers will walk up to me with nosy, insensitive questions or callous remarks while others offer unsolicited advice. Many just spew cruel and bitter criticism at me on social media. Sometimes, I'd just like one person to walk up to me and tell me their solutions to a better life as opposed to telling me what *my* problem is. If someone said to me, "I have an idea about how to end world hunger," I'd want to listen. Whether it truly was *the* solution, I would see value in that person for having given it some thought.

Look at what the verse says: Critics ("haters") are so because you have something they want. And because they don't possess it—and, I might add, *nor can they steal it from you*—they turn to harsh criticism. It's such a ridiculously simple truth, why don't we believe it? Instead, we internalize the hurt, pain, and anguish; some of us go over it and over it in our heads so often, we start to think maybe they're right.

It's not worth it. God gave you value and what they're seeing is His light shining through you. You cannot give them what they really want—all you can give them is your attention and self-esteem, which is pointless. We have more important things to accomplish—we have a world to change, and your presence is requested!

....

DAILY DIFFERENCE-MAKER

What was your favorite subject in school? (If you say "lunch" or "P.E.," then you'll have to adapt this one.) Volunteer to tutor school-children once or twice a week in your favorite subject.

.... Notes ....

55

Simplify

Let your conduct be without covetousness;

be content with such things as you have.

For He Himself has said, "I will never leave you nor forsake you."

—Hebrews 13:5

What is simple living? How can we be content with what we have? Does this mean we give up on any goals to improve our standards of living? Of course not.

To begin with, simple living begins in the mind. It takes discipline and focus. Most coffeemakers have automatic timers; get in the habit of setting yours the night before instead of a frantic morning run to the overpriced coffee house every morning. Wouldn't you rather spend a few leisurely minutes at home, anyway? Saves you stress, saves you money. Simplified.

Maybe you are envious of your neighbor's kitchen or car. Did you know that over 600,000 people in this country remain homeless*, and I believe that's a low estimate. The next time you look at your neighbor's new car with envy or think you need a new house because your bathroom is too small, think about the homeless people who would trade places with you just to have a roof over their head.

When we increase our focus and dependency on the Lord, we realize we have everything we need. He does provide, and He provides in the most unusual, highly personal ways; He does this so that we know, in our hearts, "this can only be from Him." If we're too busy scurrying around to keep up with our neighbors or think more, more, more material possessions will make us happy—we will miss the precious blessing of His provision. We can't outperform Him, I promise you.

So as your mind and heart shift to a simplified living mode, I'll leave you with one final thought: Merry-go-rounds spin and spin, but take you absolutely nowhere (except to the queasy farm). The same is true when we chase after money, power, and prestige, because it will never be enough to satisfy what only God fulfills. Aren't you tired yet?

....

DAILY DIFFERENCE-MAKER

Find an old appliance or power tool that has done nothing more than collect dust. Give it away, donate, or sell it for five dollars (no, I don't care if it is that high-power, high-dollar juicer you bought before you realized you liked steak—get rid of it!).

.... Notes ....

*Source: "The 2013 Annual Homeless Assessment Report AHAR) to Congress," The U.S. Department of Housing and Urban Development, Office of Community Planning and Development.

WEEK
TWELVE

Say No to NO

And shall God not avenge His own elect who cry out

day and night to Him, though He bears long with them?

I tell you that He will avenge them speedily.

–Luke 18:7–8

One of my favorite quotes is: "I am thankful to all those who said *no* to me. It's because of them I did it myself." (I think the Internet has attributed it to Albert Einstein, and the quote is mentioned in Wayne Dyer's book *You'll See It When You Believe It*, but actually no one knows for sure where the quote originated.) I like this quote because it reinforces persistence in pursuing our passions.

If you're a person who stops at the first *no*, then you really need to pay attention to what I'm about to say here: If God has instructed us to do something, *no human being can put a stop to it. Not a single one.* They may thwart, circumvent, or delay it—but God is always, always in control. If your desires are aligned with His, if He has placed this vision and passion in your heart, then He will not drop you on your carcass just because someone told you no!

Does that excuse you from working hard to fulfill this vision? Does that excuse you from using discernment and constant prayer?

Absolutely not. There is no such thing as a passive activist. You're not going to just wake up one morning and discover God has knitted this nice little vision together for you—He expects your focused attention and energy to be working right alongside Him.

There's an issue that has gnawed at you for years; your heart pangs anytime you read about it or see it on the streets of your town. What is it? What is your proposed solution? Before you convince yourself that it's a crazy idea, pause and consider if it's *the* idea. (If you aren't convinced, others will not be convinced!) As you move forward, remember there will be a lot of *nos* . . . but it makes each *yes* all the more precious.

....

DAILY DIFFERENCE-MAKER

You've heard of a canned-food drive? How about a can *opener* drive? Collect manual and electric can openers for seniors—some electric models cost only $10.

.... Notes ....

Barn-filling

Even so you also outwardly appear righteous to men,

but inside you are full of hypocrisy and lawlessness. . . . See!

Your house is left to you desolate; for I say to you,

you shall see Me no more till you say, 'Blessed *is* He

who comes in the name of the LORD!' "

—Matthew 23:28, 38–39

At some point, we will lose someone in our lives suddenly and remark, "But I just saw them last week, and they looked fine!" Or "they ran three miles each day—they were so healthy!" We find out later they had cancer or maybe ate a lousy diet . . . but based on their appearance, there was no way to tell.

Ours is a culture obsessed with outward appearance, and we make judgments on a person's health, wealth, and success accordingly. How many television series, both fiction and non-fiction, have been created around this obsession? How many publications are devoted to how our homes, cars, gadgets, and bodies look? We love the beautiful and shiny, and many of us spend entire lifetimes creating a beautiful, shiny life.

Well, here's a thought: How about creating a life that feels good on the inside—not just one that looks good on the outside? One that illuminates from the inside? Much like the rich fool found in Luke 12, we are all guilty of filling our own barns before we fill those of others. And you know what happens when the barns are filled? We worry that if we start filling others' barns, we might run out ourselves. So we just build more barns, and keep throwing pity at the less fortunate! What a waste. And what hypocrisy.

We cannot out-give God. And most of us have plenty. Let's not tarnish our Lord's name by keeping up appearances when He wants us to start giving up appearances. Your stuff does not make you a better person; your behavior does. Once we cut through our material trappings, His light will outshine any 'false light' we try to buy.

DAILY DIFFERENCE-MAKER

Many stores have revived the layaway plan option. Research the stores in your area that offer a layaway plan and go pay off someone's account anonymously.

Notes

Remain Calm

He who is slow to wrath has great understanding,

but *he who is* impulsive exalts folly.

–Proverbs 14:29

Sigh . . . there's no point in me pretending otherwise: I do know a thing or two about flaring tempers. I've had insults and rude remarks directed at me over the years and can feel my temperature rise. And even though I haven't always crafted my responses perfectly, these experiences have taught me a thing or two about managing my own emotions instead of letting others do it for me.

Now what I'm about to say isn't intended as a how-to for manipulating an argument to your favor. Nor am I encouraging you to engage someone who is bullying or threatening you. You have a choice as to whether or not you will respond to someone, so I'm not going there. No, I am simply unpacking what this proverb means in practical, every day terms—a biblically based response, no matter what another person verbally throws our way.

First, no matter how much you may be churning on the inside, don't raise your voice. Raising your voice doesn't make you right! Many people think talking over someone or interrupting them before they can make a point is the way to stay in control of the conversation—and really, all this does is show how out of control they are. Staying calm is extremely difficult when someone is screaming in your face, but make every effort to do so.

Next, do not interrupt. Let the other person make their statement, even if it is ludicrous. You may even ask, "Are you finished? Now I'm going to talk."

Third, listen to what's being said to you. Don't go to your happy place to conjure up your next impulsive zinger; pay attention to what they are saying.

And finally, when you do speak, do not reduce your argument to personal insults or attacks, even if the other person does. Speak calmly, speak slowly, and always, always be polite. Don't forget to smile—that will really throw them for a loop. Yes, this may make them even angrier but that's on them—don't let it get on you.

DAILY DIFFERENCE-MAKER
Get in the habit of remaining calm before you really need this skill—make a point to speak in soothing tones in your every day life, whether you are greeting a stranger on the street or making a return at the mall.

Notes

Go Pro

I can do all things through Christ who strengthens me.

–Philippians 4:13

D
o me a favor—read today's verse aloud. Re-read it, each time placing emphasis on a different word. Has its message sunk in yet? We'll see.

Do you dream about writing a book? Starting a food hub? Adopting a child? Launching a new career? Why are you still dreaming about it? Have you taken any steps to move this dream into reality? What are you so afraid of?

Failure.

"No, it's not that!" you protest. "I have all these responsibilities. I have bills. I have . . ." *a fear of failure,* that's what you have.

We need to get past the 'what if I fail?' moment and ask, 'what if I succeed?'. Well, for starters—you may write something that will inform, educate, or entertain readers; you may feed hundreds of hungry people in your lifetime, and leave a legacy for thousands more to do the same; you may save a child's life; you may be fulfilled with a new career in ways unexpected.

Re-read today's verse. This is a promise. To not claim this promise is to doubt God's power; when you coward to your fear, you are not showing humility, you are showing doubt. God is Who He says He is—so why would He give you a dream and then drop you on your keester? I'm not saying it won't take time, hard work, and a few screw-ups; but there's only one way to find out.

Full disclosure time: When we wrote our first book, *In A Heartbeat*, I was very nervous. When it became a *New York Times* Bestseller, all I could think was, "I bet my high school English teacher never saw this coming!" God's plan was much bigger than mine.

You see, mistakes and failure don't matter unless you don't continue to move forward and keep trying. Anyone who hasn't had some type of failure in their life is an amateur. Act like a pro and go for it!

DAILY DIFFERENCE-MAKER

Join a group or organization that relates directly to your 'impossible dream.' Wake up at least thirty minutes earlier than usual each day to work on this dream.

Notes

An Unexpected Payback

He who has pity on the poor lends to the LORD,

and He will pay back what he has given

—Proverbs 19:17

Sometimes, those who have seen *The Blind Side* will often ask, "Leigh Anne, are you *really* like that?"

"Oh yeah," my family will respond, "It's worse. The movie could only capture about an hour-and-a-half of her." *Ahem.*

Subjectivity aside, I often respond that my son Michael gave us so much more than we gave him. This often confuses people, because Michael had such a rough sixteen years; he was homeless, having run away from many of the twenty or so foster homes he'd been placed in, had a biological mother who was an addict, and a biological father who was murdered . . . yes, we gave Michael a home, but he gave us a more cohesive, centered family—he completed the puzzle when we weren't aware a piece had been missing. We offered support and gave advice, but he opened our eyes, making us much more aware of a bigger world than we knew. Whatever we've given Michael, he's given us back ten-fold in blessings.

When God places people in our paths who need help, at some point, hopefully, we realize that it's not a one-way street; we also needed something that they have. We may have food, clothing, shelter, knowledge, skills—but they may have other knowledge, skills, or ideas that we won't acquire unless we interact with them. It's a setup? You bet! A Divine setup.

So back to the question: Am I *really* like I was depicted in the film? Possibly. Maybe? One thing's for certain: Thanks to Michael, I was never the same. When you invest in someone's life, you not only change their life—you change your own. Are you ready to risk that? Trust me . . . it's a risk worth taking.

. . . .

DAILY DIFFERENCE-MAKER

Take a stack of coupons with you to the grocery. Leave each one near the product it applies to as a nice surprise for someone who needs it.

. . . . *Notes* . . . .

WEEK
THIRTEEN

Quit Yer Whining!

For a righteous *man* may fall seven times and rise again,

but the wicked shall fall by calamity.

—Proverbs 24:16

Sometimes, you do what you have to do to keep your dream moving forward. On days that I need that reminder, I look no further than my own mother's example.

Having put herself through a series of interior design courses at the University of Memphis, she landed a job at Sears as an in-house designer . . . and almost lost her job because she refused to work on Saturdays (the only full day she had to spend time with the family). She insisted she could make Sears more money than the designers who worked six days a week; turns out, she was right. She had to work that much harder during the week to have her family time on Saturday. Eventually, she opened her own business and she never looked back. At times, she made three times what my father made and other times, the family finances were so short she'd work evening shifts at a family jewelry store. Designers have to earn a certain number of continuing education credits to renew their licenses each year, and she somehow managed to work those in, too. She did what she had to do to keep her business and family intact. Without a single complaint.

We've become a nation of whiners because we don't realize just how good we have it. Somehow, our collective thought has shifted and we think things should just be handed to us; when it gets too hard, we crumble. We're so caught up in our whining, we forget that some homes don't have electricity, or running water, or adequate insulation. And some families don't have homes at all.

There is no shame in supplementing your income to pay off bills or to pursue a dream. If times are lean, maybe you should deliver pizzas, stock shelves at a big-box store, or even bag groceries until things are back in the black. If you've longed to learn animation, maybe you should sacrifice one of your big toys and use the money to enroll in some classes. So quit your whining, put your big-boy/big-girl pants on, and do something about your situation. Easy success isn't really success; real success must be earned.

DAILY DIFFERENCE-MAKER
Take a step toward changing your situation—enroll in a class, apply for a part-time job, and plan to take another step tomorrow. You never know whom you might meet along the way.

Notes

Cheerful Giving Is a Process

I have shown you in every way,

by laboring like this, that you must support the weak.

And remember the words of the Lord Jesus, that He said,

"It is more blessed to give than to receive."

—Acts 20:35

Now, I'm under no illusions about giving—it can be painful, it can be fruitless, and it can be a chore. Initially. But the Bible is clear—we are to do it. And something will shift inside us when we do it, because the Holy Spirit is working on our hearts.

We can be selfish and stay caught up in our own dramas and so-called emergencies, or we can be bothered by a world beyond our comfortable one. A world where the complaint isn't about buying a new hot-water heater, it's about having no water at all. A world where the pain isn't about not liking what's for dinner, it's hunger pain from having no food at all. A world where you're shivering, not because you wanted to show off your new sundress at the football game, but because a sundress was all that someone gave you to wear.

Let's develop minds and hearts that are focused on loftier pursuits that don't involve making fun of someone's eye makeup or free throw. Let's get beyond the superficial in our lives—missing a hair appointment or tee time are *not* tragedies—and get into the habit of smiling, holding doors, and being kind. Let's get our egos out of the way so the Holy Spirit can transform us into cheerful givers. That can only happen when we *start to actually give*—and once you start, you cannot stop. Never forget that to whom much is given, much is required; you may need a breather to refuel and refresh every now and then, but at some point, He will make giving a part of your DNA. Please, please do not miss this special blessing—it requires you to move before He will.

....

DAILY DIFFERENCE-MAKER
Donate blood today—it doesn't cost you anything but time, and is one of the most life-giving donations you can ever make. I don't care if you don't like needles; close your eyes. If the sight of blood makes you nauseous, look away while it's pumping. So many out there are in desperate need of good, clean blood—please do not deny them the chance at life!

.... Notes ....

Suck It Up

Humble yourselves in the sight of the Lord,

and He will lift you up.

–James 4:10

From a very young age Michael knew that he *was going* to succeed. You see, self-determination has nothing to do with race or economic status, so Michael had already settled this matter long before he met us.

As a top recruit being courted by many colleges and universities, he had one last hurdle to clear: his grade point average. Michael was determined to do whatever was required of him to get to where he needed to be to get into college; he never wavered.

It wasn't easy. It wasn't done single-handedly. We enlisted every form of support we could find to help him reach his goal—tutors, advisors, etc.—and for every three steps forward, Michael never took one single step back. He worked the extra hours, took the extra course load, completed the extra projects. And yes, there *may* have been a time or two I had to say, "suck it up."

Too many of us give up on our dreams at the first sign of difficulty instead of sucking it up and plowing on through. And while it's ultimately up to us, we also need support in our efforts—particularly friends and family who love us enough to tell us to suck it up when we don't feel like it.

And no one wants us to succeed more than the Lord. We give Him full access to change and transform our hearts and minds so that our idea of success aligns with His. He will give you the tools, give you the people, but it's our free will as to whether we take Him up on His gracious offer. So when we succeed beyond our wildest imaginings, we know that this comes directly from Him—and therefore, won't take success for granted.

Whatever you're determined to do today—don't give up. Have your "suck-it-up" friends in place *before* you need them, and by all means, submit it all to Him. You are not too weak or incapable—but nor are you meant to travel this road alone.

....

DAILY DIFFERENCE-MAKER

It's ironic that pride is self-determination's killer. Start your day fifteen minutes earlier a few days each week, focusing on what's positive, purposeful, and productive. Today, we're going to admit we've been too proud to ask for help, submit our pride to the Lord, and accept help when it's offered. Admit, submit, accept, suck it up . . . and succeed.

.... *Notes* ....

Shine in the Process

Arise, shine; For your light has come!

And the glory of the Lord is risen upon you

—Isaiah 60:1

Sean's father, "Skeets" Tuohy had been a legendary basketball coach before his health took a bad turn. Every year, Skeets insisted on buying new uniforms for his team, a point the school's administration would complain about every year when budget talks came around. But Skeets knew a thing or two about pride in a garment and the effect it could have on young people.

"The way I look at it," he would say, "it takes about fifteen years to become a good basketball player and about fifteen minutes to look like one. And we're going to look like players every day, if we do nothing else." Well, of course they did more than look the part—under his leadership, the Isidore Newman School's basketball team took home three state titles and fifteen straight district championships. The players grew into the pride they wore every time they put on that new uniform each year.

So we have kept Skeets's legacy alive by helping other athletic teams in the same manner. The talent was there, without question;

but something about wearing a crisp uniform or having the right equipment and accessories unifies a team even more, and they intend to play as good as they look.

What about hunger? You may be thinking. Or, *shouldn't we be more concerned about making sure kids are warm in the wintertime than whether or not they have matching new uniforms on a basketball court or football field?* Preach, people. Preach. But as hard as some of these kids work—not just at their respective sports, but in school, and otherwise—a nice, new uniform is a small way to tell them they've been acknowledged and to keep going. *Keep at it. You matter. You are getting somewhere, and you're further along than where you've been.*

Feed them food, yes, please. But feed them wisdom, too. Let them know they are on the right track, give them a sense of pride in their pursuit, let them shine even while they're doing it. Skeets Tuohy knew the impact a crisp new uniform could make on a child; it's money well-spent.

DAILY DIFFERENCE-MAKER

Maybe you can't buy a whole team's worth of uniforms. But you could probably buy one jersey. Or some socks? Or offer to have their uniforms cleaned? If there is an inner-city soccer league, t-ball league, or something similar, offer to pay for the shirts or caps they wear.

Notes

Adopting an Adult

Beloved, if God so loved us, we also ought to love one another.

—1 John 4:11

Government programs are great. I don't care if that statement makes you upset; nor do I care if you're Democrat, Republican, or anything else. Get over yourself! It's not about you or your politics. So my feeling is, if you're upset by it, then you're painfully unaware of the government programs that have helped you. As U.S. citizens, each one of us has received benefits—some programs, however, seem to get more media and political attention. I don't have time nor arrogance to argue this—we need a safety net, and there's no denying that.

One thing the government cannot do, however, is look lovingly at someone and say, "I love you, and I want you in my home." We have met many young people who have been in government child-care; many of them "aged out" and are now working professionals . . . but they still yearn for a family. Someone to send them a birthday card; a place to come home to at Christmastime. Think about the casual calls you make to your family, or how your mother complains that you don't visit—these kids, many of them even in their late twenties, don't have someone to check in with or to argue with about why they don't call home more often . . . because there is *no one* and there is *no home.*

Of all the many gifts we received from Michael, the greatest one was that he brought our family closer during a time when many families lose touch—those dreaded high school years. He didn't do this in a demanding way, but his presence ushered in this sort of centrifugal force—we started eating more meals together at the table, spent more quality time together as a family, and just enjoyed hanging out together, doing absolutely nothing. Yes, Michael needed this—and for a different set of reasons, so did we (I miss those times dearly).

You see, you can age-out of a government program, but you will never, ever age-out of needing a family.

DAILY DIFFERENCE-MAKER
Be on alert for the young adults you encounter who never mention a parent, or going home to visit family. They may be orphaned, have no relationship with their family, or never had a family at all—make them a part of yours. Include them in holiday plans, invite them to family meals, remember their birthdays.

Notes

WEEK
FOURTEEN

While Our History Is Still with Us

Likewise you younger people, submit yourselves
to *your* elders. Yes, all of *you* be submissive to one another,
and be clothed with humility.

—1 Peter 5:5

Maybe it's our nation's youth and inexperience, but more than six million seniors face the threat of hunger, right here in the wealthiest nation in the world. How can that be?

We have a lot to learn about cultures that uphold their elderly in the highest regard; they are revered for their wisdom and experience, ensured that someone will tend to their needs. At some point, these caretakers learned to value those who have lived many years and someday, if they should be just as fortunate, someone will value their wisdom in the same way.

The philosopher George Santayana is credited with the saying, "Those who cannot remember the past are condemned to repeat it." When we ignore the work of previous generations, no matter the scale, we are falling into Santayana's warning. Whether it's the now nearly blind grandmother who sewed your childhood clothes, or a great philanthropist who is suffering from dementia, these are people who spent their entire lives taking care of others—and this treasured group is reluctant to make others aware of their own needs.

I know this firsthand. My own mother, who will assuredly read this, hates to bother my brother and me for help. She often masks her own needs or tries to do a difficult task on her own.

Senior citizens need to know that we have not forgotten about them. We need to institute a personal system to ensure the seniors in our lives don't feel they are imposing. Today, go out and give of your time, your energy, and your resources to this wonderful generation. You might be the only voice that they can depend on, so be loud and proud for them! They are our most prized possessions, our national treasures, our history; they are the invaluable people who got all of us to where we are today.

DAILY DIFFERENCE-MAKER

Forego your expensive cup of coffee, and use the money to pick up a sandwich for an elderly neighbor. You don't have to suggest they might be hungry; let them keep some personal dignity. Offer to sit and visit with them for a bit, listen for any other needs that might come up in conversation. Kiss their wrinkled cheek, let them know they still matter.

Notes

No More Ifs

Go out into the highways and hedges, and compel *them*

to come in, that my house may be filled.

–Luke 14:23

Michael's and Collins's high school football team won the state championship. At the football banquet that year, Coach Hugh Freeze said, "It feels great to not have to answer any of the wouldas, couldas, or shouldas, because we did it!"

So many opportunities get lost in the shuffle of woulda, coulda, shoulda. Most of my days are so full that sometimes, I just want to pull the covers over my head and never get up. But I do. Then at the end of the day, as I drag myself back to that same spot in my comfortable, welcoming bed, and can be very still for the first time in many hours, I recycle the day in my head and still come up with too many 'ifs': If I had done this, if I had taken the time to . . . you get my point.

But today is a new day, one that presents a brand-new set of "would have," "could have," and "should have" directly in our paths. Let's turn around and take them down, each one, with even just the least little thing that might be life-altering to someone else. We can only accomplish this if we stop treating these moments as afterthoughts of regret and start making them a priority. Look, it's not about us—let's make it about your neighbor, your old classmate, your friend at church, your child's coach, even the little girl on the poster at the grocery store who is battling cancer.

If you are reading this and you think I am not talking to you, either because of your age or because you already did something and have patted yourself on the back for it, you are wrong. No one is taking themselves out of this game. We are all valuable players that can all make a significant difference. Yesterday's done, whether you did something or not—today, it's all-new again.

....

DAILY DIFFERENCE-MAKER

Go buy some basic cleaning and paper supplies, like toilet paper and paper towels (dollar-store brands are fine). These are items every household needs and uses. Take them to a halfway house, housing project, or community center that is willing to give them to families in need. Ask what else they may need (if the person is elderly, for example, they may need help cleaning—given how much I love to clean, consider this professional advice!).

....Notes...

A Personal Sabbath

For *in* six days the LORD made the heavens and the earth,

the sea, and all that *is* in them, and rested the seventh day.

Therefore the LORD blessed the Sabbath day and hallowed it..

—Exodus 20:11

What do you do to recharge? Even God rested—so why do you think you can't? Let me see if I can guess what's in your head right now as you read this:

"Leigh Anne, you just don't understand—I have too many depending on me!"

"That laundry ain't gonna do itself."

"Oh, she just doesn't get how busy I am; her children are grown."

Hear me on this: The best leaders, game-changers, wives, husbands, Girl Scout leaders, pastors, mothers, and fathers create routines, learn patience, listen a lot, and always set aside some time for themselves. We all need a personal Sabbath—where we unplug from everything (literally, figuratively, and metaphorically!).

Now I'm not talking about 'date night' with your spouse, though I highly recommend that, too. No, I'm talking about a hot bath that can make even the worst issue not seem so bad. Or a pedicure, cup of coffee in solitude (Diet Coke® for me), meditation, a long walk, golf game, a half-hour on your porch, guitar lessons . . . just a few minutes each day or time out each week that reminds you that you're not only a parent, or spouse, or team leader, or volunteer, or manager . . . you are *you*. You have your own likes and dislikes, your own hopes and dreams, and you still have a few things you'd like to discover about yourself. A personal Sabbath gives you the opportunity to dream, relax, recharge. When we take that time out of today, tomorrow suddenly looks much brighter. Remember, this is a journey . . . pace yourself.

DAILY DIFFERENCE-MAKER

Where does your town distribute SNAP (food stamps)? Purchase a gift certificate for a manicure at a location not far from there, and the day the coupons are distributed, pick a woman at random and hand her the certificate. Introduce yourself, offer to drive her if she needs transportation, or help her make arrangements if she has young children at home. Make a point to make that person's day magical!

Notes

Talk, Talk, Talk

But now you yourselves are to put off all these: anger, wrath,

malice, blasphemy, filthy language out of your mouth.

—Colossians 3:8

Did you know that we spend one-fifth of our life talking? Maybe that's on average, since I'd say, "Whew . . . Ms. Sue spends a lot more than that!" Talk shows saturate the airwaves, podcasts are available on just about every subject we can think of . . . we all have something to say. Sometimes we say the wrong things but regardless, we continue to talk!

Our mouths have tremendous potential to either damage or delight, and we need to take responsibility for what comes out of our own each day. You see, our words are quite powerful—they can build confidence and have a positive impact on someone or something, or they can have a detrimental and damaging effect.

Take another look at today's verse. How often do you hear any of the above? Now for the uncomfortable part—how many of these infractions have you contributed to, just in the past forty-eight hours? (Ugh, I'm so busted—guilty as charged!)

Maybe we were in a mood, maybe it was something off-the-cuff that we didn't really mean or thought no one heard us . . . but we said it. We put it out there. If you read Colossians 3, it's all about putting on the new self and focusing on the eternal. In fact, it says we are to "keep seeking"—so this is a life-long practice, thank goodness! And while you may be forgiven for your words, it's very difficult for others to forget them . . . lessons learned the hard way often make the deepest impact, so let the lesson sink in real deep to avoid as many next times as possible.

There's a lot of talking going on in this world, and not enough listening (can I get an *amen?*). If you must speak, do so with humility, humor, and motivation. Speaking this way enhances communication, builds relationships, solves problems, or even pushes a positive message to the public!

....

DAILY DIFFERENCE-MAKER

Make two commitments today: first, to not complain about one, single, solitary thing. No matter if someone is rude, your wait is excessive, or your dinner is cold. Second, practice sincerity and respect by saying "good morning" or "good afternoon" to as many people you encounter today, whether you know them or not. A simple smile and warm greeting shows recognition—and it will definitely brighten their day.

.... Notes ....

Coming Together

For as we have many members in one body,
but all the members do not have the same function.

–Romans 12:4

When's the last time you felt totally alone in a group of people? If you haven't experienced it already, at some point you will. There is nothing more deflating to a newcomer—at school, at church, in a support group, at work, in a volunteer group, on a team, in a new neighborhood, even in a new land—than to be ignored and not welcomed. That person has a role and a contribution to make, regardless of how they arrived there.

When S.J. arrived at Loyola for the first time, I'll admit I was just a bit panicked. Maryland is a long way from Memphis; my son sounded different than most people there, and knew very few people . . . I was a nervous wreck. And of course, it all worked out just fine.

We all have different styles, tastes, tongues, and traditions—when we encounter this in a group setting, what is our response? Do we smile through pursed lips and say, "that's not going to work because it's never been done that way before," or do you say, "I'd really value your input on this, since you're new and can give us a fresh perspective"? A wise leader knows how to bring all the differences together and accept that one person cannot handle it all.

What about you? If you have experience in a particular group, are you lending a helping hand? Are you helping and encouraging newcomers? Are you uplifting, gracious, and nurturing to them? If you're the newbie, do you listen and absorb what's being said before communicating your ideas and expectations? Are you respectful of those who have been there for a while? Regardless of the type of group, it will only achieve optimum results when everyone contributes and stays committed to its purpose—including the team of life, of which you are a member!

....

DAILY DIFFERENCE-MAKER

Different shouldn't always equate with bad. Think of the many groups you belong to—are there any members in any of them who seem to be struggling to fit in? Go to that person, spend some time with them, and privately see if you can figure out why.

.... Notes ....

WEEK
FIFTEEN

We Can Always Have Another

Two *are* better than one . . . For if they fall,

one will lift up his companion.

But woe to him *who is* alone when he falls,

For *he has* no one to help him up.

—Ecclesiastes 4:9–10

How many times has someone asked you what you look for in a friend? Did you know how to answer?

Friendships seldom happen in a hurry. Statistics show that people with friends are less likely to develop physical impairments, and as a bonus, are likely to lead a more joyful, productive life. Friendships also don't develop overnight. They require time, energy, loyalty, listening skills, and unselfishness.

When you meet someone for the first time, your history together is like a blank book. You will be the one who fills in the pages; you can be the hero of the story or you can be the villain. It's up to you. Real friends are true treasures—they'll love you for you, and love you in spite of you. (Thank the Lord!)

If you look around and are thinking, "You know, I don't have a lot of friends," it's probably because you're too busy. So hit the pause button because you are missing out on the good stuff. You should savor each and every opportunity you have to make a friend or to be a friend—because when that chance is over, it may never pass your way again.

Who is that special person in your life who you call a friend? Do you have one? Do you wish you had one? Do you know how to be one?

....

DAILY DIFFERENCE-MAKER

Who is that person you pass in the hallway at school or church, the neighbor who's always in their yard when you're out for a run, or the person in your spin class that—when you stop to say hello—you always talk about getting together? Guess what? Today is that day—contact them and set something up!

.... Notes ....

Be Inspired to Inspire

For you are all sons of God through faith in Christ Jesus.

–Galatians 3:26

Where do you get your inspiration? What excites, enriches, and engages you? What drives you to achieve your goals? Goals will or will not be achieved according to how we, as individuals, are inspired. Let's aim higher than accumulating more wealth, larger houses, more land, stocks, bonds, or pursuit of fame.

As insignificant and trivial as this may sound to you, especially in terms of the bigger picture of "saving mankind," I'll tell you what motivates me to get out of bed on those days when I'd rather pull the covers over my head: The fact that we all put our pants on exactly the same way. Sure, maybe one person puts a little different spin or unusual twist on the process that the next person doesn't share, but the same basic principal still applies . . . one leg at a time.

And at the end of the day, I am simply an interior designer and motivational speaker who, along with my family, did one random act of kindness because my inspiration comes from the fact that we are all created equal—far beyond however we put on our pants. God puts each one of us here, so each one of us has the potential to fulfill His purpose.

If the playing field were totally level, what would truly make you better than the next Joe? Maybe you're better at certain tasks and skills than Joe—but are you truly entitled as *better?* Nope. So that's what I find fulfilling, trying to make sure that everyone has a shot at making it, whatever their "it" is supposed to be. If we each put aside our selfish pursuits and insecurities to help or inspire someone—as a parent, a mentor, a coach, a teacher, a caregiver—we might be helping the one who will finally cure heart disease; the one who will serve as a member of Congress or U.S. president; or maybe someone who will compose beautiful music. There's only one way to find out.

DAILY DIFFERENCE-MAKER

Which school in your town has the highest percentage of poverty? Each month, draw the names of two students to take to a sports event, even if it's a high-school game. Do not let it hinge on grades, citizenship, attendance, or any other requirement—just let those kids be selected by equal and fair chance. Pack extra hats, coats, gloves, etc., if you'll be outdoors and it's chilly; let them keep those items.

Notes

Cleaning Out

Let all bitterness, wrath, anger, clamor, and evil speaking
be put away from you, with all malice.
And be kind to one another, tenderhearted,
forgiving one another, even as God in Christ forgave you.

–Ephesians 4:31–32

We are not working to full capacity until we can leave the negative feelings and bad emotions behind; those emotions do nothing but bring us down and keep us living in the past.

No one knows your heart but you and the Lord. Look at yourself in the mirror and ask yourself, *Am I happy with my choices? Do I need to make better choices?* Are you guilty of fudging, fibbing, padding the numbers, glossing over, falsifying, cheating, or any other number of ways we justify doing the wrong thing? Then change direction. No, don't tell me it's not that simple—it is! We must make that conscious decision to do the right thing. That's where it starts—that single decision, that choice.

Then, you start moving forward with that choice. Beginning with in your own home, make some improvements. All those things left undone, those "Someday, I need to . . . " projects? Yeah, that's what I'm talking about. Be mindful there may be more repairs than just the obvious leaky faucets and curling paint—you may have some relationships that need work, too.

Now move outside to your street. What's left undone there? If a neighbor's grass is too high, offer to cut it; if there's dumping in alleys or yards, don't play the blame game, see if the city is willing to haul it off. If there's unwelcome graffiti, install some solar-operated, motion-activated security cameras. And don't forget about those relationships that need maintenance and repair as you move forward, eventually to your block, and then your city.

It's never the wrong time to do the right thing. So first and foremost, let go of the bad—it's the only way you can make room for the good! Instead of wasting time re-hashing the past, you can put more purpose into your life and impact the lives of others. Who has time to plod through negative muck when they are advocating for the homeless, the weak, the uneducated, the young, the abused, and the ones not loved by anyone? Hear me on this: "Someday . . . " can always be today.

....

DAILY DIFFERENCE-MAKER
Clean something out today—old files, a closet, a junk drawer, your email box . . . you'll breathe easier and your mood will lighten.

.... *Notes* ....

A Three-way Marriage

Marriage *is* honorable among all, and the bed undefiled; but

fornicators and adulterers God will judge.

—Hebrews 13:4

Why do we fall in love with the one person and not another? Do we see a certain person and the head tells the heart this is just a crush, or this is the one who will be the lasting and deep attachment?

Most of us have been on the rollercoaster phases of love, from puppy love to everlasting love, and even the love of your life. I think your head analyzes the situation and surroundings, and then, with God's help, your heart puts it all into perspective.

Your head is the one that asks, *How does he look? Is she dependable? How does he handle his finances?* Then the heart has its own set of questions that are laced with emotions such as sacrifice, commitment, honesty, and passion. So while all these complexities are zinging back and forth between the heart and the head, the reality of the situation sinks in . . . and you realize there are really no guarantees. It's not like buying cars or blenders, that come with warranties; there's no guarantee of longevity, nor refund of time.

This is where our culture becomes unraveled. We rush into things, make unwise choices, and aren't concerned with long-term consequences. We seek our own happiness and pleasure, resenting the other person when they can no longer provide it at the level we expect it.

That's why I'm a big advocate of the three-way marriage. Oh, get your mind out of the gutter—I'm talking about God, husband, and wife . . . with the latter two always submitting to the former. When a committed couple consults with and follows the Lord, even at the dating phase of a relationship, they can make wiser choices as to whether the relationship has what it takes to sustain a marriage. And it's detrimental to replace God with anyone or anything else in the three-way marriage, so if you say "I do," the head and heart should close off all the escape routes, throw away all the keys, and keep love captured until death do you part!

....

DAILY DIFFERENCE-MAKER

DTR means "define the relationship," a conversation that usually happens after a couple has been dating for a period of time. When's the last time you and your significant other had a DTR? Whether you're courting or still courting after fifty years of marriage, it's time to do a check-in—and listen to what your partner has to say.

....Notes..

What Are You Shaping?

But you must continue in the things which you have learned and
been assured of, knowing from whom you have learned *them*,
and that from childhood you have known the Holy Scriptures,
which are able to make you wise for salvation
through faith which is in Christ Jesus.

—2 Timothy 3:14–15

My grandmother did her spring cleaning during all four seasons, and my mother had a thing for vacuum cleaner marks on the rug. I suspect both women even cleaned the soap.

As for me, I wait until after Easter to start my spring-cleaning, because I don't want to seem too eager. Nonetheless, I pretty much have a Windex bottle attached to my right hand at all times. It is like an accessory to me—my watch, my earrings, and my Windex bottle. It's in my DNA and, as much Windex as my children have inadvertently consumed thanks to my spritzing it, it has no doubt seeped into theirs.

Truly, your children are typically mirror images of you. If you're not happy with the choices they're making, take a step back and look at your own life. If your daughter is obsessed with her looks or her weight, how often have you complained about your own in front of her? If your son's school principal keeps calling you because he is picking on other students, how many times have you poked fun at others in his presence? A child is not born a racist, a bully, or even an obsessive cleaner. These are not "sudden" behaviors they've acquired, and don't claim you have no idea where they picked them up—they learned them.

From as early as they can equate your expressions with specific emotions, your children are absorbing thought patterns, behaviors, and attitudes that will closely align with your own. Let that sink in for a moment, because too many of us continue to have children on the basis that "it's time." We're not considering the full impact and responsibility of parenting. You are responsible for shaping the generation who will be caring for you and this nation—at this stage, you can choose to give it full definition or you can warp it. I'm not talking spritzing-with-Windex warping, I'm talking skewing their perspective into permanent distortion. Which will you strive for?

DAILY DIFFERENCE-MAKER
Tell a child he or she is handsome/beautiful today. It may be your own child or someone else's but they are bombarded with messages that they are ugly—make sure yours is heard loud and clear.

Notes

WEEK
SIXTEEN

Another-Mother's Day

She opens her mouth with wisdom,

and on her tongue *is* the law of kindness.

–Proverbs 31:26

It was just after Mother's Day, and I spent a moment or two checking out the leftover cards on the sale rack, the ones no one wanted. Each message that I read was rather bland; they were pretty generic phrases, or a corny poem that wasn't working. Perusing these unselected, unwanted Mother's Day cards, I wondered about the ones who have acted as a mother to so many. I know from personal experience that you don't have to carry children for nine months to love them, or to be a mother to them. Love can grow in your heart, just like it can grow in your abdomen.

Mary Magdalene comes to mind as someone who supported and encouraged many. We know she was a wealthy woman; while there is no biblical account that says she was a prostitute, there's also no indication that she had children, either. After the Lord cast demons out of her, however, she expressed her gratitude by supporting others, including Jesus and His ministry. If you recall, she was the one who delivered the Good News of Jesus' resurrection to the remaining original disciples.

Let's seek out those women who might not have birthed us, but have had an impact on our lives. Who instilled confidence in you when none was there? Who knew that—even though on the outside, you always looked like a beautiful, graceful duck swimming elegantly across a lake, on the inside you were paddling like crazy to stay afloat? Who is that person who always desires the best for you, encourages your dreams and hopes right along beside you? Whether it was a grandmother, an aunt, a sister, a next-door neighbor, guidance counselor, a foster mother, a boss, a teacher, or someone else, how will you honor her today?

DAILY DIFFERENCE-MAKER

Reach out to the woman or women who mothered you; if they are no longer with us, donate to one of her favorite charities or causes in her name.

Notes

The Leave-behind

And I have been with you wherever you have gone . . .

I will set up your seed after you, who will come from your body.

. . . He shall build a house for My name,

and I will establish the throne of his kingdom forever.

−2 Samuel 7:9–10, 12–13

Have you ever seen a life changed from the results of your labor? It is truly one of the most rewarding moments you will ever have, but what about investing your time in something that you will not live to see completed?

That was where King David was, a man after God's own heart, and a leader who worshipped through song, dance, anguish, prosperity . . . and alas, wanted to build something more substantial than a tent for His God to dwell in. It seemed self-serving for David to live in a fine home without his God living in a finer home. But God said no. David was to continue building a strong kingdom and serve God by conquering lands and continue building Israel as a strong, unified nation. It would be Solomon, David's son, who would ultimately build God's temple.

This seems like a rejection, but David accepted his God-given role in the ultimate building of the temple. Yes, David had a vision and a goal; but God had a different, greater plan. David already knew he would not live to see the temple, but obeyed God's instructions to pave the way for it.

Irish-Canadian pioneer and World War I veteran Nelson Henderson said, "The true meaning of life is to plant trees under whose shade you do not expect to sit." Not reaching your goal is not the end at all, but *not* having a goal is. If you have been moved by the Lord to accomplish something, be mindful that you may have a role in it, but it will ultimately be someone else's mantle to pick up and complete. Accept that it may be a work in progress, and pray about your portion in it. Stay open to this idea, because if you're pushing too hard or scheming other ways to accomplish your goal, you may actually be thwarting it. Give your motives a check.

You see, a legacy is etched into the minds of others and the stories they share. So carve your name on hearts, not tombstones and realize your goal may not be reached today, tomorrow, or next week, but it's a work in progress started by a small seed you planted.

DAILY DIFFERENCE-MAKER

Gather some friends and plant a few seedlings or young trees. Stay committed to mulching, watering, and caring for them. If you're not sure which trees will grow best in your area, contact your county extension agent.

Notes

Keeping Honest

But those things which proceed out of the mouth
come from the heart, and they defile a man.
—Matthew 15:18

One little lie does a whole lot of destruction. For starters, it puts an automatic barrier between the person who lied and the person who is lied to; a vine of distrust begins to crawl up that barrier, fed by accusations, hypersensitivity, and second-guessing. It really creates a mess, so heavy and thick, the liar twists things around, accusing the other person of the very things they themselves are guilty of doing!

Today's verse is Jesus' response when His disciples tell Him He offended the Pharisees. His point was that what we put *in* our mouths, we eliminate; but what comes *out* of our mouths comes from our hearts, which can be far more offensive than anything else we do, whether we leave our dirty socks lying around or—to use Jesus' illustration—eat with unwashed hands. Once evil thoughts, lies, manipulations, schemes, etc., exit someone's mouth, they are put into action, intended to harm or hurt, and reveal that person's true character.

Let's just not go there, people. Can we agree to tell the truth? To be honest? To keep honest? It's a much easier way to live. When we "fudge," "fib," or gloss over the truth, we're still lying—we're just trying to spin it. Politicians deceive, athletes cheat, people plagiarize, and magazines airbrush; when are we going to call a spade a spade? It's time we insist on honesty. When someone lies to us, particularly someone we care for, it is a hurt unlike any other—it is such a violation, and it just spirals into all of the things I've described above.

Look, honesty really is the best policy; it shows respect and care for another person. And if someone lies to you, they think you are not worth the truth. Chew on that for a few minutes!

....

DAILY DIFFERENCE-MAKER

Okay, this one's going to be tough but we all have at least one of these: You are going to come clean with someone today. Maybe you made up an excuse as to why you couldn't get together or why you couldn't help someone; maybe you borrowed something of theirs without asking; perhaps you broke something of theirs and didn't tell them; or maybe you even stole their crayons in the third grade . . . but you are going to confess, apologize, and figure out how to make it up to them ten-fold. They may reject, laugh at, or appreciate your honesty—but your heart will feel much lighter!

.... *Notes* ....

Prioritize Those Cries

Jesus wept.

—John 11:35

Not only is today's verse the easiest verse in the Bible to memorize, it reinforces that it is okay to cry. As Christians, we seem to think we must always have our 'game face' on: a fixed smile, bright eyes, and perfectly coiffed hair. Well, not only is that just one scary visual, it's simply not realistic.

Jesus' friend Lazarus had died; in fact, he'd been dead for several days. He wept for his friend openly, and people remarked at how much Jesus must have loved His friend. This isn't the only time His weeping is referenced in the Bible; John 19 accounts for Jesus weeping over Israel's unbelief. *Jesus wept.*

We should never feel ashamed to cry, even the big, old, ugly cries. The Lord gave us a spectrum of emotions, and it's our job to express and manage them.

Weeping over a lost nation or a lost friend is justifiable, as the Lord demonstrated; those are big-ticket weeps and justifiable sorrows. We should weep the same over lost nations and friends today; hungry children who live in the wealthiest nation in the world; rampant abuse of the elderly; people strung out on medications and illegal drugs they abuse . . . I could go on. As a nation, we have much to cry over. And there are those deeper, painful, more personal hurts—a cheating spouse, losing a child, hurting for a friend—which words cannot adequately express, but tears can.

There are also personal hurts that may not "justify" a cry, but we've certainly done it—when someone breaks our heart who didn't deserve to have it in the first place; when our team didn't win; when we're not invited to the party. And let's not forget tears of joy that usually surprise us as much as they surprise others who see them streaming down our faces. (Each time they announce Michael Oher starting at right tackle, I teared up. When Collins won homecoming queen in high school, I cried. When S.J. would hit a home run in baseball, I cried!)

Nutshell: God gave us emotions and tear ducts; every now and then, they should commingle. Men, women, children, hear me on this—it really is okay to cry.

DAILY DIFFERENCE-MAKER

Who is grieving today? Is it a friend? Is it a family member? Is it a complete stranger you happen to encounter? Take a moment to weep with them. I'm not saying weep crocodile tears—I'm saying let your heart be tender enough to hurt for and hurt with that person enough that you are moved to cry—even if that person is yourself.

Notes

Listen (and Think!) Before You Speak

So then, my beloved brethren,

let every man be swift to hear, slow to speak, slow to wrath.

–James 1:19

We all know people who sound off at the slightest infraction without checking all the facts . . . and chances are, we see those people each time we look in a mirror. I liken some of it to part-laziness/part-instant gratification.

Think about how quickly we draw conclusions based on inconclusives. Did your good friend really say that about you? Was your coworker really trying to take credit for your idea? Why was your spouse seen somewhere other than where you thought? Is it possible that your 'perfect' child is lying about the rebellious child's actions to save his own behind?

God gave us two ears and one mouth so we would listen twice as much as we talk. I know that's not the first time you've heard that, and it won't be the last. Let's be careful not to make assumptions based on third-party information or whatever we've dreamed up in our heads. Deal with the facts in front of you, yes—but be sure you've vetted them out as thoroughly as you can. That means doing a lot more listening than talking, and when you do speak, choose your words carefully. If the outcome still makes you angry, manage that emotion appropriately so your subsequent actions are not regrettable. When we repay hurt with hurt, we're not accomplishing anything—particularly if it turns out we are wrong. And once you've put it out there, well . . . it's out there. It cannot be taken back. You may be forgiven but the words are never forgotten.

And if it comes out in the wash that you were wrong, please admit it. There is nothing more obnoxious than a person who refuses to admit when they're wrong. Commit these three sentences to memory: "I'm sorry. I was wrong. Will you forgive me?" Repeat that one more time: "I'm sorry. I was wrong. Will you forgive me?" Very good!

DAILY DIFFERENCE-MAKER

Are you still angry about something that happened a while back? Do you feel the alleged culprit hasn't been 'punished' properly for his or her actions? Is there also some cringe-worthy moment of your own that you wish you could erase? Does it still bother you that the victim wants nothing to do with you? Today, seek peace in both situations. It may require a phone call or a handwritten note, and it will definitely require prayer for you to release them fully.

Notes

WEEK
SEVENTEEN

Yes, Let Them Eat Cake

Sometimes, we stray from our walk with the Lord. This is where Israel was, having realized just how far they'd strayed. They were full of remorse and grief, ready to rebuild what their rebellion had destroyed.

And what was God's response? "Get to work!" "You oughta be ashamed!" "That'll teach you!" Nope. None of that. God instructed them to celebrate!

Now this had to be confusing—where was God's punishment? Where was the fire and brimstone? What about the guilt and shame? ""Eat the fat"? "Drink the sweet"?" Are you kidding me?

Israel had been wallowing in sin for decades, hardened to the point there was no remorse. Finally, finally, they were convicted; finally, finally, they saw clearly their need for God; finally, finally, they understood why His ways were always best. Is that not reason enough to celebrate?

You may find yourself today in a financial hole that you created. Or perhaps you're debating whether to take bread or a fancy cake to the homeless shelter, wondering if you're sending the wrong message. Or maybe you've been involved in a sinful relationship and you're facing the reality of its destruction.

Listen, every now and then we need to dress up and light some candles. Yes, even before the hard, healing repair work commences. Feeling convicted is always reason to celebrate, because we are acknowledging our need for a Savior. And just because a person needs a loaf of bread every now and then doesn't mean they don't deserve an occasion for cake. We are to love lavishly, just as He loves us lavishly—and celebrate that He does! Cheers!

DAILY DIFFERENCE-MAKER

Take a cake, tablecloths, cloth napkins, and candles to a homeless shelter—just because. Enlist a few friends (and yourself) to dress as servers and wait on the residents.

Notes

Take a Snooze

And suddenly a great tempest arose on the sea,

so that the boat was covered with the waves.

But He was asleep. Then His disciples came to *Him*

and awoke Him, saying, "Lord, save us! We are perishing!"

But He said to them, "Why are you fearful, O you of little faith?"

Then He arose and rebuked the winds and the sea,

and there was a great calm.

–Matthew 8:24–26

Hey, guess what? The world didn't crumble while you slept/ tossed and turned last night. God was at work the whole time. In fact, your company, your household, even your church will not fall apart simply because you take a break. Someone else can take the helm in the interim, if necessary.

Folks, we are not battery-operated. If you do nothing but put your nose to the grindstone, eventually you will be ground up and useless—it's not healthy, not productive, and not necessary for you to work nonstop. If someone asks, "How will we manage without you?" well, here's a newsflash: *They will.* Things might not get handled the way you would have handled them, or it may be less organized, but the world will not grind to a screeching halt or implode simply because you aren't there. (Note to my assistants: I know you enjoy a little time away from me, and I see that slight smile on your faces when I tell you I need a little R&R. It's all good!)

The disciples were convinced their world was about to end. As the waves tossed them about, they knew they were going down, and taking Jesus with them. Now Jesus was taking a nap—yes, even Jesus slept—and the disciples woke Him, because they thought they would drown otherwise. I wonder if they thought He'd grab a bucket and start bailing water; or if He'd be shocked and panicky, like they were. I don't know if Jesus was one of those who got grumpy when woken up, but He did call them out on their lack of faith; even asleep, He was in control. He was not leaving this world by water!

Do you need a break today? When you've tried to take one before, do the panic-stricken expressions of others stop you? Don't wait for your body to rebel against fatigue—rest easy, knowing that God is at work while you sleep!

....

DAILY DIFFERENCE-MAKER
Make arrangements to sleep in tomorrow. And start planning a long weekend, whether you leave town or not.

.... Notes ....

Respect the Call

For wisdom *is* a defense *as* money *is* a defense,
but the excellence of knowledge *is that*
wisdom gives life to those who have it.
—Ecclesiastes 7:12

learned more about interior design from my mother than I did from my formal education. She's a wheeler-dealer who can spot a diamond-in-the-rough antique and have it restored and in a new home, within a week. She can walk into a room and can size up its needs within minutes (complete with mental calculations of what it will take to get it done, down to the number of yards of fabric and rolls of wallpaper!).

I can run my little formulas I learned in school and still come up short, or with too much surplus; whereas, my mother is spot-on with her mental assessments. Why? Because formulas can't see a room's idiosyncrasies, a client's taste or apprehension, or a customized way to do business. So whenever she and I have a professional disagreement, I'll say, "I'm the one with the degree," and she'll respond with, "I'm the one with forty years of experience." There's no arguing with that. My mother has had forty years and counting to accumulate this sort of professional wisdom, and I'd do well to glean as much as possible.

We can get so worked up at the way things have to be that we forget to take into account the wisdom of knowing how things really are. We dig our heels into formulas, numbers, facts, and forget the purpose and people involved. The 'hard facts' have value, but it's quirks and characteristics that make the task unique . . . when a community declines donated planters for their garden because the residents would prefer to build their own . . . when a neighborhood would prefer to hold on to older, smaller homes, instead of shoving new shotgun houses on to a lot . . . when an elderly person turns down the offer for a brand-new smart phone . . . maybe these decisions don't make sense to us, but if we have stated our case, we need to respect and trust the reasoning behind their decisions. In time, it's possible we'll understand, but for now, just respect the call that has been made.

....

DAILY DIFFERENCE-MAKER
Learn the name of someone you see often, but don't know!

.... Notes ....

Support Education

The heart of the prudent acquires knowledge,

and the ear of the wise seeks knowledge.

—Proverbs 18:15

Whether your children are in private school or public school, every school needs help. They need tutors, they need donations, they need mentors and volunteers . . . they need parents *involved*.

Sean and I both attended college thanks to the generosity of others, and it's true that some students need full scholarships while others need various expenses subsidized. Parents should be proactive and keep their ears open to needs in their schools—whether it's students, the building itself, programs, or teachers, all schools need assistance.

Which brings me to another point—we're losing excellent educators because they cannot make ends meet. Many of them spend their own money on their classrooms and help students with personal needs that cannot be provided for at home. Do not assume health insurance is provided or, if it is, that their premiums are paid for, either. Teachers need our support, too, beyond classroom needs—ask, prod, and do not let them tell you they don't need anything!

Education is a three-prong process involving the student, the teacher, and the parent. If one or more is not engaged, no one wins. Don't deny a child his or her full benefit of a good education. Whether you volunteer your time, your money, or both, make sure you are in regular contact with your child's school—a proper education is not up to them, it is up to all of us. Remember, it is easy to sit up and take notice; it's more difficult, however, to get up and take action.

DAILY DIFFERENCE-MAKER

Pay a child's application fee to take the ACT or SAT. Set up a benevolence fund for children who cannot afford class trips or supplies. Locate the child who doesn't eat lunch or whose clothes are dirty—those are glaring signs they need help.

Notes

The Right Equipment

That the man of God may be complete,

thoroughly equipped for every good work.

−2 Timothy 3:17

Do you remember a few years back, during March Madness, when Lehigh beat Duke? I would have wagered that Duke's shoe budget is more than Lehigh's entire basketball program's budget, but that particular year Lehigh delivered one of the tournament's biggest upsets.

We all have this small, inner voice that talks to us; and too often, we pay attention to its negative messages: *It's impossible; useless to try; too risky and time-consuming; pointless to attempt*, etc., etc. So we listen, even agree with it, and follow its lead.

What if Lehigh had listened to that inner voice? "Lehigh, you can't beat Duke; they are bad to the bone. They are past National Champions. You can't be serious about playing them."

If Lehigh had only done the sensible, logical thing—based on the evidence at-hand—they would have just dropped out and handed Duke the *W* on the bracket. But those of you who follow basketball know what happened instead; they'd practiced, they'd worked hard, and they decided they had just as much chance as Duke to win . . .

turns out, they were right. They believed in themselves as individual players and as a team, realized they put on our uniforms the same way as Duke, and they were just as capable.

If God has invited you to join Him in something huge, do not let the little voice intimidate you. This is an opportunity to join the Creator, the One who knows everything . . . and He wants you along. He has a task for you, and He intends to equip you for it. Because thanks to Him, we have value. We have worth and purpose. Do not discount what He has put in your heart. Do not think you aren't enough—you are, because He is.

What good work has He equipped you for today?

DAILY DIFFERENCE-MAKER

Rally some local businesses, friends, and donations to host a carnival cookout for an inner-city housing project; rent concessions, some bounce houses . . . sky's the limit. Encourage residents to schedule these events, offer to help keep them going.

Notes

**WEEK
EIGHTEEN**

86

Role Reversals

Comfort each other and edify one another,

just as you also are doing.

—1 Thessalonians 5:11

The first semester of their freshman year at Ole Miss, Michael seemed to adjust quicker than Collins. In fact, Collins was ready to pack it up she was so homesick.

Thankfully, Michael took great care of his sister during those days. When Collins developed migraines, it was Michael who took her to the doctor and got the help she needed. By second semester, we couldn't have pried Michael or Collins away from Ole Miss if we'd tried.

While Michael may have had an easier time adjusting, he was very committed to Collins's comfort; when she wanted to come home, he was going to come with her.

During high school, Collins took care of Michael and helped him adjust; now, the roles were reversed. We never know when we may be in need of help; and we never know when we're helping someone if, down the road, they may be somehow helping us. That's the beauty of loving on and helping others; it's rarely one-sided. Someone may have more resources, but if that person is in danger, their money and prestige won't help them—they will be just as dependent on someone's kindness as someone who is penniless. True need can be a great equalizer.

I like how George Bernard Shaw put it in *Pygmalion*: "The great secret, Eliza, is not having bad manners or good manners or any other particular sort of manners, but having the same manner for all human souls . . . where there are no third-class carriages, and one soul is as good as another."

Let's not discount others we've helped. When you find yourself in need of comfort and encouragement—and one day, you will—they may be exactly the ones the Holy Spirit sends to intervene.

....

DAILY DIFFERENCE-MAKER

If you witness a kindness—particularly if it's done without the person's awareness of your presence—acknowledge it with a thank-you.

.... Notes ....

Aging Parents

Honor your father and your mother, that your days may be long

upon the land which the LORD your God is giving you.

—Exodus 20:12

few years ago, my mother was intent on going to Israel; my father passed away many years prior, so I had my reservations about her traveling without him. There's a lot of walking when one tours the Holy Land, and you're doing it in hot weather. Born and raised in the South, my mother has experienced her fair share of heat and humidity—but she also has air conditioning at her disposal. When I expressed my concerns, she replied, "God knew on the day I was born the day that I would also die." Well, she kind of had me there.

I look at it this way: My mother still has the rationale to present a fair argument. She still dresses impeccably, stays involved and engaged in what's going on, and still forgets more than most of us will ever learn. I don't take for granted that my mother has made it fairly easy for me to honor her, as God commands.

What about those whose relationships are fractured by neglect, dysfunction, or emotional abuse? Or those whose parents suffered from addiction or mental illness? Or those parents whose bodies are still functioning, but their brains are failing, or vice-versa? Sometimes, they become irrational and bitter, lashing out at the ones who care the most. As difficult as it can be, it's important to remember the most positive memories you can—even if it's simply the reminder that they brought you into this world. Make every effort to ensure they have proper care—even if they are hurling accusations and criticisms at you.

None of us wants to lose our freedoms, and when your joints and muscles no longer work like they once did, it's a double-whammy. At the same time, we cannot force our parents to throw out their old magazines, take their medicines the way they're supposed to, or eat properly. Be sensitive to their aging process, and stay alert to any changing conditions. In this way, you will honor them in ways that please the Lord.

Remember, Lord willing, you will be there, too—someday.

....

DAILY DIFFERENCE-MAKER

Get in the habit of bringing your parents healthy food (already cooked or oven-ready, so there's no prep involved). Bring enough for leftovers, and ask them if there's any tidying up you can do while you're there. If they have a microwave, go ahead and clean that. Change the sheets on their bed, and wipe down the bathroom.

.... Notes ....

Each Look After Another's

Be ready in season *and* out of season.

Convince, rebuke, exhort, with all longsuffering and teaching.

. . . be watchful in all things, endure afflictions,

do the work of an evangelist, fulfill your ministry.

—2 Timothy 4:2, 5

Reed Sandridge worked at a nonprofit in our nation's capital and was laid off in 2009. Rather than be discouraged, the then-thirty-six-year-old walked the streets of Washington, D.C., giving away ten dollars to random strangers. According to Sandridge, his mother had taught him that when you're going through tough times, that's when you need to give back the most.

The world is changing at a rapid pace, and I don't know about you, but I have a difficult time keeping up. The choices seem greater, the consequences bigger, the temptations stronger, and the expectations different. One thing I have concluded, however: There will always be someone whose blind spot needs protecting.

Each one of us has a blind side, and they're not always obvious to the naked eye. In terms of football, a left tackle cannot do his job effectively if he's always looking to his own left, watching his own blind side. His job is to mind the left side of the quarterback—the quarterback's blind side. When he does his job effectively, someone else can mind the left tackle's blind side effectively; in fact, they can do it better because they have a better perspective on the vulnerabilities.

What are your unmet needs? Maybe like Reed, you need a job. Or perhaps you're more like Michael—you need a family to love, and have them love you right back. I don't know what your unmet needs are, but keep looking after someone else's blind side—someone out there is looking after yours.

....

DAILY DIFFERENCE-MAKER

Maybe you can't hand out ten-dollar bills—but you can stop and offer help to the driver on the shoulder of the road. When cooking dinner—or like me, ordering take-out—you can make a bit extra dinner for an elderly neighbor. You can provide a warm, sincere smile and friendly *hello* to someone who looks like the world has been kicking them around. You can quietly make sure the person in the wheelchair crosses a busy intersection safely, or anonymously leave cans of formula or diapers on the porch where a new baby resides. Be the angel on someone's shoulder.

.... Notes ....

Grow Up, Already

Do not be children in understanding . . .

in understanding be mature.

—1 Corinthians 14:20

My father had this quote attached to a file cabinet in his office: "I wish I was, what I was, when I wished I was, what I am now . . ."

One day I asked him to explain it. He said, "Well, when you become an adult, it means you will look back to the time you were a child and think, 'Wow, now that I am a teacher or a lawyer, I wish I were that child again and not the adult I am.'"

Was he kidding? I couldn't wait to be a successful, contributing member of society—a *real* adult. Now that I am *almost* there, I never dreamed this would be my path; this was not the plan, not on our agenda, nor did we ever imagine it; this applies to the good *and* the bad.

So how do we "be mature" in our thinking, as Paul instructs? What does your life reflect? Well, for most of us, life's path is rarely straight; it has many curves and hills and blind spots (no pun intended). But it's time to shift our perspectives and look beyond the ends of our own noses; let's transition from 'what can you do for me?' to 'what can I do for you?" The task of helping others seems very daunting to most of us, but each one of us is capable and each one of us has something to offer. So many people need a hand or kind word in these uncertain times; they just need a little extra push or polite gesture. One of the hardest decisions to make is whether to walk away or try harder—so how hard are you willing to try?

We're there, people—we have that adult strength now, the kind we dreamed about as children. Free time is extremely overrated; when you give your time and yourself, lives will be changed—including your own. So grow up, already. It's time!

....

DAILY DIFFERENCE-MAKER

Your time will be infringed upon today . . . a telemarketer desperate to stay employed, a samples clerk or cologne-sprayer at a store . . . someone is going to interrupt your day. Let them do it. Answer their questions, sample their food, wear the stinky stuff . . . smile, ask their name, ask how long they've had the gig, allow yourself to be inconvenienced. They will remember (and hopefully, imitate!) you.

.... Notes ....

The Lure of Internet Free-for-all

And whatever you do in word or deed, *do* all in the name of the
Lord Jesus, giving thanks to God the Father through Him.
—Colossians 3:17

If you can't say something nice, then don't say anything at all. How
many times did your mother tell you that growing up?

I am Southern from the tip of my head to the tip of my toe. I
believe in good manners, using china and crystal, dressing up every
day, lighting candles, sending handwritten notes, and being nice to
everyone. I believe in making every effort to be a positive force in my
community. (But in the interest of full disclosure, one of the very few
things I truly dislike is the color orange.)

Now in a community, you build each other up, help those in need,
share information, provide positive feedback, and answer questions.
So that 'being nice' part extends to the online communities . . . or
should. Yet for some reason, there are people who demonstrate very
poor etiquette online. Whether it is from provocation, inebriation, or
just plain stupidity, they think that the Internet protects their ano-
nymity and they can say and do things they would normally never do
in the light of day . . . that they will suffer no consequences or face any
repercussions.

NEWSFLASH! That is one-hundred-percent inaccurate. There are implications to everything we say and do, and every word you put on the social web is permanent. The 'delete' button really doesn't; your potential employer, future client, or new friend could see what you have posted any time down the road.

A card laid is a card played, and something on the Internet is forever. My son S.J. used to call those online trolls who talk trash "Internet gangstas." I just call them idiots. Don't ruin your character, along with everyone else's online experience; it's okay to dislike and disagree, but there's no need to be rude and nasty. Before you hit that 'send' button, let's all agree to pause and ask, *Have I used proper etiquette?* After all, what would our mothers say?

· ·

DAILY DIFFERENCE-MAKER

Now we're all guilty of putting a foot in the mouth. Think about a time you did that; if you still cringe at the thought, then it's still an issue for you. Call that person up, drop them a line, whatever you have to do, and apologize. Ask for forgiveness, even if it happened twenty years ago. You are not responsible for their response; you are only responsible for your apology.

· Notes ·

WEEK
NINETEEN

Time to Party

For You formed my inward parts;

you covered me in my mother's womb.

—Psalm 139:13

Why does August always matter to me? Well, August is the month that the good Lord brought me into this world and each year it gives me pause to stop and reflect on what I've done, where I am now, and what is down the road. I'm such an advocate of practicing random acts of kindness, community service, and social responsibility, however, that I often forget to genuinely celebrate with the people who matter the most, the ones who are always around me.

If you're one of those, "oh, birthdays are not such a big deal," rethink that—yes, they are. God brought each one of us into this world with a purpose in mind. He knew everything about us before we were even born, paying extraordinary attention to detail, since not even identical twins are exactly alike! Anyone who has a birthday has made another trip around the sun, having survived whatever they encountered along the way. Shouldn't that be reason enough to make a fuss over someone you love, even if that someone is you? Every family has different ideas about this—some have parties, some have quiet dinners, cakes, presents—but birthday celebrations are wonderful ways to create family traditions and memories. Don't miss that boat with anyone, particularly with little ones.

Make a point to acknowledge birthdays, even among acquaintances—particularly those who may not have anyone to celebrate with. It doesn't have to be anything elaborate; a simple card, phone call, or even a text lets the recipient know that they matter to you.

Birthdays are important for two reasons: Everyone has one, and everyone deserves to be celebrated. Don't neglect your own, and make every effort to acknowledge others'.

DAILY DIFFERENCE-MAKER
Do you know someone at your church or in your community who is now living in a nursing home? Or a younger child who has a multitude of siblings? Find out their birthday and bring them a bouquet of balloons on that specific day—don't wait a week or even a day, do it the day of! Since balloons are now located in the floral section at most supermarkets, they're fairly convenient to come by.

Notes

Mouth Management

Let your speech always *be* with grace, seasoned with salt,

that you may know how you ought to answer each one.

—Colossians 4:6

During the filming of *The Blind Side,* my son S.J. would occasionally inform Sandy (Bullock) that she didn't exactly deliver a particular line "how my Mom would have." And after she'd ask, he'd feed her a few lines that his sweet, tender ears heard his Mom say over the years. After this incident occurred several times on the set, someone laughingly suggested that "S.J.'s Mom" needed "mouth management." Yeah, I'm not gonna even pretend like I don't!

If we don't manage our mouths, none of our words will be headed in the appropriate direction. So break it down with me into what that means in the day-to-day stuff. We need to manage our mouths when:

- Someone gets your parking space
- You get cut off in traffic
- You have bad service at a restaurant (never, ever at a Taco Bell!)

Or, as in my case, you hear someone say an unkind thing about your child at a sporting event.

Bam! before your know it, you're irritated, frustrated, and aggravated and lose your composure! You may be the greatest person in the world—you pay your taxes on time, go to church every Sunday, and kiss your spouse good-bye every morning . . . but you let someone take that parking space you were waiting on and all that integrity flies right out the window!

Profanity is epidemic in this country, along with hateful words used to bully others. So how do we season our words with grace? Today's verse indicates that when we do so, we will know how to respond to each person. What we say can influence and affect someone or something—and when we manage our mouths inside the realm of grace, even during those times we must admonish someone, we can rest easy and have peace in our hearts.

It's important to engage your mind before you put your mouth in gear. Remember, all of our words make a difference. The question is, *What kind of difference do yours make?*

DAILY DIFFERENCE-MAKER

Someone's going to cut you off today—in traffic, in conversation, in a store. Don't seek to cut them off in response; if both sides keep cutting the other, eventually there will be nothing left to salvage. Instead, be gentle in your response. Let them in your lane, let them finish their point, let them wait on another customer even though you were next.

Notes

Haves and Have-nots

We then who are strong ought to bear with the scruples of the weak, and not to please ourselves. Let each of us please *his* neighbor for *his* good, leading to edification.

–Romans 15:1–2

There is a fine line between the *haves* and the *have-nots*. You'd be surprised at how much the haves actually have in common with the have-nots. From a Christian perspective, we really can't explain why some can spend as much on a winter coat as others make in a year; wealth is acquired in a variety of ways, but not always to the most intelligent, hardest-working, or most-deserving people. Why some are born into families that have insurance, use libraries, have cars, or even clean water to drink while others never have any of these things? Only God knows.

Everyone doesn't have the opportunity to be the quarterback, point guard, or pitcher, but that doesn't make the rest of the team any less important. Each member plays a role that makes the team stronger and each position has responsibility. The wingback will have a different perspective than the center; the catcher sees what the pitcher can't.

In the same way, no one person can do everything, but everyone can do something. We all have something to contribute, and at some point, each one of us will need some sort of assistance. Today, you may find yourself uncertain of where you fall; let me assure you that right now, some sees you as a have and another as a have not. So even if you feel like your life isn't completely together, someone out there needs what you have. Maybe it's a few extra bucks, maybe it's your time, maybe it's your encouragement, or message of hope—but someone out there needs what you have. And in fact, that same person may have what you have not—there's only one way to find out. What will you offer them today?

DAILY DIFFERENCE-MAKER

Who in your community doesn't drive? Maybe they're elderly, have physical limitations, or perhaps they've even lost their license for some reason. Offer to take them grocery shopping, or to do their shopping for them; offer them a ride to the polls on Election Day, or drive them to church.

Notes

Plant More "Trees"

And let us consider one another in order to stir up love and
good works, not forsaking the assembling of ourselves
together, as *is* the manner of some, but exhorting *one another*,
and so much the more as you see the Day approaching.

—Hebrews 10:24–25

After *The Blind Side* released, it was so interesting and comical to me how many "acquaintances" asked me about the scene where Sandra Bullock was having lunch at the country club with a group of ladies. They would strike up an awkward conversation with me and, in an attempt to be nonchalant, ask, "That wasn't me in that scene, was it?"

I got such a kick out of that, and still do. Those individuals are not friends, or at least they do not fit my description of a friend. So if you are someone who asked me that question, you are not on my Christmas card list!!

True friends are rare, and speaking from personal experience, they leave their imprints on you and become a part of you. There are people in my life that, from the moment I laid eyes on them, I loved them and appreciated them for being special. Just knowing that they are out there somewhere doing good puts a smile on my face. I know they are being a great source of joy and putting other's needs ahead of their own. They prioritize their own agendas by putting them last, as opposed to first.

There are too many broken, lonely, desperate people who need you as a friend. They don't have to be your best friend, but they need to know someone in this world cares. A kind word to someone can spark a friendship. Then, lead by example; you are the one they will look to for direction. When you plant that small seed and nurture it, the seed becomes a huge, healthy tree. In return, trees provide shade, exchange carbon dioxide/oxygen that's vital to humans . . . some trees provide fruit and homes for other living creatures. Given this analogy, you never know where your budding friendship may take you, take them, or take your community—so let's plant more "trees"!

DAILY DIFFERENCE-MAKER

Seek out one person in your ever-widening circle who is either much younger or much older—someone you might not know very well, but for whom you feel great affection. Offer to buy them dessert and coffee (or, if you're a baker, invite them over for dessert and coffee).

Notes

Never Too Old

Whoever receives one little child like this

in My name receives Me.

—Matthew 18:5

You're never too old to be adopted.

Sean and I spoke in Washington D.C. recently, and a twenty-three-year-old handsome young man named Derrick, beaming, introduced us to his parents—he'd been adopted just the week before.

When I could stomach looking at Michael's child services records, the words that hit me in the face were the notes written by counselors: "difficult," "hard to place," "runner" (meaning, of course, he was a flight risk). Just in case you missed the movie, here's a newsflash: Michael Oher, just like thousands of others, was extremely adoptable! (Oh, and he's not adoptable now—you can't have him. He's mine, all mine. And maybe a little bit Sean's, too.)

Michael Oher, much like Steve Jobs, Dave Thomas, Faith Hill, and names you might not even know are contributing members of society because someone took a chance on them. The adoption picture is painted so incorrectly; it doesn't have to be a week-old baby or toddler (and admittedly, I was fine skipping the whole toilet-training phase!).

If our Father is willing to adopt us into His family at *any* age, why are we so reluctant to follow His example? Look, we have a flawed system. Thousands and thousands of kids age out of childcare each year, and most are victims of abuse, neglect, or abandonment. They didn't ask for any of it, nor could they do anything about being on the receiving end of a world of grief, loneliness, and always longing to wake up each day and thinking today might be the day someone tells you that you have worth and are loved.

And on the other side of this: you're never too old to adopt, either. Did you know that one out of four kids is adopted by a person over the age of fifty-five? We as adults are responsible for *all* children. These kids deserve a better shot than what we are giving them. Over one-hundred thousand kids just like Michael, just like Derrick, are still waiting . . . still hopeful . . . folks, that's a number we can cure.

....

DAILY DIFFERENCE-MAKER
Get involved in the life of a child—an orphan, a mentoring program, scouting, after-school club. Let them know they matter to you. Someone needs your personal support and encouragement—not just a signed donation check.

.... *Notes* ....

WEEK
TWENTY

96

keep at It

But those who wait on the LORD shall renew *their* strength;

they shall mount up with wings like eagles,

they shall run and not be weary, they shall walk and not faint.

–Isaiah 40:31

I read somewhere that when we get to the place that has all the answers, the questions won't really matter anymore. Sometimes, we are rejected and there's simply no plausible explanation as to why.

Nobody likes rejection—for a job, for a loan, for a date, for a party invitation. It's human nature to want acceptance and approval, and when it doesn't happen, it can kill our self-esteem.

Yet at some point, we will all experience some form of rejection. And just because the ball doesn't bounce in your favor doesn't mean you're no good, and certainly shouldn't keep you from trying again— because it's possible that next attempt it might bounce back to you!

One of Satan's greatest tricks is to prey on our vulnerabilities; and yes, he knows what they are. We can listen to his lies—we're worthless, why bother, we're stupid to think we can do whatever it is we're attempting—or we can trust in the Almighty who has our best interests, always, in mind. We are valuable because the Lord gave us value; we are precious, each one of us, because He treasures us!

If you're facing some sort of rejection today, let me assure you that there will be other opportunities. The Lord has not forgotten you—He may be rescuing you from a disaster, or it may not be time yet—and I can promise you that He has something better in mind. I can tell you from personal experience that the rejections I've experienced turned out to be the biggest blessings of my life. Don't believe in luck—believe in Jesus. Trust in His timing and keep at it. We have no guarantees, of course—unless you don't try at all; then, you'll already know the outcome.

DAILY DIFFERENCE-MAKER
Speak to someone today who continues to reject your friendship. Ask them how they're doing, what's going on with them, and do not attach any further agenda beyond simply being nice. If they are disinterested, simply smile and tell them to have a great day.

Notes

Evil Days

See then that you walk circumspectly, not as fools but as wise,

redeeming the time, because the days are evil.

—Ephesians 5:15–16

We labor over the preservation of fine furniture and take such precautions to protect expensive jewelry; but do we do the same for life's precious moments?

Now I'm not talking about worry—worry is a useless activity that prevents us from doing much of anything constructive. I'm talking about mindfulness of moments that need to be etched in our minds and hearts: the expression on your child's face when they discover something new; the joy of a friend seeing the ocean for the first time; or the gratitude expressed by an elderly parent when you provided them a meal. Maybe it's the delightful squeals of orphans whose names you don't know, but for whom you purchased Christmas gifts. Perhaps it's the tender lick you received rescuing an abandoned dog or cat, or watching a robin feeding her young babies. Or savoring the dish your elderly neighbor finally showed you how to make. Or the family vacation where you and your spouse changed a tire in the rain.

If we don't take time to stop and capture these moments, we forget them. We need to observe, listen, smell, taste, and touch because they are fleeting; the only way we can grasp them is by making them into cherished memories.

Paul calls the days "evil"—so much out there vies for our attention and too often, we're focusing on the wrong things. We get stuck in worry or chase after things that won't matter next month, next year, or ever. So where are you walking these days? Are you on a wise path? Will your steps make a difference? Will they be the sorts of steps you want to cherish and remember, or will they fill you with regret?

....

DAILY DIFFERENCE-MAKER

Go buy a slew of pizzas at the five-dollar pizza store; maybe ten or fifteen, all varieties. Gather up some paper plates and napkins. Drive around town, offering a slice to anyone who appears hungry or homeless. If you usually see a number of homeless children in your town, be sure to purchase several plain-cheese pizzas, since young children often prefer it. Remember how the pizza smells, the reactions you receive, what you observe, and the joy in your heart.

.... Notes ....

Same Blame, Different Day

Now let no man contend, or rebuke another;

for your people *are* like those who contend with the priest.

—Hosea 4:4

Seems like in situation after situation, when we mess up we tend to blame it on everyone but the person with whom the blame really lies: ourselves.

Many times life can be very difficult, and it is definitely not always filled with cupcakes and cartwheels. Inevitably we all stumble across pain and suffering in our lives, whether it is through the economy, our health, our relationships, or simple human stupidity, but no one is immune from suffering.

In Hosea's day, God's people were so far removed, even murder was taken casually. Verses two and three identify swearing, deception, murder, stealing, and adultery, and violence as commonplace . . . even the ecological environment was suffering, as the land, animals, birds, and fish were dying off. Because everyone—including the "priests" who were not God-ordained—was to blame, there was no need to finger-point. All of the Israelites were guilty, and so are all of us.

On the flipside, however, we make the choice to allow ourselves to be miserable and remain unforgiving, or to release it. Find a healthy way to grieve what you've lost—a job, a friend, your pride—but don't wallow and linger in it. Consider your role and responsibility in what occurred, and accept your portion . . . then give it to the Lord, Who can dispose of it permanently.

If you want to change, if you want to improve (and we all have room for improvement!), in order to change your community, then get on your knees and ask the Lord for help. Remember, your life won't get better by chance . . . only by change. Misery is easy; change is not. Guess which one yields the better reward?

DAILY DIFFERENCE-MAKER
Buy some men's undergarments in various sizes and take them to a homeless shelter.

Notes

On Mothering

Strength and honor *are* her clothing;

she shall rejoice in time to come.

—Proverbs 31:25

We don't have to limit "mother" or "mothering" to the person who carried you around for nine months. That really was nothing more than a mode of transportation. A mother is one who raises you, teaches you, feeds you, inspires you, lets you know when you are being difficult, challenges you to be better, soft-pedals your wrong-doings and loves you unconditionally. Do you see 'giving birth' anywhere on that list? The birthing process is the easy part—it's the day after that the real challenges begin!

As humans we have a need to pigeon-hole everything and wrap it up in a defined package. There is not enough wrapping paper in the entire world to wrap up the who, how, why, or when you are called upon to be a mother. Every time we encourage someone, we give him or her a shot of our mothering. Keeping someone balanced in this difficult world of ours or helping someone reclaim joy or renewing someone's perspective when that person thought that was not possible . . . *that* is mothering.

Ladies, whether you hope for a child, long for a child, or have been told having a child may not be possible, or maybe your children are grown, there are children all around us who need your wisdom. You may be the only one who teaches them how to balance a checkbook, how to apply for a library card, about the joy of reading, the importance of understanding current events, the value of a good education, or any number of life lessons that no one else has been willing to share. Demonstrate your strength, your confidence, your dignity so that they will not fear the future—regardless of whether you gave birth to none or nineteen, you have an opportunity to be a mother.

....

DAILY DIFFERENCE-MAKER

Take a random Saturday every so often to set up your own complimentary lemonade stand with cookies. If you live in an apartment building, post flyers up the night before and either arrange with management to set it up in the lobby, clubhouse, or another common area. Parents and children will get to know you if they don't already, and will that know you are a safe, go-to person if they need someone.

.... Notes ....

Face-to-Face

The hearing ear and the seeing eye,

the LORD has made them both.

—Proverbs 20:12

Eighty-percent of Americans identify themselves as Christians. Even though over half are thought to be steeple dropouts, they continue to identify themselves with the faith into which they were baptized.

So while this country is decidedly blended spiritually, the dominant flavor of that blend remains Christian. So how does a Christian base of Americans let child abuse, foster care, homelessness, and any other injustice that we see on the news each day continue to go on without getting involved? The Bible is very clear where children are concerned; Jesus issued a stern rebuke to the disciplines when they tried to shoo the children away (Luke 18:15–16); Christ Himself was a child on the run at one time (Matthew 2:13–14), because their mentally ill king was slaughtering baby boys.

As a fellow Christian, are you content to sit in church each Sunday, comfortably receiving its benefits, while out there is a child who needs you to actually *give*? "I give to my church," you protest. "I teach children's Sunday School. I do the shoebox thing at Christmas." And those are beautiful ways to give back—but in each case, how many face-to-face encounters are you having with a needy child? I get it, it's ugly—the welts and scars, the malnourishment, the neglect, the smell, the lack of warm clothing . . . you don't want to live that way, but what about the five-year-old who knows no other life? No child ever asked to live in a situation like that.

When we connect face-to-face with these issues, we can no longer look away. At that point, it gets personal and it gets real. Sometimes, the parents work very hard and simply cannot make ends meet; sometimes, there are addictions that take priority; sometimes, the child is simply unwanted and they hope he/she will just go away.

Don't let another one remain invisible—they need you to see them.

....

DAILY DIFFERENCE-MAKER
Find a playground or empty lot in a low-income neighborhood or within a housing project. Bring cupcakes and offer them to children; introduce yourself, ask them how they're doing. The next time—and there will be a next time—add little gift bags of soap, shampoo, and small toys to your offering. Keep going back, and try to befriend some of the parents and long-term residents who may be able to tell you more about their neighbors and needs.

.... Notes ....

WEEK
TWENTY
-ONE

Fixing the Cracks

And God will wipe away every tear from their eyes;

there shall be no more death, nor sorrow, nor crying.

There shall be no more pain,

for the former things have passed away."

—Revelation 21:4

What's motivating you in this broken world? The persuasive dollar? A child who counts on you? A girlfriend you're pursuing? The Super Bowl (hey, you never know!)? Is it the promise of heaven? The fear of hell?

Take a look around you. Turn on the news. You don't have to look very far to see pain in our world, or pain in your own life. The Bible is very upfront that there will be a series of events in our lives that are painful. Some of these are based on bad choices while others are just out of our control, and we will never know this side of heaven why they were inflicted upon us.

But look at what eternity holds: He dries every tear. Cancer and other awful diseases no longer exist. We will not hurt any longer, physically, emotionally, or spiritually because it's gone. Wouldn't it be awesome to catch a glimpse of this right now?

There's a story about a nun who asks God how He intended to take away disease and poverty and God says, "I created you." Have you ever watched a hungry child—one who hasn't eaten a full meal in days—gobble up a balanced meal? Or a senior citizen gifted with a much-needed motorized wheelchair? Or a teenager who finally 'gets' algebra? Their expressions—of satisfaction, joy, relief, hope—are what motivates me. When I see a change and get to be a part of it—I am motivated to do more. The Lord has entrusted us to mend some of the broken spots in this world—get to it!

....

DAILY DIFFERENCE-MAKER
Are you a couponer? Start a couponing group in a low-income neighborhood using donated coupons. It teaches math skills, how to save money, and families can put saved money into healthier food and possibly even the bank!

.... Notes ....

Are Y'all Dating, or Just Friends?

Flee also youthful lusts; but pursue righteousness, faith, love,

peace with those who call on the Lord out of a pure heart.

—2 Timothy 2:22

Dating sure has gotten blurry in recent years. People will jaw on and on about this shift, and I don't intend to get into any of that—so you're free to keep on speculating on where, when, or how the shift occurred. But what I can't wrap my mind around is why this coy game has become accepted as a normal way to do the dating business. When did someone's personal dating habits become primetime entertainment for the rest of us? How are you supposed to find the right person, the right companion, without privately stating the intentions?

This business of "oh, we're just talking," or "yeah, we hang out"— what the heck is that? And even worse, this idea of collecting hearts— that is, leading someone on—is cowardly and narcissistic. Are you really that insecure? Get a grip. And for those of you who are caught in this quagmire of confusion: Don't let someone hold your emotions captive or keep you from finding the right person.

I'm not suggesting anyone rush into anything; there are some people who are so in love with the idea of love, they don't have a very good screening process in place, and wind up with regrets. But if you're spending time with someone alone, you need to be clear and upfront about your intentions. Do not leave room for any ambiguity—each person needs to know exactly where they stand with the other.

There's this saying: "Hate the game, not the player." While I'm not advocating any sort of hate, I would steer clear of anyone who thinks dating, particularly among adults, is a game. If you are not treating your dates with respect, if you think it's fun to keep them guessing, please stop dating until you grow up.

....

DAILY DIFFERENCE-MAKER

If you have hurt someone in the past with your ambiguity, find a way to apologize to that person because you did some emotional damage. Hopefully, they worked through it—but until you apologize, you are still responsible. If you are in an ambiguous relationship, end it; if you're the one doing the hurting, you'll only make it worse sticking around and if you're the one being hurt, you're not being fair to yourself.

.... Notes ....

When Life Makes No Sense

Yea, though I walk through the valley of the shadow of death,

I will fear no evil; for You *are* with me;

Your rod and Your staff, they comfort me.

—Psalm 23:4

f you're around me much, you'll often hear me say, "Don't take everything personally," and "Life's not fair." Sometimes, the two phrases intermingle into the same situation.

* When you go on a third interview and still don't get the job.
* When a friend suddenly has nothing to do with you.
* When your wife leaves you.
* When you're diagnosed with an illness.
* When you finally pay off a loan . . . and your home suddenly needs a new roof.
* When you're laid off from your job, and your lazy coworker isn't.
* When your home is broken into, and what little you have is taken.

"Okay, Leigh Anne," you're probably saying. "My wife walks out on me, and you're saying it's not personal? My possessions are stolen, and I'm just to shrug and say, 'oh well, life's not fair'?"

I'm not saying some of these things don't have a personal effect on us—but unless you have harmed or wronged the other person, there is usually something going on with the other person, not you. If you care, reach out and let them know. If you lose your job due to downsizing, you cannot control the company's budget; bashing and threats will not earn your job back for you. If you are robbed, by all means call the police; but thank God your life was spared.

There are just some things in life we will never be able to explain; sometimes, these things hurt or cause us strife without justifiable cause. These are symptoms of a fallen world, yes, but we're the ones enduring them. As believers, we have a choice: to find comfort in Him or insulate ourselves into bitterness. So before you cry to the heavens, "why me?" ask yourself: *Why not me?* Don't you know the One who can truly give you comfort and peace? The One who will cradle you in His arms? The One who is just and loving?

DAILY DIFFERENCE-MAKER
Put your life's metaphor into practical terms: Go purchase bandages and healing ointments of all kinds and donate them to a daycare or free clinic. No matter how much you're hurting today, someone is hurting far worse. Do not let the Enemy get even one finger grasped around your heart today.

Notes

One Father, One Family

There is one God, the Father, of whom *are* all things,

and we for Him; and one Lord Jesus Christ,

through whom *are* all things, and through whom we *live*.

—1 Corinthians 8:6

One of the most beautiful mysteries of the Bible is The Trinity. Today's verse gives us a bit more insight into the relationship within the Trinity and our relationships with the Trinity and each other. Creation is born *of* the Father, and eternal life is possible *through* the Son. Wisdom and knowledge comes *from* the Holy Spirit.

Prepositions aside, I want to focus on this first part: All creation is breathed into existence by God. Yes, even snakes. Yes, even rats. Human beings are all members of the same family because God created each one of us. This statement sounds so peaceful and harmonious until we realize that this also includes humans who commit crimes and harm others. God loves them, too, and offers the same gift of eternal life through the Son . . . but not everyone accepts this gift. Though He is grieved, God still loves them as part of His creation.

If we only had to love the ones who look like us, live like us, agree with us, and show us love, it would be so easy, wouldn't it? And we wouldn't recognize what godly love is, because the 'love' wouldn't challenge and stretch us beyond what we already know.

But if God created us all, then we need to love those who are different. Don't hate what you don't understand—with love comes understanding.

Jesus took it even further and said we are also to love our enemies (Matthew 5:44). Now 'enemy' is very subjective—but according to Jesus, it doesn't matter. We are to love them.

There is someone you've snubbed or even lashed out at who needs to see Jesus through you. They may not know Jesus, and you can't force them to know Jesus—but they need to experience His love. So much of our prejudices are fear-based; remember, perfect love drives out all fear (1 John 4:18).

DAILY DIFFERENCE-MAKER

Today's the day to get real—what stereotypes or prejudices have you bought into? Maybe you have friends who find a way to 'justify' these prejudices, but they are counter to Jesus' instruction. Find a program, lecture, workshop, or house of worship that will educate you on this group—commit to making at least one new friend from this group who might be willing to help you combat your fear.

Notes

Lose the Agenda

Take heed that you do not do your
charitable deeds before men, to be seen by them.
Otherwise you have no reward from your Father in heaven.

—Matthew 6:1

After many years of attending church, our family realized that spontaneous giving was a powerful tool created by God. As our faith increased, God showed us that we had the choice to be generous and make ourselves available for His use by serving others.

This also meant getting our hearts right, which meant releasing any agendas that we may have been harboring. No recognition to seek, no awards to lobby for, no demographic formulas to base our giving upon. If we were the only ones helping and no one noticed (or thought it was important), we had to arrive at a point where we were okay with that. It sounds silly until you make a conscious effort to truly release all that junk.

When it comes to giving, agendas aren't necessary; in fact, they can be detrimental. Nearly ninety percent of American households give to charity—but it averages out to be less than two percent of our income*. What are we waiting for?

If you're waiting to save Africa, impress your boss, receive a big check, ease your conscience, look good at church, earn airline miles, or whatever, then you're missing the point. Ask God to help you get your heart right so your eyes can see the needs right there in front of you . . . the ones He purposefully places in your path. As you work with Him, your field of vision widens and you'll see more and more opportunities to give.

You have a choice—and someone's life could hang in the balance. Lose the agenda and gain some eyes that truly see!

....

DAILY DIFFERENCE-MAKER
Arrange with your local Little League or child's soccer league to pay anonymously for a needy child to play—uniform, shoes, socks, photos, the whole bit.

....Notes..

*Source: National Philanthropic Trust

WEEK
TWENTY
-TWO

Get Dirty

For as the body without the spirit is dead,

so faith without works is dead also.

—James 2:26

My family tells me I have "Truth Tourette's Syndrome," meaning I pretty much say what's on my mind. I'm all about getting things done, so I think lip service is actually pretty cheap. Anybody can get up and talk, quote a few scriptures, and appear holier-than-thou. But in the end, doesn't it matter how you walk and live your days?

Growing up, we had a distrust of false piety. I credit my maternal grandmother with instilling this discernment. Every evening she read her Bible, had a devotional, but never sermonized. She simply lived according to the gospel, and often remarked, "Don't talk about it, sister. Live it." My mother acquired the same habit, reminding me that God was most important, above anything and everything. She and my father faithfully tithed, no matter how lean things were. "Things are not important—people are," she'd remark. They also gave beyond the ten percent that went to the church. While there wasn't much to spare, they helped various organizations.

The Tuohys were no different, which is why Sean and I shared a common vision: We believe that both of us were born to try and make a difference. We came from a long line of givers and we learned that giving required action—not just talk. Neither of us is afraid or above getting our hands dirty, if it means planting some seeds in someone's mind, heart, and future.

How about you? Do you 'delegate' the action portion of your charitable talk, or do you get down to it? What sort of message are you sending to those around you about giving? This whole notion of being an 'idea person, not a details person' is hogwash. It's time to get down, get dirty, and into the details.

....

DAILY DIFFERENCE-MAKER

As a reminder of what all-talk-and-no-action is, take a load of compost to a community garden in your city. The good news is, your compost will actually help grow something useful. While you're there, ask if you can help weed.

.... Notes ....

Learn a New Language

He who answers a matter before he hears *it*,

it *is* folly and shame to him.

—Proverbs 18:13

Observation and listening are so much more important than talking; they provide the sort of input that filters the information we're taking in. My husband Sean is an exceptional listener; he knows the language of the needy almost fluently, because he often spoke it as a kid.

For example, he'd observed Michael in the school cafeteria and knew that he was hungry; when he quizzed Michael about it later, Michael responded, "I ate in the cafeteria."

"I didn't ask *where* you ate, I asked *what* you ate," Sean responded, because he knew better and had been listening. He knew how Michael would skirt around the hunger issue, just like Sean did at his age. And no one's pride ever satisfied a hunger pain.

I can't say for certain that I would have picked up on Michael's skirting, but I'm not sure very many of us would. But Sean knew, based on observation and his own personal experience.

Your life has given you a 'language' and signals you can look for to determine if a person could use your help. If you've suffered at the hands of abuse, for example, you might be able to spot someone who is in a similar situation—but it's time all of us learned a few languages, even those that are 'foreign' to us. We need to learn how to listen carefully and read between the lines.

Each day, we encounter people who need help and do not know how to cry out for it—people whose gaps we can fill. And if we're not paying them proper attention, we will miss the signals. We may need to buy them an occasional meal, take out their garbage, offer them a ride, or even adopt them into our homes, but we can't go about gap-filling if we don't know where the gaps are.

The more we observe, the more familiar faces and behaviors we'll see. And from there, can engage. Learn to listen, watch for clues that something might be bubbling just beneath the surface. And by all means, don't give up; we should all be on alert.

....

DAILY DIFFERENCE-MAKER

Meet all of your neighbors—in your building, on your block, on your floor, in your wing, or on your quad. Learn the languages that they speak, listen for signs that they may need your help. Introduce those in need to those who can offer support.

.... Notes ....

Storing Up Treasure

For where your treasure is, there your heart will be also.

—Matthew 6:21

What do we treasure? What are our treasures? Some of the most valuable treasures don't cost anything—yet only the best eyes and hearts can spot them.

Here are some things to consider: If we diverted our political campaign contributions to house the homeless, we might just solve that problem (not to mention we wouldn't have to watch grown people acting like first graders on a playground!). And if we diverted the amount of money spent betting on the Super Bowl—last time I checked, that number was 90 million just through Las Vegas alone—every child in this country might go to bed with a full belly and our elderly might live out their final years in comfort and with dignity.

Sadly, we all know that is not going to be the reality. We simply don't treasure the right treasures. Our faith is lacking, and our selfishness makes a futile effort to make up the difference. We aren't willing to let go, and take the Lord at His word—He promises to provide, yet we think it's all up to us. We don't see how fragile our man-made security blankets truly are, and we remain blind to how snug and safe God's is.

Maybe you think your contribution wouldn't move the needle. If I'm reading the 2013 Census data correctly, if each adult between the ages of eighteen and sixty-five donated one dollar, it would be about $120 million that could go toward the homeless, hungry children, and senior citizens. One dollar. You can do the math for two- and three-dollar donations.

Invest in someone who is hungry or neglected. No, it's not as shiny as a new car, renovated home, or elaborate vacation—its brilliance cannot be seen as much by the human eye as by the human heart. But it is priceless!

....

DAILY DIFFERENCE-MAKER

Do you know someone who has a sick loved one in the hospital? Make arrangements to stock their fridge and, if you know them well enough, keep their home cleaned. Arrange vases of fragrant flowers throughout the home as a welcoming touch.

.... Notes ....

Do Love

Let all *that* you *do* be done with love.

−1 Corinthians 16:14

ove is a verb. Love is proactive, alive, flexible, and works best when applied to others.

I love how Paul puts it to the Corinthians: What we do, do with love. He doesn't say do with sacrifice, do so we can tell others, do out of obligation or peer pressure . . . nope, we are to be motivated by love to love. What we do should be the way we love.

This is not about seeing the latest fashion trend or newest this or that and calling it love at first sight. Nor is this puppy love. Those are momentary infatuations that will pass; don't be fooled.

So when we hand a stranger a twenty-dollar bill, or buy a bicycle for a needy child—we love on that stranger, we love on that child. We do not sacrifice for that stranger or feel obligated to that child. We don't do this so we get the "Hands Out Twenties and Bicycles" award and our picture in the paper. When we spend time with an elderly person or help them with light cleaning and taking them to doctor appointments—these are manifestations of love. This is the way Christ showed us to love—not just some warm, fuzzy fond feelings we keep locked away.

I'll say it again: *Love is a verb.* How will you love today?

....

DAILY DIFFERENCE-MAKER

Get a stack of five-dollar bills and stand near the entrance of a drive-through (preferably Taco Bell or KFC, but you probably already knew that would be my preference!). Hand 'em out, knowing you are feeding several someones today.

.... Notes ....

Lost in Complacency

I will search Jerusalem with lamps,

and punish the men who are settled in complacency.

—Zephaniah 1:12

That person you just walked past? That's the person who could change your life. Every once in a while, you have to stop and turn around to find out about that person.

Sean and I were not out roaming the countryside looking for a third child; a miracle simply hit us in the face and we didn't run from it. We can tell you from up-close, personal experience that the child or person you're not looking for may be the most surprising blessing in the world. I love how God works that way!

Had we not turned around, had we not persisted, I believe Michael would have still made it—but the four Tuohys might have suffered an unknown loss! Now if you know how crazy life in the Tuohy family can be, *complacency* probably isn't the first word to come to mind; but complacency can take many different forms. And that's why it is a dangerous thing.

When we settle into complacency, we're not gaining any sort of security—we are rotting away. We are content with life as usual, to each his own, I'll go my way and you go yours . . . all the while we're growing bad roots, dulling our minds, and boarding up our hearts. We lose our sight and our worlds become distorted. It's a slow decay, and we are sadly unaware that our inactivity is the source of our suffering. To paraphrase Jesus, we are losing our saltiness.

Don't miss out on the treasure of connecting with others—it is not the easier path, but it is the most blessed. When we connect with another person through activity or need, everyone's edges are filed down to a precision fit; we learn, we grow, we bond. Someone is counting on us, and we discover we count on them, too. Turn around—that person may be the one your life has been missing. When we invite someone to come along with us, we may have to move slower—and many times it's three steps forward, two steps back—but I can assure you, the journey is much, much richer.

DAILY DIFFERENCE-MAKER

Is there a familiar face you pass each day? Do they work in the neighborhood, or live nearby? Find out why your paths intersect each day. Here's a script to nudge you: "Man, I see you just about every day, I'm [insert your name here]. How are you?"

Notes

**WEEK
TWENTY
-THREE**

Strong and Courageous

Be strong and of good courage,

for to this people you shall divide as an inheritance the land . . .

Only be strong and very courageous,

that you may observe to do according to all the law . . .

Have I not commanded you? Be strong and of good courage;

do not be afraid, nor be dismayed,

for the LORD your God *is* with you wherever you go.

—Joshua 1: 6–7, 9

How often do we truly consider our freedom? When we're on a holiday picnic, or watching fireworks? When we're enjoying time with friends and family? How about when we're in a heated debate with someone who has a different opinion? Or when we walk through our church doors, or openly take issue with any of our leaders? How many of us have signed a petition in our lifetime, when we feel our elected officials aren't listening or it's required in order to make some sort of change? Some countries would imprison or put to death anyone who even appeared to be involved in such activities; here in the U.S., we take this sort of freedom for granted.

It is a blessing and a privilege to be a U.S. citizen, but we don't come by these freedoms "just because." We have a great and powerful force called the United States military that ensures our freedom is protected. Our cookouts, our worship, our churches, our disagreements, our political debates . . . all are protected by the U.S. armed forces, who uphold our laws and freedoms. They are strong, they are courageous, they are bad to the bone! (Please tell me you remember in your prayers!)

And we are often told to thank them for their service—and no doubt, a simple thank-you is appreciated—but how do we show our thanks? Are we caring for families affected by a deployment? Are we sending care packages or letters to those deployed? What happens to their pets that are left behind? Do we send a card or note to a grieving military family, or greet the ones who return home with a hero's welcome? And finally, are we keeping their legacies alive by teaching our children to respect their awesome responsibility and service?

Let's honor and remember, friends. We have our freedom—let's show our gratitude to the ones responsible: the strong and courageous members of our armed forces. And God bless the U.S.A.!

DAILY DIFFERENCE-MAKER

Did you know that military families stationed overseas can use expired coupons at their base's PX? Hold a coupon drive specifically for that purpose.

Notes

Fingers and Tongues

Death and life *are* in the power of the tongue,

and those who love it will eat its fruit.

—Proverbs 18:21

Okay, the rumors are true: I'm a woman who doesn't mince words. I am a straight-shooter and I've been known to take people down a peg or two if I see an injustice. But let's get straight on this: There is a difference between truth and disrespect, constructive criticism and taking someone's dignity.

Now before you say, "well, *duh*, Leigh Anne!" just hang in here with me. Do we consider our typing fingers—the ones that type our e-mails and social-media posts—an extension of our tongues? Do we hit the 'like' button on crazy, undocumented political comments; post photos and make comments on the physical appearance of an unassuming bystander; or rant on someone whom *you've* deemed suspect before getting all the facts? (Of course I'd be lying if I told you I had a clean online slate; our family has often been the subject of social media posts that make me want to do some bodily harm to the poster. Ninety-nine percent of the time, I'll choose the high road but if you happen to catch any of my one-percent posts, let me just apologize in advance. Sometimes, it's in reference to the color orange.)

Legal consequences of your online life aside, Proverbs 18 is pretty clear that we don't go out there half-cocked. Your posts can be polite, supportive, and not-so destructive. Use basic common sense, think first before you type, and always take the high road when someone else wants to tear someone down. When we're honorable, accountable, and responsible, people will respect us whether they agree with us or not.

Contrary to what some think, there is accountability on the Internet, and inflammatory language, tasteless comments, and inappropriate photographs bear a certain kind of fruit. The detrimental effect goes both ways . . . not only on the ones being talked about, but the ones doing the talking. The sooner in life we learn this, the better our world will be—so have a conversation with your kids about this while you're having it with yourself.

Character and integrity are so important; both are difficult to acquire and so, so easy to lose. So share your thoughts and opinions, listen to those that are different than yours, but always preserve your dignity. Based on the actions of your fingers and tongue, what fruit will you be eating today?

DAILY DIFFERENCE-MAKER

Choose five individuals from your list of friends, followers, or e-mail address book, and message them personally—either recounting one positive quality each one possesses or simply thanking them. And if you see a social media post that totally inappropriate, report that user—get involved.

Notes

Pay Attention

As for me and my house, we will serve the LORD.

—Joshua 24:15

Our faith, our family, and our work are all a balancing act. With the complex issues that life tosses us each day, we need to remember we are bound by our choices. Let's strive to make good ones, starting within our own homes.

It's essential that we make those who are right under our noses first priority before we help those on the other side of town. Trust me, if we're not paying attention, you can be sure that someone else will . . . and not in ways we may like. Hold your spouse's hand, take your kids out for ice cream, send your best friend a note in the mail (yes, I'm talking about the U.S. Postal Service—go old school!). When the family eats together—which means you need to plan some meals where the family actually eats together—make everyone put down their cell phones. Talk about quality family time—that'll get everyone's attention! Keep an eye open for those little magic moments to nurture your nearest and dearest, moments that keep communication open and honest—because when life starts placing all its demands on us, those moments are what will carry us through the stresses. We're also sharing very valuable lessons about God, grace, and gratitude. Remember, when we serve them, we serve Him.

....

DAILY DIFFERENCE-MAKER

Plan a surprise meal for your family that includes at least one favorite dish for each family member. If you're a cook, feel free to make each and every dish from scratch; if you're not, then take the time/trouble to hit as many take-out places necessary to ensure each family member has a favorite dish to comprise the meal. Then, for goodness sake, put down the cell phones, unplug the gadgets, and enjoy the meal—later, watch a movie together!

.... Notes ....

Smile—Your Integrity's Showing

Better *is* the poor who walks in his integrity than
one who is perverse in his lips, and is a fool. . . . What is desired
in a man is kindness, and a poor man is better than a liar.

–Proverbs 19:1, 22

What is "integrity"? When I hear the word, I think of actions, values, principles, expectations, and outcomes. We've grown too accustomed to short-term relationships that have attached agendas, situations where we (or others) don't want to get involved unless we know "what's in it for me?"

Now integrity factors into all sorts of things, from business practices to relationships to how/if we pay our taxes, but one of the biggest indicators of integrity are the words we speak each day.

How we give and receive hype, for lack of a better word, is very telling about our integrity. When we gravitate toward anything that might give us an edge, get us ahead—career-wise, socially, community recognition, or yes, even at church—we have a tendency to flatter others, accept flattery, and abridge our own versions of "the truth" in order to make it so. One that you hear most often starts out, "I can't say whether it's true, but I heard . . ." Well, if you can't speak into its truth, why speak of it at all?

Take another look at that verse at the top of the page—this behavior is perverse in God's eyes. This is lying—the opposite of truth. This does not demonstrate the integrity of God's children, nor does it honor the Father. It is better to do without and keep your integrity intact than to grovel at this level in order to run with a perceived 'A crowd'. Oh, we can make so much better use of our time!

Our words are a projection of our integrity—and they will reveal your character. We live in a world of half-truths, rumors, flattery, and negative speech—as Christians, this gives us a wide berth to be different, stand out, speak with distinction . . . yes, we have many options to show our integrity, but only one choice: to stand with the popular opinion or assumption, or to stand with God. Which one has eternal benefit?

DAILY DIFFERENCE-MAKER

Call someone who has recently been the subject of a group's verbal assault and invite them to lunch. You don't have to become their best friend, but let them know they have a friend in you.

Notes

Defender of the Defenseless

You shall do no injustice in judgment.

–Leviticus 19:15 NASB

When it comes to doing the right thing, we have all blown it at some point . . . in elementary school, when you could have taken up for your friend who was being bullied; in high school, when you didn't stop the rumors about the introverted new student; perhaps in college, when someone else wrote your paper for a class; or at work, when you looked the other way from the sexual harassment in the office. Maybe you exchanged some inappropriate emails that might affect your marriage, or didn't embrace a friend you encountered while running with a different crowd . . . the list could go and on and on.

Dr. Martin Luther King once said, "The ultimate measure of a man is not where he stands in moments of comfort and convenience, but where he stands at times of challenge and controversy." If we are going to affect change, then we have to be accountable for those past actions—or lack thereof—and take a hard look at ourselves in the mirror. We could have done something; we should have done something; and we didn't do anything. And folks, I am guilty of all of the above.

Silence is perceived as condoning, lack of action makes injustice permissible. We must stop being heroes-in-waiting and get on with making a few waves. I'm not talking about ruffling a few feathers— I'm talking about plucking the whole chicken. Each day a child goes hungry, a teen is raped, a woman is victimized, a man dies from exposure, and a senior is robbed is another day that someone else could have stepped in and changed the story . . . and created a different outcome of hope and security. It's time to be the voice for the voiceless. Defender of the defenseless. If we don't pick up the mantle on behalf of others now, who will be left to defend us? And that should keep you up at night!

DAILY DIFFERENCE-MAKER

Look back over the list of infractions in the first paragraph—do any of those strike a memory? If you were indifferent in a situation, even if it happened thirty years ago, make an effort to find the victim and apologize. Don't worry about what they'll think, even if you haven't spoken to them since that day! If the list above instead strikes a nerve because you were the one being bullied or harassed, please give that situation to the Lord and ask the Holy Spirit to help you forgive.

Notes

WEEK TWENTY -FOUR

It's Not Quittin' Time

Let us not grow weary while doing good,

for in due season we shall reap if we do not lose heart.

–Galatians 6:9

T.S. Eliot said, "It's never too late to be what you might have been." I think, we were made for something far greater than watching cable news in the recliner and collecting shells on the beach. Ms. Sue is one of the greatest examples I know of someone who changed courses, intent on changing lives. She'd retired after thirty-plus years of teaching; when we called her looking for a tutor for Michael, she could have said, "No, I've done my hitch. I want to catch up on some television." Thankfully, she didn't; she reinvented her day and started changing lives.

Maybe life hasn't worked out for you the way you thought it would. Maybe your career was littered with mishaps. Maybe your marriage ended in failure. Maybe you never finished college, or worked in the field you wanted, or . . . maybe you think your life isn't the example for others to follow. Okay, then—three points I need to make here:

1. **You're reading this.** This means you are here for at least one more day to make a difference. Every day we are alive and

aware, we are victorious. Now go take a victory lap! Raise your arms if you're really feeling brave.

2. **If you want someone to learn from your mistakes and missteps, then you are going to have to share these regrets with someone who needs to hear them.** You know the George Santayana quote, "Those who cannot remember the past are condemned to repeat it"? Well, it goes double for those who have never been *taught* the past.

3. **Sometimes, we have to create what we want to be a part of.**

We have significant work ahead of us; use your time in a meaningful manner as opposed to a menial manner. Don't think that you can't make a difference—even all the broken dreams, hurts, heartaches, shames, drudgeries, and pains have value . . . God makes sure of that, so the only way you can really fail is to quit!

....

DAILY DIFFERENCE-MAKER
Take a roll of quarters to a bus station, or anywhere that has people waiting. Leave coins in all the vending machines.

.... Notes ....

Get Infected

Yes, brother, let me have joy from you in the Lord;

refresh my heart in the Lord. Having confidence in your obedience,

I write to you, knowing that you will do even more than I say.

—Philemon 1:20–21

Kindness is contagious, and our communities desperately need to be infected—it's the one epidemic I pray we all come down with.

A caring community only happens when we *care about* and *care for* our communities. A situation or a life-gone-bad is easier to endure when there is support—even if it's just a friendly face, or someone there to hold a hand. A caring community doesn't just leave it up to the teachers, pastors, counselors, coaches, or family member to handle while everyone else stays safely in their bubbles. Nor do we leave it to chance, to work itself out. No way! A caring community takes care, gives second chances, is sensitive, empathetic, and optimistic.

Philemon's servant Onesimus ran away because he'd stolen from his master. He fled to Rome, located Paul, and came to faith in Christ—just as Philemon had done back in Colossia. The entire book of Philemon is actually a letter penned by Paul to his friend, begging mercy on behalf of Onesimus. Paul had two requests: that

Philemon not only forgive Onesimus, but accept him and care for him as a brother—as part of his community. The story not only illustrates heartfelt restoration and new relationship among all of us in Christ, but how that care and concern renews in each one of us when we obey in kindness. Paul could have used his position and forced Philemon's hand—but that would risk instilling pride in Paul, more fear in Onesimus, and resentment in Philemon. By Philemon taking the initiative to do the right thing, *all three men would benefit*.

Any of us can jump into action to help an elderly couple find their car, or a mother struggling to put her stroller in the trunk. There's so much opportunity to invest in our communities without spending a dime, and let the teachers, counselors, coaches, etc., have enough respite to return to what they are trained to do. Let's infect our communities with kindness and spread it as thickly as possible—no hazmat suits allowed! By the way, I would not even look good in one of those.

....

DAILY DIFFERENCE-MAKER
Is there a neighborhood or place where kids hang out and look bored? Start up a baseball, football, or soccer game. You don't have to have fancy equipment, just the right ball and some imagination.

....Notes...

Greater and Still More Excellent

But earnestly desire the best gifts.

And yet I show you a more excellent way.

—1 Corinthians 12:31

What are the "greater gifts" Paul's talking about? He spends most of this chapter discerning spiritual gifts and why one isn't superior to another, but then he throws this zinger in at the very end!

In the preceding passage, Paul mentions that the Spirit has distributed gifts to each one of us, and in our diversity, we are unified by using them for Christ. The "greater gifts," then, are the ones used to serve the body of Christ.

So we are given a gift that we can, in turn, give to others. One that's less valuable if we keep it to ourselves. Oh, I like where this is headed . . . we could start a revolution by engaging in some non-traditional gift-giving options!

Many of us can keep our gifts local; that is, we can find plenty of ways to use them in our own communities. We can give gifts of service—those gifts require nothing but your time. Volunteer to baby-sit for a young couple to allow them to have a date night; offer to clean at a homeless shelter; spread mulch on a school playground. And if your own children can't remember what they received last Christmas or for their last birthday, then they definitely need to be a part of this!

As a family, you could serve a meal at the local soup kitchen, volunteer to walk the dogs at the animal shelter, pick an item off your child's own wish list, purchase, and deliver it to The Boys and Girls Club to give to a child their age. I can tell you from personal observation that S.J. serving as a Big Brother in the Big Brother/Big Sister program has had as much of a positive effect on him as it has the child he mentors. Kids are never too young to be active members of a caring community.

And finally, what does Paul mean by "a still more excellent way"? Well, the next chapter is 1 Corinthians 13—the "love" chapter, quoted most often at wedding ceremonies. Paul wanted to make sure the Corinthians understood the definition of love, because the more excellent way to serve Christ by serving others with our gifts would be to serve with love. Do not serve for show; do not serve to tell others how you serve; serve because you love your fellow human beings and because Christ gave you the power to love and to care.

....

DAILY DIFFERENCE-MAKER

Gather a group of your friends and in lieu of exchanging birthday or Christmas gifts among each other, sponsor a family in need or load up a few angels from an angel tree.

.... Notes ....

Personal Fouls

My brethren, count it all joy when you fall into various trials,

knowing that the testing of your faith produces patience.

—James 1:2–3

We all commit personal fouls each day. Unfortunately, there is no ref to blow the whistle and charge us with a penalty for bad behavior because things didn't go our way. Nor will we hear an official call a penalty or throw a flag for unsportsmanlike conduct because someone wronged us.

As adults, we need to take to heart that *everything* we do counts! The importance of doing the right thing does not vary from circumstance to circumstance. Most of us know what would be the right thing to do, but are we doing it? Even when life is not fair?

I recall a very important NFL game where certain well-known player's equally well-known wife was caught making a very unsportsmanlike comment as she was leaving the game. Yes, she knew what would have been the right thing to say, but she was upset about the game's outcome and chose, instead, to say something inappropriate. This gorgeous and seemingly 'perfect' woman wasn't perfect when faced with something that wasn't favorable.

Listen up: the call's not always going to go your way; at some point, you will be grabbed by the facemask of life's unexpected demands. Situations will arise that are beyond your control, you will experience major crises, and bad news will, at some point, knock the wind out of you. Even so, you still have options. A victory dance is still a real possibility. This is just a mere delay of game!

Respond graciously, then huddle up and regroup. Reevaluate the situation and recommit to yourself, your plan, and your goals.

It's very difficult to differentiate who we really are when things are going our way; it's how you handle life when it is unfair that reveals your heart and your character. Handle these moments in a godly manner: Respect rules, refuse to engage in mean-spirited, disrespectful behavior, sacrifice personal gain for the benefit of others, and hold others accountable for only what they are responsible for. Remember, every play counts—including the ones made off the field.

....

DAILY DIFFERENCE-MAKER

Have you been holding a grudge, or blaming someone for something that was out of their control? Have you been blaming yourself for things you couldn't control? Take a moment today to unpack all of it—make apologies with whomever necessary, and leave every bit of it behind. It's easier to travel light.

.... *Notes* ....

Vanishing Vapor

Whereas you do not know what *will happen* tomorrow.
For what *is* your life? It is even a vapor that appears for a little
time and then vanishes away. Instead you *ought* to say,
"If the Lord wills, we shall live and do this or that."

—James 4:14–15

Let me be clear: Do not *ever* regret aging. It is a privilege so many people never get to experience! We need to adjust our attitude, our way of thinking about getting old, and what we can do or want to do with the new opportunities available to us.

As James writes, we have no idea what tomorrow may bring. It's sobering to think that we are a vapor that *poof*! can be snuffed out. We get cocky, think our tomorrows are guaranteed . . . and forget that only One truly knows for sure.

So no matter what your age, if you're still here then you are to make every moment matter "as the Lord wills." Age is not discriminatory when it comes to tight budgets, illness, loss, hunger, or any other travesty that comes in this journey we call life. Just because you have reached a certain age doesn't mean you can't use the Internet, have a smart phone, download music, practice yoga, try online dating, or take a continuing education class.

For some reason—again, perhaps because we are cocky and forget Who is responsible for each of us seeing another day—we are one of the few cultures that do not truly value those who were here before us and who paved our way. This is hogwash, and we are doomed to repeat past mistakes if we don't take into account those who are trying to help us learn from them. Seniors have vast amounts of knowledge; they have history in their heads. They have been there, done that, and have lived to tell about it . . . but they won't be around forever to tell us. At the same time, their minds need the exercise, so give them the opportunity to work them out! I am approaching this "Senior" title very quickly and all I can say is here I come, because I'm going to be the one that people look at and say "That lady is too old to be_____" you fill in the blank. I'm going to refuse to let my age hold me back. Does that surprise you?!?

DAILY DIFFERENCE-MAKER

Do you know someone who has lived in your town for over sixty years? Take them on a tour of your town; ask them questions, let them recount memories, and visit old haunts (or whatever is standing where the old haunts used to be).

Notes

WEEK
TWENTY
-FIVE

Give It Away

Let us not grow weary while doing good,

for in due season we shall reap if we do not lose heart.

—Galatians 6:9

Did you know that National Volunteer Week falls every year in April? It's a call for each one of us to drop our routines and take a week to help someone or some cause.

So much of our life is pre-planned and scripted; we are creatures of habit. We are list-makers, planners, taskmasters, goal-setters . . . and we certainly get angry over insignificant things, become passionately involved with stuff that doesn't really matter, and invest ourselves in pursuits that are truly self-serving. Yet an act as simple as volunteering could provide assistance and would serve so many.

When's the last time your to-do list included the following: *Stamp out hunger; eliminate illiteracy; provide electricity for all; love those whom no one loves; don't litter; march on the courthouse steps for injustice;* etc. We should be angry that families live in cars, intelligent teenagers don't have the opportunity to attend college, students don't have adequate school supplies, and some Americans still don't have quality health care. These are big problems, huge injustices that cannot be left for the next person to hopefully tackle; de-clutter from your personal dramas and start tackling!

There is a difference between kicking up dust and slinging mud; when you sling mud, you lose ground! So be aggressive, but do it in the right manner. And we don't have time to wait for one week out of the year to roll around before we do something—let's start today. Start asking the tougher questions and have the guts to make a difference! If it is something that will change lives or did change lives . . . please share it with me!

....

DAILY DIFFERENCE-MAKER

Gather up a load of inner-city children and take them to a farm near your town. Let them see gardens, cows, horses, chickens, pigs . . . perhaps they'll see hay being harvested or grain being picked. Most importantly, they get to see life lived in a completely different way.

.... Notes ....

122

No Drama Distractions

Beloved, do not avenge yourselves, but *rather* give place to wrath;

for it is written, "Vengeance *is* Mine, I will repay," says the Lord.

–Romans 12:19

We have to learn to let go and move in a forward direction. Forgiving someone will not take away the memory or really the pain but without it, things tend to get worse. We become bitter and callous.

So the next time your coworker throws you under the bus or you get blamed for something you didn't do . . . remember, only you are responsible for your actions. One of the Enemy's greatest tricks is to preoccupy our minds and eventually, our hearts with worldly drama—when we are distracted, we have no time for God's work.

Instead, let's use our energy to fight the real injustices of the world. Let's be loud and proud for those who are being bullied and treated poorly. Let's try to find a home for every foster child and a bed for every baby. Don't let your emotions cause you to do foolish things. Use those emotions for the good—make changes that are so badly needed in our society. It's time to kick up some dust—if we use our common enthusiasm collectively, the pettiness melts into some faraway horizon and real difficulties disappear, and obstacles vanish.

When our only response to petty dramas is to kill them with kindness (and forgiveness), we're headed in the right direction to focus on the stuff that really matters . . . leaving the Enemy so, so frustrated. And guess what? We win!

....

DAILY DIFFERENCE-MAKER

Give away an umbrella to someone today, particularly if it's raining.

·· Notes ··

Don't Discount Others

Bondservants, be obedient to those who are your masters according to the flesh, with fear and trembling, in sincerity of heart, as to Christ; not with eyeservice, as men-pleasers, but as bondservants of Christ, doing the will of God from the heart, with goodwill doing service, as to the Lord, and not to men, knowing that whatever good anyone does, he will receive the same from the Lord . . . And you, masters, do the same things to them, giving up threatening, knowing that your own Master also is in heaven, and there is no partiality with Him.

—Ephesians 6:5–9

Do you know the names of the people who come to your house each week and collect your trash? Or the name of the postal worker who delivers your mail each day? For most of us, it is the same people week in and week out, so if your answer to that question is you have no idea of their names, shame on you. (Goes double if you live where curbside-recycling pickup is also available.)

Today's verse is sound advice for business owners, employees, service providers, and any human on the planet. When we serve, we are to serve each person as though they were Christ because ultimately, that is how He would serve. And if we are in the position of business owner, customer, or the recipient of a service, such as trash collection, we are to honor those individuals by treating them with respect and dignity. In both cases, the Bible is clear: we are not to do this just when we are being observed. We are to do this full-time, all the time. In other words, we don't turn a friendly smile to those who are picking up our unwanteds and discardeds and then turn up our noses in our hearts or if we run into them elsewhere.

When we associate a name and a face with a service or an issue, it can be a game-changer. Look, I'm not telling you that you are going to have to become the Welcome Wagon, but we all need to figure this out—not one of us is "better" than another; we are all sinners, we are all created by God. Always act with integrity and be polite to everyone.

....

DAILY DIFFERENCE-MAKER
Pick a random day and leave a tightly sealed treat for your trash collection team with a note, wishing them a great day. More than likely, they will return a note of thanks with their names, and *bingo*! You're making new friends.

.... Notes ....

Gold Stars and Check Marks Won't Work

For by grace you have been saved through faith,

and that not of yourselves; it is the gift of God, not of works,

lest anyone should boast.

–Ephesians 2:8–9

Here's my translation of the above: Keeping all the rules don't getcha into heaven.

Now my platform and mission has been to turn around and care for those you've passed over, passed by, and disregarded. We should all practice kindness, be respectful, help the less unfortunate, not judge, not bear false witness, not covet thy neighbor's . . . wait a minute. Yes, you see where I'm going with this.

Many of us have a list of rules, some of them rooted in the Ten Commandments while others have more root in cultural norms, like attend church every Sunday or pretend to listen to the preacher and either cut a check or serve a meal once a year to the homeless. We hit our marks, do good, and think that's Christianity. Newflash! *You're wrong.*

If you've even so much as attempted to read the book of Leviticus—it's a tough one, I know—surely it dawns on you how desperate we are for a Savior. We can't hit the marks to save ourselves, and we won't know the marks we've missed without knowing the rules first. But when we realize we can't earn our salvation, He is our only hope. It starts with a relationship with Jesus Christ. Now I'm not talking about a statement that you believe God exists, or even that Jesus walked the earth—even Satan himself can attest to that—I'm talking about the most intimate relationship you've ever known, that has a love so pure and so joyful we cannot fathom its entirety. A tender Savior who cradles us in His arms, listens through our tears, and comforts in ways we cannot explain.

John 14:15 says, "If you love Me, keep My commandments." I'm not saying it's going to be easy, but it is so worth it. Because we love, we obey. We've had it backwards all this time.

....

DAILY DIFFERENCE-MAKER

Is there an inner-city or low-income neighborhood where many children walk to school, crossing some streets without a crossing guard? Help the guards and the parents by helping them cross some of these streets safely.

.... Notes ....

They're Just People, Like the Rest of Us

Woe to those who draw iniquity with cords of vanity,

and sin as if with a cart rope . . . Woe to those who call evil good,

and good evil; who put darkness for light, and light for darkness;

who put bitter for sweet, and sweet for bitter! Woe to *those who*

are wise in their own eyes, and prudent in their own sight!

—Isaiah 5:18, 20–21

You've heard the tongue-in-cheek expression, "Do as I say not as I do." Honestly, it's good advice to give . . . to ourselves. Sometimes, I receive social-media messages from people saying they want to be just like me, or they admire me; it's flattering, and they mean well, but it scares me. Trust me, I'm a big mess! We have become a nation that worships any form of celebrity. Too often, someone famous turns our heads, and we immediately adopt their views because we've allowed our admiration to seep into the spiritual pipeline that should be reserved for God only. How many athletes, politicians, actors, and even ministers have had their images completely ruined amid some sort of scandal? Why are we following ordinary human beings who are known for extraordinary things, when our perfect Creator has power over all of them?

Human beings will fail; the first two who ever inhabited our earth put that in motion. And the Bible encourages us to spend time with fellow believers for encouragement—so this is not a plea for us to stop admiring certain people or seeking wise, godly counsel from others. But when we put too much stock in another person—whether they are known internationally or they are a personal, local hero—at some point, they will fail us. And then our 'god' has failed us.

Just because someone has won numerous Academy Awards, puts on the best concert, is the most vocal member of Congress, or holds the record for three-pointers doesn't mean they know everything. And just because someone you've long admired has pulled you into their inner circle doesn't mean they know everything, either. Keep God's pipeline free from the debris, noise, or sludge of others who compete for your time—He has given you His word and His Spirit to help you filter all that stuff out.

....

DAILY DIFFERENCE-MAKER

Comfort someone today who's been burned by another person's "flame." Help them build their self-confidence by pointing out the things you sincerely admire about them—their kindness, their cooking skills, their sense of adventure, their woodworking skills—we all have God-given special talents and gifts that no callous opinion or off-hand remark can take away.

.... Notes ....

WEEK
TWENTY
-SIX

When It Seems Hopeless

We are hard-pressed on every side, yet not crushed;

we are perplexed, but not in despair; persecuted,

but not forsaken; struck down, but not destroyed—

always carrying about in the body the dying of the Lord Jesus,

that the life of Jesus also may be manifested in our body.

–2 Corinthians 4:8–10

What are you struggling with today? Is it something in your own life, or someone else's? Is it an idea that would resolve many issues, yet you can't seem to get traction? Is it a financial setback, illness, a strained relationship, or all of the above?

The attacks and circumstances seem to come out of nowhere, like darts being hurled straight into your heart. You may be convinced God isn't listening, so you turn up the volume, crying for help.

To paraphrase Paul's words, we are not crushed. We have not been forsaken. We are not destroyed. As long as we have Jesus in our hearts and minds, we have hope. I get it: this doesn't pay your light bill. My words do not cure your ailing parents nor repair your broken relationship. But He can—and whatever He chooses to do, you can trust it is for your best interest. He is taking you somewhere deeper . . . and you will live to tell about it. Look, I'm not all-seeing, all-knowing (but don't tell my three kids that, since I have them convinced I am!); I don't know where, when, or how He will make His presence known but I do know the teacher is always quiet during the test. Stay faithful—He knows and He cares.

Remember, when life knocks you down, you're in a perfect position to pray. His vision for us is often hard for us to see; make your struggle purposeful, stay obedient, and continue to release it to His care.

....

DAILY DIFFERENCE-MAKER

Someone out there needs to hear your struggle and you need to start telling it, even if the ending isn't fully formed from your vantage point (trust me, He knows even when we don't!). Share it with someone unexpected today; let others see your vulnerability.

.... Notes ....

It Doesn't Make the World Go 'Round

Now godliness with contentment is great gain.

For we brought nothing into *this* world, *and it is* certain

we can carry nothing out. . . . But those who desire to be rich

fall into temptation and a snare, and *into* many foolish and

harmful lusts which drown men in destruction and perdition.

–1 Timothy 6:6–7, 9

Life would be so much easier with money, right? Wrong! In fact, when you gain material wealth, your troubles are just beginning. You suddenly have a million new best friends who could use a little help; distant 'relatives' from faraway lands embrace you; seedy investors want you to bankroll their incredible business opportunities ('incredible' being the operative word, since they lack credibility!). Every so often, we hear about lottery winners who lost their entire fortune due to leeches and bad spending. Even our family was petitioned once by another family, wanting us to send them on a cruise because they'd never been on one (you can't make this stuff up!). We get all sorts of crazy requests, constantly. No, life is not easier with an abundance of material wealth.

In fact, you aren't really wealthy until you have something money can't buy. Your health; a loving family; real friends; fresh air; a bird's song; a walk in the woods to view the little miracles that occur in God's creation. Or a heartfelt hug and tears of gratitude from someone you've just helped. Those beautiful treasures are not for sale—and can get overlooked if you're obsessed with money.

Let's live lives that value people over profit. Let's do all the good we can, to as many as we can, as often we you can! Let's not let the things we want make us lose sight of the things we have. Be grateful for each day the Lord gives you to do something wonderful for someone and take Him up on the offer to do so—after all, the smallest act of kindness is worth more than the grandest intention.

DAILY DIFFERENCE-MAKER

Insert bills of different denominations into some balloons, along with pieces of paper containing uplifting messages or Bible verses. Release them to symbolize your own release from the love of money, and to trust the bills will fall into hands that need it more.

Notes

Prove Me Wrong Today—Please!

He who has a generous eye will be blessed,

for he gives of his bread to the poor.

—Proverbs 22:9

I don't cook. There, I said it. I am a Southern woman who does not cook. Let me be clear—I *can* cook, I just don't like to. I know I have a sisterhood out there of non-cooks, so don't judge. (Non-cookers, unite!)

S.J. loves to tell the story about a program our local grocer started where—for every fifty dollars you spent—the store would give four dollars to the school or charity of your choice. In one year, the Tuohys racked up a whopping seven-dollar donation, pretty much based on our Diet Coke® and Gatorade® consumption. And it's true, our lovely home pretty much has a galley kitchen that's barely touched. Initially, I didn't want a kitchen at all, but Sean insisted we have something that resembled a kitchen. So a small hallway became our kitchen—strictly for resale purposes!

Now my fridge has all the food accessories: sauces, condiments, seasonings, drinks, all ready to go should someone actually bring in some food. You know, so I'll be prepared for some home-cooking that was cooked in someone else's home. But the Tuohys live this way by choice—I can go pick up food any time I want, as can any member of my family.

Nearly fifty million Americans live in food-insecure households; almost sixteen million of those are children. The circumstances vary, but the bottom line is that nearly *sixteen percent* of our nation does not have access to good food*. They cannot hop in the car to go purchase because maybe they don't have a car or cannot drive; they cannot ask someone to pick up food, because they cannot afford to pay for it. There are many other reasons, of course, but certainly no excuses as to why the wealthiest nation in the world has hungry people. Hunger affects your mental and physical health, which impacts a person's ability to learn and grow. Think about that when you see the person standing there with a sign, or a child that is peeking in someone's garbage can. How will you stop hunger today? Make my statistic inaccurate—at least take it from fifty million to 49,999,999, please—and thank you!

DAILY DIFFERENCE-MAKER
Commit to feeding one person who is not a member of your family each week. Invite them to dinner or hand them a burrito out your car window—just keep that person from going hungry.

Notes

*Source: FeedingAmerica.org

Complementary, Not Complimentary

Put on the whole armor of God,

that you may be able to stand against the wiles of the devil.

—Ephesians 6:11

There's no question that Sean has a greater influence on me than I probably do on him. When we were younger, we came at things from the opposite perspective; whereas, I'm going to tell you what's wrong with something, Sean will tell you what's right with it. Over the years, he has tempered my judgments (believe it or not!) and helped me learn how to think before I speak. Mind you, this is over thirty-three years of work, and still a work in progress!

Sean has always seen value in others, and underscored we cannot judge a person's worth based on their appearance. One of my favorite sayings of his is, "Everybody starts on the same page and we're all going to end on the same page." On the basketball court, you'd see a competitive, cocky player but off the court was a humble, caring, considerate man with a keen intelligence.

When we bicker, he'll often say, "I'm not going to win. So if I can get to tie, I'll take it and call that a victory." He has a way of making me seem in charge, even during those times I'm not. (He gets a forty-nine percent vote, and he exercises it each day!)

If you desire growth, complementary relationships are much more important than complimentary relationships. We need people in our lives who are decidedly different; in appearance, in faith, in approach, in perspective . . . they have something to teach us, and we have something to offer them. Folks, if your social circle doesn't include someone who is decidedly different, then shame on you. If, instead, you're insulating yourself with complimentary relationships, you're narrowing your mind and shrinking your world.

While our approaches were decidedly different in the early years, we both had one very important value in common: to make a difference in the world. And God is always in charge. Always. Do not fear those who are different—put on the armor of God and carry on!

....

DAILY DIFFERENCE-MAKER
Smile at everyone who doesn't look like you or sound like you . . . in fact, just smile at everyone!

.... Notes ....

Level the Playing (and Cheering) Field

The righteous considers the cause of the poor,

but the wicked does not understand *such* knowledge.

–Proverbs 29:7

'm not sure if this has clicked as you've read, so I'll just put it bluntly: We are a sports-loving family. I know that doesn't shock you. Many years ago, my daughter Collins drew the line at cricket and bowling, but we'll watch just about any sort of match there is to watch at any level—Little League, junior varsity, high school, college, professional. We're not picky in that respect, I guess.

But for many kids, attending their school and league games is a luxury; many of them cannot afford to be fans. Five dollars or whatever the cost of admission is just not possible when it could go toward a can of beans or a bag of rice. I know, I know, I spend a lot of time talking about feeding the hungry and clothing the needy, fulfilling basic needs . . . but when I talk about providing "opportunity," school events are a great example of how we can close the gap—these events are part of the education process, and as a result, there's a certain percentage of students not receiving the full benefit of their education. Yes, we need to be mindful to feed, clothe, and shelter those in need—but is that all? Is there more we can do to level the field?

What opportunity could you provide a student today? Think about that . . . a ticket, transportation, your time . . . don't miss the opportunity! You may never know what results from your involvement, but one thing is certain: If you do nothing, there will be no results.

....

DAILY DIFFERENCE-MAKER

Check the athletic schedule of a low-income neighborhood who could use some fan support. Buy a bunch of tickets and hand them out to random students—not just the ones with the good grades or perfect class attendance. The only requirement needs to be that they will attend and cheer for their school. If the game is away, check into the price of renting a van or gassing up a school bus—enlist other parents to help if the cost is too much. Ice down the sports drinks (heck, even purchase the sports drinks!), make some snacks, and let these kids know they are valuable and their futures matter!

.... Notes ....

In Deed, Indeed

My little children, let us not love in word or in tongue,

but in deed and in truth.

—1 John 3:18

How many Mondays, New Year's Days, first of the months, etc., have you woken up and determined that is the day you start fresh? No more past behaviors or bad habits . . . you're getting on a right path, a good mind-set, a healthier perspective. And by the time your feet hit the floor, you're already back in your old routine.

Well, I'm not going to reveal five steps to healthier living or have you add blueberries to you daily food pyramid. Nor am I going to tell you to drink more water, eat less red meat, walk faster, or sleep more (however, all those are excellent recommendations; I should try them myself).

What I am going to ask you to do is choose. Choices are what define us as individuals. We are such a "woulda-coulda-shoulda" culture; we have these things we're thinking about doing, need to do, going to do . . . and then we don't. In football, you have two options—either get in the game, or stand on the sidelines. Life is the same way, and the choice is ours to make.

Look at what John writes: let's not love with words or talk, but love with our deeds and truth. To put it bluntly, enough with the lip-service about what we're "thinking about doing"—get on with it! Make an impact! Be the one to help build up the community! Be the one to create positive memories! Make an impact beyond ourselves and our own personal agendas—the sort of positive impact that will be felt for generations. As S.J. likes to say, "it's time to put some time into the gym. Become a gym rat!"

....

DAILY DIFFERENCE-MAKER

Take children (from a low-income neighborhood or a low-performing school) on a career tour. Arrange in advance to bring a group of interested children to visit places like a veterinarian's office, an accounting firm, a television station, a hair salon, a newsroom, a science lab, a fire hall, an artist's studio, etc. Each student must bring at least three questions to ask.

.... Notes ....

Invest Wisely and Often

I *am* my beloved's, and my beloved *is* mine.

—Song of Solomon 6:3

Red hearts, flowers, mushy cards, champagne, chocolates . . . lovers in love scramble around like a rat in a maze trying to decide where to eat, how much to spend, what to buy and even what to wear when February 14th rolls around. This special day is as much about the doing, as it is the getting.

And yes, it *is* about the romance and the roses, or whatever your romantic equivalent to roses happens to be. The idea is to strengthen the bond and trust between two people; so many times the romance fades after months of dating or the honeymoon. Too often, we miss that part after the head and heart have made their decision.

Friends, that decision is only the beginning; we can't just mark the love box off the list as "done," and move on to the next item, thinking the relationship will flourish on its own. NEWSFLASH: That ain't happening!

So you may wonder what happened to the chemistry, but are *you* putting in the effort? Are you investing your emotions? Are you making sure that significant other knows he or she is worth working through the disappointments, flaws, and bad times?

Love needs nourishment, and everyone wants to be loved. We have an entire generation of kids who need to see what real love looks like—they need to see what commitment, trust, honor, and forever looks like. God has blessed you with a companion, someone who can walk this journey alongside you. When you look at this person, do you get that? Your chemistry may not be lost as much as it is buried under family obligations, work responsibilities, country club committees, tennis matches, and shopping excursions . . . when reality sets in, it's not quite as smooth sailing. If real, abiding, encouraging, selfless love was easy, we wouldn't cherish it quite so much. Remember, relationships and marriage are investments, not impulse buys; the February 14th cards and chocolates won't be quite as valuable if you haven't been investing a bit each day in the interim.

DAILY DIFFERENCE-MAKER

Let your spouse sleep in next Saturday; bring him/her a cup of coffee just as they are rousing, but before they get out of bed. Let your children see you serving your husband or wife with these small kindnesses; let them see you flirt with each other.

Notes

ST. PATRICK'S DAY

Ordinary People Can Change Lives

Now therefore, thus shall you say to My servant David,

"Thus says the LORD of hosts:

'I took you from the sheepfold, from following the sheep,

to be ruler over My people, over Israel.'"

—2 Samuel 7:8

Sean Albro Tuohy is the man I sleep with every night. Well, most nights. Oh, get your mind out of the gutter—he's my one and only.

Before Sean's family entered my life, I don't even think I really knew anything about—nor did I care about—St. Patrick's Day (Sean has deep Irish roots, so that changed in short order). It's actually a beautiful story about how God uses ordinary people to accomplish extraordinary things. Saint Patrick was a real-deal person who lived in the fifth century. Brought to Ireland as a slave at age sixteen, he was credited with bringing Christianity to the Irish people. Just think, he was an average teenager, held captive—and eventually, a household name that is celebrated globally. Let's not miss the most important point, however; the impact he made was *eternal* and continues to be, even hundreds of years after his death. Isn't it amazing how God plucks people out of ordinary lives and equips them to do extraordinary things?

We see evidence of God making use of others, in the Bible and in our present day—yet we remain trapped, afraid of failure, negative feedback, and humiliation. Look, you do not have to be the mayor, or the head coach, or CEO, or any big cheese to be used by God— you just have to be you, yielding to His will.

All the money in the world cannot buy manners, morals, or integrity—and those attributes are what will change this world. Ordinary, everyday, typical, normal people are the ones who can make a difference and their lives are the ones that are being used to move the needle. We make tacos for a living! Come on! Can it get any simpler than that? Meat, cheese and a shell! Today, let's stop worrying about the critics; let's stop holding back. It won't be easy, and it's not necessarily going to be comfortable—but you're the only you in existence. Don't wait for someone to ask you for help—be bold and have some backbone. Just like St. Patrick, the story of your life might just be the story to change someone else's life.

DAILY DIFFERENCE-MAKER

Make a list of 'ordinary' persons who made an extraordinary impact on you. Write, email, call, even text—let them know they made a difference, and how their legacy will be passed down through you.

Notes

EASTER

Forgive, as We've Been Forgiven

Who Himself bore our sins in His own body on the tree,

that we, having died to sins, might live for righteousness—

by whose stripes you were healed.

–1 Peter 2:24

A shiny new pair of shoes, a new Easter outfit, hiding colorful eggs, the big furry white bunny, a basket of candy, the Resurrection . . . what is your first thought of Easter?

Well, for starters, Easter is a Christian holiday. I understand other faiths celebrate Christmas and Easter with many of the exterior trimmings, but for Christians, these holidays are not rooted in superstition or ancient custom; with Easter in particular, Christ's resurrection offers us the greatest hope ever known. Now along those same lines, let me be clear—regardless of your church creed, denomination, whether you have a robed choir, whether you sprinkle or dip—without Christ, Christianity would be just another one of those man-made, dead religions.

Easter is a beautiful reminder of forgiveness, mercy, and grace . . . and we should take time to pause and consider if we're following Christ's example. There is so much hurt and sadness infecting our world, and forgiving others opens the door to many possibilities. It is such a difficult thing to do; admittedly, I can be the worst at it, but it is a powerful thing when you truly forgive. It brings about unconditional love, real understanding, renewed trust, stronger relationships, and the kind of hope that heals.

Are you grateful that He bore the sin you committed earlier today? What about the one yesterday? What about the one last year? He bore every single one of your sins that day He hung on the cross. He bore mine, too. All of the ugly, horrible, shameful, embarrassing acts we have committed. Thanks to Jesus, we can go to the Father for forgiveness. We can go in anticipation that we will be showered with love and grace, and we can heal.

This is what has been extended to us—surely we can extend the same to others?

DAILY DIFFERENCE-MAKER

Forgiveness is more about you than it is the person who needs forgiveness. Today, quietly forgive someone who hasn't asked for it nor deserves it—remember, neither do we, yet Christ made it possible. You've not held that person hostage like you think you have; your own heart has been imprisoned all this time. Release the situation and your heart. Be free.

Notes

Using our Freedom to Make a Positive Change

For everyone to whom much is given, from him

much will be required;

and to whom much has been committed,

of him they will ask the more.

—Luke 12:48

Every July 4th, I stop and think how similar the correlation is between our country's deep and storied history and helping others hundreds of years later. All that history is what allows us to never be afraid to stand up for what we believe in, and to never be too timid to speak one's mind. We've been given this thing called *freedom*, and we need to collectively use that freedom to work in a positive way to make improvements.

Think about the dreams, goals, and plans of previous generations; our forefathers managed to explore and face each challenge with a spirit of gratefulness, knowing they were making a new, good life for themselves and the future generations to come. They did it without cell phones, microwaves, and Internet searches. They didn't just 'post' about their grievances. We need to take a lesson from the ones before us, who gave tirelessly of themselves. They had a sense

of adventure, and never hesitated when it came to serving and helping others.

We owe them, and future generations, the commitment to not
get lost in the shuffle of everyday life. We need to push our pause
buttons for a minute and explore our options. Renew our sense of
awareness about injustice to others, our willingness to be bold, and
our desire to get a message out. Make a decision to lead by example
and inspire those around you to volunteer. Our society is one of imi-
tators, so go do something worthy of imitating! Let's leave a legacy
that says we helped those around us overcome obstacles, we enabled
their dreams and did everything we could with the cards we were
dealt to make life better for those now and those who will come after
us. What are we doing today to ensure someone has a better future?

I will close with a quote from the great American Teddy Roosevelt, "Do what you can, where you are, with what you have" and
God Bless America!

....

DAILY DIFFERENCE-MAKER

Have some courage when you pass a street person. Smile at them,
look them square in the eye. Depending on the weather, offer a
street person a cold bottle of water or a hot cup of coffee. Ask their
name, and shake their hand. Help them look forward to tomorrow!

....Notes...

In Marching Phalanx

Do not forget to entertain strangers,

for by so *doing* some have unwittingly entertained angels.

–Hebrews 13:2

n 1884, President Grover Cleveland designated the first Monday in September as Labor Day as an official federal holiday. In 1898, Samuel Gompers, the first and longest-serving president of the American Federation of Labor, described Labor Day as, "The day when toilers' rights and wrongs may lay down their tools for a holiday . . . and touch shoulders in marching phalanx and feel the stronger for it." (Yeah, I had to look up the word *phalanx*, too—basically, a military formation. Who knew?)

My father was a police officer; I know from experience that he was overworked and underpaid. Yet he did his job with a happy heart. With fourteen million unemployed workers in this country—the most privileged country in this world—and other workers who put their lives on the line each day and still struggle to make ends meet, we need to take more than a day to respond to this iniquity. Someone is responsible for driving the school bus, collecting our garbage, and protecting us from crime and catastrophes. Do we know their first names? Do we know anything about them? Their responsibilities are huge, and they are the backbone of our communities—angels who protect us, our children, and our properties. We have depended on these workers all these years to teach us, help us, and provide for us, and we should not wait for Labor Day to give back. We should be "marching in phalanx"—shoulder-to-shoulder—with them, forming a strong shield that not only protects our communities, but protects our protectors.

Get to know people like my father—the workers who quietly, faithfully serve your community. They have fulfilled your needs for many years—it's time to fulfill theirs.

. . . .

DAILY DIFFERENCE-MAKER

Bring lunch to your local first-responder precincts; doesn't have to be elaborate, could be just a deli sandwich tray and a jug of tea. Don't just drop it off—offer to serve them, or at least pour the tea or lemonade and bring it to them. Learn their names, learn about their lives, learn what they need—and meet those needs.

. . . . *Notes* . . . .

THANKSGIVING

Release the "Thanks-getting"

Offer to God thanksgiving,

and pay your vows to the Most High.

—Psalm 50:14

While it is accurate that Thanksgiving only comes once a year, I think Thanksgiving is more of an attitude that we should live by than a one-off holiday. Thanksgiving promotes an attitude of gratitude; I apologize for the cutesy-ness of the rhyme; merely a coincidence. You know I am not the cutesy type.

Our perceptions of words like Thanksgiving, blessing, giving, etc. have changed, almost to a point they're unrecognizable. As Sean says, this is not "Thanks-getting," nor should it be. Ralph Waldo Emerson once said, "For every minute you are angry, you lose 60 seconds of happiness." Given that you have the freedom to read this book or any other book instead of a government-issued required text, you have much to be thankful for.

In 1863—yes, smack in the middle of the Civil War—Abraham Lincoln declared that the last Thursday of every November honor those colonists and Wampanoag Indians who sat down and shared a feast one autumn day in 1621. It bears mentioning that the original settlers sat down and were thankful for a meal, even though about half of them who traveled over on the *Mayflower* perished during the first winter. Lincoln's timing of this declaration is interesting, too—he was thankful, even though he was the leader of our nation during the biggest turmoil our country has ever had to go through.

The cheesy definition of *gratitude* is: "The quality of being thankful; readiness to show appreciation for, and to return, kindness." So it's not what we *say* about our blessings, but how we *use* them. Sure, it may be easy to sit around a table with friends, family, send a tweet, or however you count your blessings, but counting only gets you so far. Live thankfully by showing, not telling—and don't wait for some holiday to take action. A year from now you will have wished you had started today. On your mark . . . get set . . . *go!*

DAILY DIFFERENCE-MAKER

Find the department in your local indigent hospital or free clinic that has the least number of volunteers, and volunteer in that department. Delivery meals to shut-ins, and find a way to make their meals around holidays extra-special.

Notes

The B-word

Just as He chose us in Him before the foundation of the world,

that we should be holy and without blame before Him in love,

having predestined us to adoption as sons by Jesus Christ

to Himself, according to the good pleasure of His will . . .

according to the riches of His grace which He made

to abound toward us in all wisdom and prudence.

–Ephesians 1:4–5, 7–8

do not like the b-word, especially around Christmas, birthdays, and other gift-giving occasions. You know the b-word I'm talking about . . . *budget*. Nails running down a chalkboard for me to even think about, much less have to act upon.

Zoom, zoom, swipe swipe—that sound of our credit cards being used so freely as we shop, splurge, and give into the urge . . . gifts for family, friends, coworkers, business acquaintances, and those who are less fortunate. At Christmastime, we all rush around like crazy people who have a deadline to beat, grabbing this and that, waiting in a line for a store to open at 4:00 a.m. in the pitch-dark to get that item with a greatly slashed price, cheerful decorations and music to keep us in the mood . . . until we look at the cold, hard truth of that card statement, and realize there's nothing merry about January.

Remember how, as teenagers, we saved ticket stubs, pressed flowers, and other small mementos? Where did we lose that sentiment, and think that the more money spent, the more love is there? Sometimes, the best gifts are handwritten notes or small tokens that evoke a memory, letting someone know how much they've meant in our lives; a person does not know they are loved until someone tells them so. Don't waste another day assuming that person knows. Never, ever apply the b-word to your love; lavish it on others, just as the Father lavishes His love upon you. Find ways to love richly, graciously, abundantly—such love is priceless.

DAILY DIFFERENCE-MAKER

For one year, make every gift you elect to give. It may be a CD of music, a fabulous meal, flowers from your yard, or coasters made out of tile and felt feet, but make each gift with your own two hands. The recipient will cherish it!

Notes

WEEK
TWENTY
-SEVEN

Start a Family

He who has two tunics, let him give to him who has none;

and he who has food, let him do likewise.

–Luke 3:11

Just because you may live alone doesn't mean you have to *be* alone. Whether you're single, divorced, widowed, an empty-nester, or live three thousand miles away from your parents, you can still forge a family right there in your town. You are surrounded by others who need this sort of connection, and you may be the catalyst that assembles it.

My dear friend Sue Mitchell tutored Michael during his senior year of high school. That fall, she accepted a position at Ole Miss as a learning specialist; not only could Michael continue working with her, several of his teammates would have the benefit of her help, too. Once Collins settled into collegiate life, she bonded with several of her Kappa Delta sisters and fellow cheerleaders; all of us made some great memories during football season, but the synergy of all these worlds colliding achieved a much greater purpose on that cocooned cozy campus. A family was emerging, a family that closed generational, racial, and gender gaps. My kids were getting the education of a lifetime, and I couldn't be more thrilled; they were caring for themselves, each other, and others independent of Sean and me.

Who needs a seat at your dinner table? Who needs a place to go during special holidays? Who needs their birthday remembered? Who needs a friend they can count on—to cry with, celebrate with, and yes, even help them when they move? Who just wants to know that somebody cares whether they are alive or dead?

Introverted or extroverted, independent or interdependent, we all need a place to belong. If you're needing to find that place, it may be up to you to be that place for others. Never lose sight that families do *not* have to match! God equipped each one of us to interlock and not walk this journey alone; find your back-up, reinforcements, by serving in this role for others. In this respect, anyone can start a family.

. . . .

DAILY DIFFERENCE-MAKER

Do you know someone who is alone? Take that person a plant and a promise—a promise that you are there for them. Invite them over for a cup of coffee or a meal. Remind them that they matter to you.

. . . . Notes . . . .

Do More of It

He has shown you, O man, what *is* good;

and what does the LORD require of you but to do justly,

to love mercy, and to walk humbly with your God?

—Micah 6:8

When it became apparent, rather quickly, that *The Blind Side* was going to be a grand slam, we knew God was behind it. And He had a plan.

At the premiere after-party, a society columnist asked some of our friends, "Why do I not know these people?" Our friends explained that we're not black-tie people, and it's true. You won't find us on the froo-froo pages of newspapers and glossy, upscale magazines. We belong to a country club only because it provides a kitchen and "home-cooking" that I can claim as my own.

"So what do they do?" the columnist asked. Our friends said we primarily help kids in the public school system, to which he replied, "Have they changed?"

I loved my friend's response: "The only thing that's changed is that they can do more of it."

You may be a gazillionaire; you may have every judge and politician's personal number on your phone; you may be on a first-name basis with every A-list celebrity or socialite in the world; but if you're not seeking justice and mercy, you're not leveraging your success. And no matter how humble your surroundings or lifestyle, if you're not humbling yourself before the Lord, you're not meeting His requirements, either. Whatever God has entrusted us with, we are only managing what is rightfully His; He intends for us to use it for His glory. Sean has informed me he is going to form his own 501c so I will give money to him! He is such a smarty pants! But giving changes your life.

God doesn't want our trappings—our fancy cars or special shoes with the red soles—He wants our hearts. From there, He can make use of our money, power, connections—whatever it is He has blessed us with—to right a few wrongs in this world, and to show compassion to those who are in need or suffering. He's not saying, "It sure would be nice if you'd help these people." He's saying, "You have these resources for a reason. My reason."

If you're confused by this, the part you may be struggling with is "walk humbly with God." You know what is good and what is right— so get on your knees and find out how your gifts and blessings can be used to help others. It may be that you are to do more.

DAILY DIFFERENCE-MAKER

Stop and help someone today. It's not an interruption; your paths were intended to cross. Find out why.

Notes

We Can Cure This

But Jesus said, "Let the little children come to Me,
and do not forbid them; for of such is the kingdom of heaven."
And He laid *His* hands on them.

—Matthew 19:14–15

We don't know how many young Michael Ohers are out there, we just know they are everywhere. Children of incalculable worth are walking the streets, much too much alone. They aren't asking for a Mercedes or a Rolex; they just want love and opportunity.

With as many intractable problems in the U.S., the problem of children in need is curable. Recently, I heard a startling statistic: If every church in the United States would see to it that one child—catch that, *just one child*—is adopted, the problem of homeless children in this country would disappear. Now before you sit back, arms folded, indignant, and thinking, "So *there*, churches! You need to do something about this," let me deduce it further. Based on this statistic, it stands to reason that *if each one of us got involved*, then, we could wipe it out overnight. Are your arms still folded? Still blame the church? Are you still just as indignant about children who are homeless, family-less, and overlooked?

Here are a few more statistics* for you to chew on:

- Over four hundred thousand children are in foster care right now
- About two-hundred fifty thousand will be removed from their homes, primarily due to neglect and abuse
- An estimated one hundred thousand children in foster care are available for adoption
- We're adopting them at a rate of only half

Conservative results from research studies find one in five will become homeless after age eighteen; only half will be employed by the time they turn twenty-four; less than three percent will have earned a college degree; seventy-one percent of the young women will be pregnant by age twenty-one; and one in four will have experienced post-traumatic stress disorder at twice the rate of United States war veterans. Sadly enough, many are at risk of moving right back into government systems—usually jails and prisons.†

How many bright, wonderful children are slipping through the cracks because people don't notice them? If we are the hands and feet of Christ, then it's time we lay loving hands on these children, grasping them gently to save them from falling off the radar.

....

DAILY DIFFERENCE-MAKER

Smile at everyone who doesn't look like you or sound like you . . . in fact, just smile at everyone!

.... Notes ....

*Source: U.S. Department of Health and Human Services, Administration for Children and Families, Administration on Children, Youth and Families, Children's Bureau: "Trends in Foster Care, FFY 2002–FFY 2013"

†CNN "We Are Abandoning Children in Foster Care" (April 17, 2014)

Declare Your Own "Father's Day"

"Honor your father and *your* mother," and,

"You shall love your neighbor as yourself."

—Matthew 19:19

I want to give a shout-out to the guys today. All of the guys who contribute to the idea, the institution we call 'family'.

Now there is nothing more powerful on this earth than family and home. But home is not just a physical address; it's who we are and where we belong. And there are different elements that can make up a family and a home.

Family isn't just a mother, a father, and 2.2 children; we all have men who have touched our lives in a special way and have given us fatherly advice that has helped us make those good choices. Sound counsel doesn't always come from a biological father; sometimes, it comes from a coach, teacher, law enforcement official, cousin, or even a brother.

How have you thanked those wonderful men who might not have contributed to your birth, but are responsible for crafting you into the person that you are? Men who nurtured us, encouraged us, supported us, and helped us make good decisions and good choices in our own journey of life . . . it's time to put their dispensed wisdom into action.

Show them that you now care about *their* problems, listen to *their* stories, and hear *their* fears. Remember, one day you will be a memory to someone; let's honor our mentors by making sure we will be good ones. Wouldn't you rather be glad you did instead of wishing you had?

....

DAILY DIFFERENCE-MAKER

Call one of your "fathers" today; if they live far away, take time to visit by phone. If they live close by, arrange to visit them in person. Bring them lunch, take them to lunch (including transportation), bring them vegetables from your garden or a favorite dessert. Verbally tell them the gracious impact they made on your life, no matter how awkward or clumsy the words come out. Share specific stories about how you applied their inspiration to your own life. Do not leave anything to speculation—say it!

.... Notes ....

Set an Example

Come, you children, listen to me;

I will teach you the fear of the LORD.

—Psalm 34:11

After watching *The Blind Side* for the first time, my three kids left the theater and—referring to Sandra Bullock's performance—said, "Great. There are two of them running around now." My rhetorical response was, "Is there a problem with that?"

Parenting is hard, people. And at times, very thankless. But let me ask you this: Are your kids seeing you live out the principles and values you expect from them? If your kids shadowed you 24/7, would they be better because of it . . . or not?

Yes, as parents we have occasional lapses in judgment; we too, are a work in progress. But your children watch each and everything you do and say; the tiniest off-the-cuff remark or action speaks volumes to a child, and can impact them for a lifetime. Don't let your lives as a parent contradict what and how you tell your kids to live. Children are usually a direct reflection of the parents—hence, that old saying that the acorn doesn't fall far from the tree!

Yes, it takes a village—but as parents, that doesn't relinquish or diminish our primary roles in our children's lives. We're not off the hook by any means, and our children observe and absorb more of our 'little actions' than we realize. As you interact with individuals today—coworkers, grocery clerks, bank tellers, street people, etc.— ask yourself whether your behavior would inspire and educate your children, or would it teach them things that are not really appropriate or uplifting? Be the parent that you want your kids to remember when they reflect on their childhoods.

....

DAILY DIFFERENCE-MAKER

Go—don't call, don't e-mail, and please don't try to text—physically *go* to the lowest-performing school in your town and ask them what they need. Involve your own children in this effort—help them assemble boxes of supplies, take them shopping for items. It doesn't matter if you're doing this in August, December, or February, and it doesn't matter whether it's your own child's school—there's not a school in our nation that doesn't need something!

.... Notes ....

WEEK
TWENTY
-EIGHT

136

What Did You Miss?

After they had come to Mysia, they tried to go into Bithynia,

but the Spirit did not permit them.

—Acts 16:7

Sean and I were mapping out our fall schedule. Michael's NFL games were practically every Sunday; S.J.'s Loyola basketball games were twice weekly; Collins scheduled several speaking engagements and we wanted to hit a few of those; and now that Coach Freeze was at Ole Miss, we wanted to hit most of those (for obvious reasons, if you know us!). Oh, and when the Grizzlies are in season, Sean does the television commentary on occasion. . . my head was spinning, particularly when I realized how tight our fall schedule would be! There would be very little wiggle room for extracurricular activities and errors.

So when the first delayed flight happened, the plan fell apart quicker than a house of cards. As I was fretting over this, I was reminded of how the Holy Spirit postponed Paul's trips to Asia and Bithynia. Since the Bible uses phrases like, "Paul was forbidden" and "Jesus did not permit," we can conclude that there had been some desire on Paul's part to travel to those places, but he yielded to God's plans instead. So sitting there, sweating like a goat, I realized that God knew exactly what Sean and I had planned, and knew exactly where we were. He may be sparing us from an unseen danger, or needed us to tend to someone in that airport who had a need . . . there could be any number of reasons God stuck us in that airport for an unexpected period of time! So I needed to be kinder to the airline rep behind the counter (trust me, that was *not* in my original thought process!).

When life doesn't go according to plan, guess what? The sun's still gonna rise the next morning, the world will keep spinning, and Wal-Mart will be open for business. Like Paul when his plans were altered, we need to trust that God's plans are far better than ours, and have much greater purpose. We may not understand why at the time, but each step in faith puts us a little further ahead, closer to His plan.

DAILY DIFFERENCE-MAKER

Something's or someone's gonna wreck your schedule today: a call from school to retrieve your sick child, a talkative neighbor who spies you at your mailbox, or even standstill traffic. Give into the interruption as a direct appointment from the Lord; what would you have missed if you'd stuck with your own plans?

Notes

Oh, Stop It . . . Really.

A flattering mouth works ruin.

−Proverbs 26:28

My translation: Don't be a suck-up and don't tolerate them, either.

After *The Blind Side* released, I was hit with more "best friends" than I could count; many of them barely knew me, knew me thirty years ago, or had never met me. If I'd believed their hype about me, I would think I was the most beautiful, smartest, innovative, hard-working woman in the world! (Oh, and modest. I left out modest.) Perhaps I even had a halo and wings. Yeah, right!

At a certain level of celebrity, one has the power and money to surround themselves with 'yes-people' who will do anything that celebrity says, no matter how ridiculous or harmful . . . until the money runs out. Most of us regular folk can see this for what it is when we see famous athletes and movie stars arrested or, tragically, when one of them dies from addiction. Yet we fail to see the flatterers in our own lives, or even our own attempts to fast-track a friendship for some sort of personal gain or agenda.

It's very simple: Don't be fake and don't allow it, either. Had I been swayed by those flatterers, they would have eventually left me

high and dry when they met someone else who might be able to cata-
pult them further into whatever realm they're trying to reach. My
besties know who they are, and I enjoy meeting and forming relationships with others whom I've admired for years, but you just can't rush
an authentic friendship. And what's worse, people who flatter are just
as easy to bash you once your back is turned—you can practically feel
the knife going in.

Who is the friend who is there for you when you're at your lowest? The one willing to spend time with you doing simple activities
that don't cost anything? They're just as happy to go to Taco Bell as
they are to eat at an expensive restaurant? And perhaps most importantly—who is the friend who has the courage to speak the truth in
love when you're screwing up? That person is your real friend. And
remember, in order to *have* a real friend, you must also *be* a real friend.

DAILY DIFFERENCE-MAKER

Is there someone in your life who seems desperate to be your
friend? They may just be insecure and thrilled that someone they
admire is kind to them. Practice your God-given discernment, and
trust your instincts. Be kind, sincere, and set boundaries.

Notes

Blinded by Pride

Most assuredly, I say to you,

a servant is not greater than his master;

nor is he who is sent greater than he who sent him.

–John 13:16

One day I received a call from a friend of mine who lives in Oxford, Mississippi. She said to me, "If I didn't know better, I thought I just saw your son pushing a broken car down the street." I texted Michael immediately and he confirmed that he had been, indeed, pushing a car down the street—his friend's car. I replied, "How very nice of you." Michael joked, "Well it might be, but it's not a good look for me." That comment made me laugh out loud, but also beam at the thought of Michael not letting his pride get in the way of helping his friend.

Jesus Christ knew that pride has no place in His kingdom. He's not talking about self-respect or being proud of your children—He's talking about the kind of pride that blinds us from seeing and serving others. Today's verse is taken from the account of Jesus washing His disciples' feet, and as a mother who has washed more than her share of stinky athletic socks, I still cannot imagine the smell, the dirt, and the calluses accumulated by all the miles these men had walked . . . yet here was our King, serving others in this manner.

Whom have we overlooked? Who did we think should be waiting on us, instead of the other way around? Whom have you passed by on the side of the road? Who has been dismissed, because we don't associate with "that kind"? Let's take our blinders off—let's throw pride away to make room in our hearts for humility and service.

DAILY DIFFERENCE-MAKER

What's the weather like today? If it 's hot, distribute some freezer packs or frozen water bottles to street people or children waiting on a school bus. If it's cold, purchase some hand warmers or gloves from a farm or hunting supply store and distribute.

Notes

139

Missed by an Inch

Blessed *are* the merciful, for they shall obtain mercy.

−Matthew 5:7

Leaving my house, I passed a cute little creature on the sidewalk, happily making his way to the other side with so much energy and enthusiasm. On my return trip back, I encountered this little fella once again, saddened to see it did not complete its journey.

The destination had obviously been the luscious green grass, where I'm sure the worm would have lived happily ever after in its worm world. I'm not sure whether its demise was from a heat stroke or human foot, but the worm was within inches of completing its goal. If that worm could talk, it would probably remind us that an inch really matters!

Too often, when we encounter injustice, we don't want to interfere or get involved. We turn our heads and justify it by trusting that someone else will take care of it, some agency or trained person who can handle whatever it is will be a much better fit for the challenge that's right there in front of us. A small, nagging voice asks, "How can you walk away from this?" We ignore the voice that continues to gnaw away at our conscience until we can preoccupy ourselves with something happy and easy.

Listen, if you're reading this and feeling your gut tighten, then do not dismiss my voice as easily as you've dismissed these opportunities; believe me, I can talk louder if I need to! The missed inches should make all of our lives challenging, and I hope even a bit frustrating, as you reflect on the times in your life that all you had to do was go that extra inch and you would have been the difference-maker.

But you know what? Today we can make a fresh start and hopefully finish strong, as we look for those invisible would-be losses and opportunities. When you leave the house today, insist on no longer looking away, no longer justifying the injustice by dismissing it as someone else's problem. Half-done is still undone—go the extra inch!

DAILY DIFFERENCE-MAKER

I dare you to take one act of kindness and amp it up—if you're purchasing school supplies, purchase backpacks and fully stock them; if you're purchasing for a Christmas angel or some other program, fulfill the entire list and then some; if you're contributing part of a meal for someone who is ill, tackle the entire meal . . . don't just do the bare minimum, go the extra inch, foot, yard, MILE! I double-dog dare ya!

Notes

The Boos Lose

You therefore, my son, be strong in the grace

that is in Christ Jesus. . . . if anyone competes in athletics,

he is not crowned unless he competes according to the rules.

—2 Timothy 2:1, 5

Booo . . . boooo . . . boooo . . . No, I'm not referring to Hallow-een, just all of the nincompoops who go to sporting events and *boooo.* What's their problem?

Having attended enough sporting events in my lifetime, I consider myself an expert witness to this bad behavior. Admittedly, I am stunned at the number of people who 'boo' the players. We don't go to restaurants and boo the servers for poor service; we don't stand up and boo in the movie theater if we don't like the film. People would think we'd lost our minds! So why is this mark of poor sportsmanship increasingly acceptable?

I mean, let's think this through. How would you feel if you went in Monday at work and there was a crowd pulled in off the street to watch you in action? And every report you submitted, meeting you presided over, class you taught, or delivery you made was met with thousands of bellowing *boooos?*

The players and coaches do not want to lose; getting behind in the game or losing doesn't give spectators a free pass to act like children. So many of these same people have younger children with them and of course, the children eventually act like their parents. Remember, your children are mirror images of you!

Ballgames and other sporting events can make some fun family memories, whether you are on a Little League field or sitting at The Super Bowl. They also provide an excellent vehicle for teaching children about sportsmanship, dignity, and respect. Don't blow these teachable moments; it's fine to be opinionated, certainly, but let's also be respectful at the same time. By example, let's teach our children that every individual should be treated with dignity and respect rather than acting as though every disappointment is a betrayal and a matter of incompetence. Anyone can be a bully from the bleachers—let's decide we're not going to be just anyone. Be you—not them.

....

DAILY DIFFERENCE-MAKER
Find out where a children's league is playing today—soccer field, gymnasium, baseball diamond, football field—and deliver some fast-food sandwiches to the team that demonstrates good sportsmanship. Pick a new team the following week—these kids will catch on that they are truly being watched, and will want to set an example!

.... Notes ....

WEEK TWENTY -NINE

Hand-ups

For the gifts and the calling of God *are* irrevocable.

–Romans 11:29

Some of us think the only way to help the needy is by giving money or making meals . . . well, guess what? If God had gifted each one of us to be either wealthy or great cooks, our world would be boring. And dirty. And lack clean water. And beautiful architecture, great music, art, and sports. And . . . well, I think you get my point.

The unique gifts God gave each one of us, and His calling to glorify Him are *irrevocable*—cannot be changed. He has wired you, me, the person standing next to you and each and every person in this world a particular way; and we need to determine how to use those gifts. Yes, we can offer needy people handouts, but at the same time, let's offer them a hand-up!

You already know I am not a great cook . . . as a matter of fact, I don't cook at all, but I can serve and clean up one of the best meals ever—what about you? Maybe you know how to garden, and can teach those who are hungry how to garden. Maybe you know how to maintain or make simple automotive repairs, like changing the oil, and can teach others. There are so many different ways to help others, and I've only listed a few.

Maybe you don't have a designer wardrobe to donate . . . but you know how to sew. Or shop for bargains. Or you know how to organize and arrange clothing according to size and season. There are so many ways to help clothe the needy.

Maybe you don't have a house or a car to give away . . . but you know how to do some basic plumbing repairs. Or change a flat tire, landscape on a budget, or even maximize a bus pass. So, so many ways to help those who need shelter and transportation.

Look, the discouraging statistics aren't going away tomorrow, but we don't have to be a gazillionaire to make an impact. Instead of throwing our hands up in defeat and thinking, "what's the use?" be compelled to make a difference and ask instead, "What's next?"

DAILY DIFFERENCE-MAKER

Teach someone a life skill today: how to fix a leaky faucet, prepare a household budget, sew a button, freeze or can vegetables . . . something that will improve their way of life. One person, one kindness at a time!

Notes

Complaining Is Easy

Not that I speak in regard to need, for I have learned
in whatever state I am, to be content: I know how to be abased,
and I know how to abound. Everywhere and in all things
I have learned both to be full and to be hungry,
both to abound and to suffer need.

–Philippians 4:11–12

Don't believe for one minute that you do not possess the power to create change! I get it, you've seen a lot and experienced a lot: failed marriages; job loss; abandoned families; child abuse; illness; high-school dropouts . . . sometimes, it's not "a wonderful life," is it?

Every single one of us experiences loss or sadness at some point, and yes, they do transcend socioeconomic barriers. They seem to level the playing field, and the choices we make coming out of these losses and sadness are what defines us.

It's so much easier, then, to choose to complain, criticize, whine that it's never going to get better, and guess what? We'd be right! As long as we choose to remain there, nothing will change for the better. There are two outcomes from this choice: things will remain the same, or get *worse*.

Regardless of your circumstances, two facts remain: Someone will always be better off, and someone will always be worse off than you are right now. Someone is sicker; someone is poorer; someone has more financial resources; someone's career is skyrocketing. My Grandmother Cummings used to always say, "I wept at the man who had no shoes until I met the man who had no feet." We are not mass-produced, thank God! We can be content in our present and hopeful for our future at the same time.

And in the interim, there are individuals and organizations moving the needle every day, either helping us through these tough times or, are daily trying to be there for those who are in the middle of them. Saddle yourself to them and realize you can create meaningful change for yourself and others. Or, you can just stay put and keep complaining because things are bleak, life's not fair, and you drew the short straw again. It is easier, but nowhere near as fulfilling.

....

DAILY DIFFERENCE-MAKER

Find a life skills program in your area—doesn't matter if it's for adults with special needs, teenagers who do not live at home, prisoners who are about to be released . . . just get involved. You have some of these skills; you may not have them all mastered, but you have them. You can help them not fall back into the cracks!

.... Notes ....

"How can you walk away from this?"

143

Numbering Our Days Wisely

So teach *us* to number our days,

that we may gain a heart of wisdom.

–Psalm 90:12

At least once a week, someone says to Sean, "Oh, you're that old point guard from Ole Miss." While I feel like we've been called out as dinosaurs, he tells me the best is yet to come.

I like that; the best is still to come, no matter your age. So do not be embarrassed by your age, or think you're unimportant. You remain useful until you and you alone make the call that you won't be any longer.

Now there are two sides to this equation. We need to make sure that when we see a person who is a little more seasoned than we are to seek their advice, help them plug into meaningful moments, and ensure they have access to help and security. On the other hand, if you are the person who is a little more seasoned, don't be stubborn. Ask for help, and make sure that you continue to do all that you can to help those who so desperately need it. There's an old saying, "If flowers can teach themselves how to bloom after winter passes, so can you." Each time I read it, I am reminded that I'm not too old to try something new.

As we "number our days," each one of us should think about what we'd like to witness or accomplish during our lifetime and what can be done to contribute to that vision. Whether you are a senior or a senior-to-be, this sort of mind-set deems each one of us useful; and when a vision is shared by multiple generations, the combination of wisdom, strength, and strategy could yield *real* change. If we all made this effort, our world would be better for it!

....

DAILY DIFFERENCE-MAKER

Share a personal concern with an elderly person, something that you wish you could change about your community in your lifetime. Ask them if they are aware of anyone attempting it, get their input on what your next steps could be. As you move forward, enlist their insight and wisdom while harnessing the energy, ingenuity, and enthusiasm of someone who is younger.

.... Notes ....

Because She Cared

Do not forsake the law of your mother; for they *will be* a
graceful ornament on your head, and chains about your neck.
–Proverbs 1:8–9

Usually when we think of the word *mothering,* we think of
someone kissing a baby's fears away, someone who sugar-
coats everything, or someone who never pronounces a bad
situation hopeless. And yes, that definitely describes a mother—but
being a mother is often times a dirty, stinky, thankless job and in my
world, no matter how many times we have to get dirty, we always
return for more.

Who's the person you call, not only to share good news with, but
also just to talk about your plain, old, ordinary day? Then there is
someone in this world who cares if you take your next breath, someone who thinks you are magnificent, and will also set you straight
when you need it. Whether that someone cared for you, supervised
you, or taught you, she obviously had an impact on your life. What is
her legacy? Did her influence directly impact some of your choices in
life—where to attend college, what career field, whether to relocate?
Or maybe she dried your tears when your heart was broken. Run
through the names in your cell phone, check on your email contact

list, or flip through the old-fashioned address book and find those women who mothered you—the ones who had a part in making you who you are today. Any day is a good day to hear "Thanks for being like a mom to me"—it will be happily received!

....

DAILY DIFFERENCE-MAKER

Can you locate any of your teachers from school? Be sure they receive a birthday and Christmas card each year from you with a handwritten note. Offer to take them to lunch the next time you're nearby—and follow through on that offer.

....*Notes*..

Applause, Applause

Then David danced before the LORD with all *his* might . . .
"Therefore I will play *music* before the LORD. And I will be even
more undignified than this, and will be humble in my own sight."

—2 Samuel 6:14, 21–22

There are some interesting moments of worship in the Bible, but King David by far had some of the most memorable.

I love this whole passage from 2 Samuel 6; if you read it in its entirety, David is celebrating the ark's return to Jerusalem and that it was transported correctly. Wearing part of a priest's garment, David twirled, sang, danced, and handed out food to everyone. Yes, *everyone*. It was a celebration to be remembered. What would you do if your mayor or the U.S. President came dancing down your street and handed you food?

In gratitude, in worship, in awe, here was Israel's king, dancing among his people, openly worshipping God and making sure no one went hungry. He didn't care how ridiculous he looked, nor did he care whether it was "protocol" for a king to be right in the mix of things; he was celebrating his God!

When have you given God some applause? No, He doesn't need it—but as His children, shouldn't we be doing it? I'm talking foolish, crazy, don't-care-who's-watching sort of applause . . . where you load up a bunch of tacos and hand them out to random strangers; when you see the Grand Canyon or the birth of a baby and are awestruck by the miracle and beauty of it all. Shout to the Lord . . . smile uncontrollably, giggle to God and dance with joy! Celebrate the King!

We worship a creative God; He is just, and He is kind. Our human minds cannot fathom what He does and what He has in store. How will you applaud Him today?

DAILY DIFFERENCE-MAKER

Volunteer at your local Boys & Girls Club, teen center, or after-school program. Don't be afraid to get silly with these kids! Laugh, dance, sing . . . and applaud!

Notes

WEEK
THIRTY

Be the Answer God Sent

Go out quickly into the streets and lanes of the city, and bring
in here *the* poor and *the* maimed and *the* lame and *the* blind.'
And the servant said, 'Master, it is done as you commanded,
and still there is room.' Then the master said to the servant,
'Go out into the highways and hedges,
and compel *them* to come in, that my house may be filled.

—Luke 14:21–23

The things most of us take for granted, someone else is pray-
ing for: clean water, garbage collection, food to eat, clothes to
wear, even shelter from heat, rain, and cold. Some of the more
intrinsic things, like a loving family, a real friend, or just a sense of
purpose and belonging, are also the prayers of many.

Today's verse is from the Parable of the Feast, and it illustrates
God's call to come to His banquet. Many turned down the man's invitation for various reasons, so he continued inviting others to fill his
home and eat from his table. Along with the spiritual application of
our own salvation and purpose, this parable provides a great illustration about those who need our provision as well.

Not too long ago, I was on my daily walk and an older woman stopped me with hesitation, needing directions. She was very apologetic, but I was familiar with the address; when I pointed her in the right direction, she actually teared up and thanked me for various reasons. For me, what I did was simple; I provided directions. I had no idea of what it would mean to her!

Each one of us can provide love and friendship to the unloved, and to make them feel welcome in our presence; some of us may be called to provide a loving family to someone or at least provide them shelter. Whether we're sharing half of our sandwich or feeding the multitudes, donating a designer wardrobe or buying cotton socks and underwear from the dollar store, we have a portion to provide someone who is doing without.

We may be the only Jesus someone sees today. So answer someone's prayer.

DAILY DIFFERENCE-MAKER

Purchase a $50 gift card that can be used anywhere, like those from a major credit card company. Go to a bus stop and look for the person whose face appears most troubled. Hand them the gift card without saying a word—just smile, grasp their hand gently, and walk away.

Notes

Funny People

A merry heart does good, *like* medicine,

but a broken spirit dries the bones.

–Proverbs 17:22

When is the last time you've enjoyed a really, *really* good laugh? I'm not talking about chuckling, cheap humor, or at another's expense; I'm talking about the sort of laughter where you can't catch your breath, stop the tears or preserve any energy for the next laugh. The kind that makes your sides and belly ache.

Whatever flavor of humor we enjoy, we need to spend time with people who make us laugh. Look at what the proverb says—fun and laughter is like medicine. Cancer patients and others who battle serious illnesses are encouraged to watch funny movies and laugh a lot; but laughter can work wonders on anyone!

And if it's true that we're often identified by the company we keep, wouldn't you want to capture some of that merriment from your crowd and carry it with you—for those times when you feel a bit down? Invest in some good, healthy laughs each day—your body, mind, and spirit will thank you for it!

··

DAILY DIFFERENCE-MAKER

Everyone is not a comedian—but everyone can make another person smile. Today, see how many smiles you can muster in another person—and if you're feeling really spunky, go ahead and see how many you can make laugh! :)

···························· Notes ························

Salute Through Action

There is no authority except from God,

and the authorities that exist are appointed by God. . . .

for he does not bear the sword in vain.

—Romans 13:1, 4

Thank a service member today.

- Thank them with a care package of gloves, hand wipes, hard candy, hand sanitizer, moisturizer, lip balm, shaving lotion, and anything else you can think of.

- Thank them when you see them out at restaurants by paying for their meal.

- Thank them by writing your elected officials about the care they receive while active and retired, and making sure they are properly equipped.

- Thank them by sending coupons to their families if they are stationed overseas, since the PX will honor even expired ones.

- Thank them by mailing them Christmas cards, whether you know them or not.

- Thank them by giving up your seat for them—after all, they're willing to give up their lives for you.
- Thank them by sending them your old magazines since many of them are not in one place long enough to have a subscription to any.
- Thank them by sending them gift cards to download their favorite music.
- Thank them by giving up your first-class seat and sit in their coach seat.
- Thank them by giving them gift certificates to their local movie theater or restaurant where they're stationed.
- Thank them by hosting them in your home, if there is a base nearby.
- Thank them by caring for any family members or pets left behind on a deployment.

Please, please, please, thank a service member today!

. . . .

DAILY DIFFERENCE-MAKER
Contact the Family Center affiliated with the military base closest to your home to identify five deployed service members who do not have families. Write them regularly; remember them at birthdays and holidays. The Family Center will be able to help you determine what items are needed or may be sent.

. . . . Notes . . . .

Hustle Sold Separately

Commit your works to the LORD,

and your thoughts will be established.

—Proverbs 16:3

Too often, we adopt the "apologize later" adage when it comes to involving God in our plans. We're impatient, we want something so badly that we don't want to hear any 'negativity,' or we've acted on impulse. Or, we're afraid He'll direct us in a different direction.

Always remember to fall asleep with a dream and wake up with a purpose. And somewhere in the middle of it all, we need to commit ourselves and our work to the Lord. We need to ask in advance, and don't advance if He tells us otherwise. We may not have all the answers laid out before us, but He will make things clear.

My boys always say, though, "The dream is free, but the hustle is sold separately." If your dream does, in fact, become a reality, you'll need to be ready to engage. Trust Him to provide the resources to get the job done; trust Him if your role is only part of the big picture. Nothing worthwhile is ever easy—it requires dedication and determination. Do not interfere with His plan—accept the role you are given, and commit to it.

DAILY DIFFERENCE-MAKER

Find a random stranger's public wish list from your favorite online store—purchase something from that list to send to them.

Notes

You Can't Always Win

Therefore, my beloved brethren, be steadfast, immovable,

always abounding in the work of the Lord,

knowing that your labor is not in vain in the Lord.

—1 Corinthians 15:58

There are those times when we invest in a life and it doesn't work out. Maybe we adopted a child and they still chose a life of crime or addiction. Maybe we helped someone find a job or housing and they walked out on the opportunity. Maybe we trusted someone to work on our home and they stole something. It happens. There are no guarantees.

But look at what the scripture says—if you're working for the Lord, if He is the driving force for your good works, then even all the work invested in that setback is not in vain. How the recipient responds is up to him or her, and ultimately that's out of your control. But what is in your control is your resolve to keep trying.

And be mindful of your definition of success. If you feel like a failure because the person you've helped wants to wait tables or teach school instead of becoming a five-star chef or playing professional sports, then you've still helped someone become a productive citizen and a very important contributor. That's hardly a failure!

No, I'm talking about those times when we've helped someone get back on their feet and they return to their former life . . . it's disappointing and emotionally hurtful, but for every one of those situations there are thousands more who would love the same opportunity to succeed. Just as we shouldn't let one bad apple spoil the whole bunch; the good stories far outweigh the bad, so don't let one person's setback prevent you from helping the next. If you're doing it for God, it will *not* be in vain!

....

DAILY DIFFERENCE-MAKER

Is there someone who accepted your help, then disappointed you with how they used it? Check in with that person today, and let them know you still care. And remain steadfast: Offer someone else the same opportunity they had.

.... Notes ....

WEEK
THIRTY
-ONE

Do Not Forget His Church

"Bring all the tithes into the storehouse,

That there may be food in My house, And try Me now in this,"

Says the Lord of hosts, "If I will not open for you

the windows of heaven And pour out for you *such* blessing

That *there will* not *be room* enough *to receive it.*

—Malachi 3:10

Cheerful giving begins in the heart, out of gratitude for God's generosity to us. He gave us sun, wind, water . . . and an opportunity to live with Him forever. So when He also gives us the gift of wealth, at what point do we cheerfully give our portion?

So many believe that they created—and therefore, own—their wealth. They feel no obligation nor grace toward giving some of it back—but are quite generous with their criticisms: "Losers," "good-for-nothings," "just want a hand-out," "hitting me up for money," "get a job," "cannot manage the finances," etc., etc. What's particularly disturbing is when these criticisms are pointed *at the church*.

I get it—we've all seen the scandal and opulence that characterizes so-called pastors. But for every one of those, there are thousands more who cannot make ends meet, who stretch every dollar and pinch every penny until it squeals for mercy. Yet we file in our seats each week, demanding we be fed a good word from the Good Book. Seriously?

Who do you think keeps the lights on? Who is responsible for keeping the place clean and in good repair, or providing for various programs and ministries? And are we suggesting that staff simply work for free? Would you?

The word *tithe* actually means 'ten percent,' and that's all the Lord has asked we give to His church. Now, whether you chose to give more or less is between you and God, but He has given us so, so much—how can anyone not be moved by His generosity?

And claim His promise from today's verse—whatever you give, He will give more. You'll learn firsthand that you can never, ever out-give the Lord.

DAILY DIFFERENCE-MAKER

Find a church in your city—one that you do not attend—and donate some money.

.... Notes ....

Be Persistent, Stay Consistent

Do not grow weary *in* doing good.

−2 Thessalonians 3:13

Now some people willingly accept help the second that it's offered. For others, it could take a while . . . sometimes, years.

I have a lifelong friend like that. We joke that she was the "first Michael," but we actually met as teenagers through church socials. She attended a public school nearby, and we both wound up at Ole Miss. She came from a large family with very little money; her mother struggled with various issues, so she moved in with her grandmother. When her grandmother's health was failing, she stayed with other families until she eventually stayed at ours most of the time. For a long while, however, she would decline my offers to help. We saw a similar pattern when we met Michael.

What I realized in both situations and many others: Hurt and abandonment penetrates deeper than we realize. A lot of people have had the rug jerked out from under them so much, they spend their entire lives insulating themselves emotionally, fiercely grounding themselves in self-sufficiency, and eschewing opportunities that would alleviate some of their pain and struggle. The distrust isn't intentional, but the other shoe has dropped so often, they'd just rather go barefoot.

Another thing I realized in these cases: Love and reassurance are ultimately more important than any clothes bought, food provided, and shelter offered. If you're trying to really help someone—not to be their hero, savior, or for some sort of public pat-on-the-back—please do not give up. Really check yourself to make sure you're not looking down on them, thinking they're stupid or crazy for not taking you up on whatever sort of help you're offering; trust me, they will have picked up on this long before you will.

Don't let someone's hurt or reluctance discourage you; authentic relationships take time, and everyone deserves to be treated with dignity. Be persistent, be consistent, be respectful, and be kind—people are hurting more than we realize.

....

DAILY DIFFERENCE-MAKER

Speak to the person pumping gas next to you. Without being creepy, take note if they pay with any coins, or only put in a few dollars' worth—offer to pay for their gas, if that is the case. Ask if they'd like a cup of coffee, bottle of water, or snack.

.... Notes ....

Be still

Be still, and know that I *am* God; I will be exalted

among the nations, I will be exalted in the earth!

—Psalm 46:10

Yes, I'm outspoken and yes, I'll tell you how it's gonna be . . . but not on an airplane. That's my downtime; I shut it down, take deep breaths, and relax.

Sean does this in his own special way. When we attend NFL games, he wears earphones. Want to know his shut-down secret? They're not connected to anything. They're powerful enough to muffle obnoxious fans and Sean can focus on the game and relax. I may have to try this the next time I'm on a flight!

We all need to take a time-out every now and then, where we shut the world out so we can focus. The most important 'shut-out' we can take is our daily time with the Lord; a quiet time to commune, discuss, and listen to His Spirit, without any distractions.

The Father isn't sitting perched up in heaven, lightning bolts at the ready for those times we screw up; nor is He faraway, having cast us on to planet Earth to wander aimlessly without His guidance. That said, however, I've found God to be quite a gentleman; He's more likely to speak to us through a whisper or gentle nudge, not pushing or demanding us to keep in touch. So it's critical that we reach out—and when we do, we give Him our entire focus.

What's truly remarkable is that the Creator of all things—all things including you, your neighbor, your dog, your trees, that squirrel that gets into your birdfeeder, and even the poor birds who can't get to that food—yes, *that* Creator works with your schedule. He works with mine, too. If I need to speak with Him at an odd hour, He's there. (He's also there to mend broken hearts, heal the sick, and even feed those poor starving birds . . . He is all-knowing and everywhere.)

Whatever you have to do to tune in—wear earphones, find a quiet park, rise before everyone wakes up, or stay up after everyone has gone to bed—please don't miss this precious opportunity to receive His presence. It will be the most important conversation you have today. Shut the world out so God can come in clearly.

DAILY DIFFERENCE-MAKER
Close this book. Open your heart and mind. Ask the Lord to fill it—with love, with compassion, with direction, with the names of people who need to see His love in action.

Notes

154

The Value of a Passing Game

But "he who glories, let him glory in the LORD."

—2 Corinthians 10:17

Our friend Frank Harris runs a Memphis youth basketball clinic as one of his jobs. In fact, S.J. used to play with him and now volunteers his time in a similar fashion. It's not lost on us what a profound impression Frank made on S.J.; I credit Frank for much of S.J.'s giving heart and 'make a difference' spirit.

Growing up in one of the toughest neighborhoods in Memphis, Frank dares kids to dream about possibilities, inspiring them to take any bad situation and turn it into good. His father was a custodian and his mother was a laundress for a nursing facility; as a child, Frank hadn't realized how rough they had it—it was simply the only life he knew. When you ask him, he'll tell you that the biggest mistake we make in society is that we don't believe in these kids enough; according to him, "that's too much for them to overcome."

Whoa. It's not hunger, it's not poverty, it's *how we discount them* that is too much for them to bear. So here's where Frank leverages basketball to teach ethics. Truly, he coaches children so poor they will not even receive one Christmas present, but he expects them to find a way to give. Frank knows that we can expect more from our children, and as a coach, he has the opportunity to reinforce this from a very young age. "The best thing in basketball is the pass," he always tells them. "Giving always feels so much better than taking. Give God the glory, and He'll give us the victory."

Our children follow our example, not our advice. So what kind of game are you playing these days? Is it a passing game, or are you fouling out? What part of your character will the children in your life still be carrying forty years from now?

DAILY DIFFERENCE-MAKER

Find a creative way to teach the word and value of *assist* to a child. If you're involved in sports, this should be fairly easy, but remember courtesies and manners, like holding doors open for others and wearing a smile can be taught at a very young age. You're never too young to be a giver, and they will learn how to recognize greater needs as they age.

Notes

Going Jael

Then Jael, Heber's wife, took a tent peg and took a hammer

in her hand . . . and drove the peg into his temple,

and it went down into the ground;

for he was fast asleep and weary. So he died.

−Judges 4:21

At the time of this writing, the NFL is swathed in domestic violence scandals. In fact, I've given a few statements and interviews, underscoring the same message: *It's never too late to do the right thing.*

Now today's verse may not be the most uplifting thing you've read, and admittedly, it's a curious choice; but it relates to a little-known, powerful, Old Testament story during the reign of Deborah. When Barak wanted to alter God's instructions, the Lord told Deborah that Sisera's defeat (the leader of the Canaanite army) would go to a woman. Given the culture at the time, this would have been a low-blow for any man.

Jael, the wife of a Canaanite sympathizer, took an enormous risk to do the right thing—defying her husband, his politics, and their culture—in one single stroke of a hammer (that is some powerful aim, y'all!). She did a man's job—or at least, what God had intended for Barak to do.

Women, we are at the forefront of this domestic violence issue, and we don't need men to do the fighting for us (though we certainly want them *with* us). Doing nothing has only made this situation worse. Are we raising our kids to respect or objectify women? Now before you answer that . . . what sort of threshold do they observe when we interact with our husbands, boyfriends, male coworkers, or other men? Hitting a woman is *never* okay, *ever*—no one comes out of the womb hitting women. When our actions (and inactions) don't jive with our words, the message we're sending our kids gets lost in translation.

Jael didn't have time to wait on whether or not her husband changed his mind, or whether she should let someone else handle it. She seized the opportunity and took control of the situation, giving Israel a much-needed victory. Domestic violence that's just curtailed or cut-down isn't a victory; elimination is the only victory. Ladies, it's time to 'go Jael' on this issue.

DAILY DIFFERENCE-MAKER

Take some make-up, hair color, perfume, and nail polish to a battered women's shelter. Find out what happened to the victim's abusers—did they get away with it because of some law's loophole? Was it never reported? Encourage them, but resolve to help them take up the fight.

Notes

WEEK
THIRTY
-TWO

Follow the Rules

Train up a child in the way he should go,

and when he is old he will not depart from it.

—Proverbs 22:6

Now before you call me out, I'll call myself out—when it comes to the human condition, I am a rule-breaker (you'll probably read that admission a lot in this book). There are too many children and others who do not have the luxury of time—they need our help *now.* They're slipping through the crack so fast, I don't have time nor use for whatever somebody else has deemed an appropriate route for a middle-aged Southern woman to take to help them. So yes, when it comes to individuals at-risk, I'm a rule-breaker. Feel free to join me any time.

But what I'm talking about here is the parental responsibility of establishing and enforcing rules. You can be sure our household had rules to follow. It was pretty simple in our eyes: If you followed the rules, then everything would probably work out for the best. Occasionally, the kids courageously broke the rules and Momma was not happy about that! My first instinct was to tear into them, but the reality was we had to pick them up, brush them off, hug them, explain the seriousness of the infraction, and reassure them that tomorrow is always a new day, a get-it-right day!

You see, love and stability are two of the most important factors in raising a child, and setting boundaries encompasses a large part of establishing both. Many kids think if they play by the rules they won't have any fun in life, and many parents think going easy on the rules is love. Neither is true.

Let your children know that life has so much to offer and that rules are a good thing. And as a parent, sometimes it's easier to lax on the rules, but we are ultimately doing our children a disservice. Here's some advice: My house. My rules. It's not a democracy. Set rules, enforce them, and follow through on discipline . . . then hug them and remind them that tomorrow is always a brand-new day!

DAILY DIFFERENCE-MAKER

Are your kids itching for a new toy, gadget, or item of clothing? That's fine. Now go with them to their closets and toy boxes—which items are they willing to part with to make room for the new? There are some children out there who would love them!

Notes

Now What?

Turn Yourself to me, and have mercy on me,

for I *am* desolate and afflicted.

The troubles of my heart have enlarged;

bring me out of my distresses!

—Psalm 25:16–17

Our plans had been interrupted and it was nothing that we could control . . . so I asked Sean if he had a Plan B.

Sean replied in his serious voice, "Did Michael Jordan have a Plan B when he was cut from his high school basketball team?" Sean has a way of lightening the mood while getting his point across. "Get out!' I responded. "He was cut? " What a blow!

Even now, we still have occasion to tell our kids, "Life's not always fair." When they were younger, we'd tell them this usually if they didn't win a class election, win the big game, or get the job they wanted. We'd talk about how each let-down was a character-builder and hopefully, would enrich their lives for the better. So sitting there with Sean as our plan unraveled, I realized this is actually an ongoing, life-long lesson. Not just something we tell our kids . . . something I needed to tell *myself*. And ask God, "now what?"

We can learn so much from rejection and disappointment if we take it to the Lord. Today's verse is just a sample of what David was doing in Psalm 25, which in its entirety shows a fairly raw outpouring of David's heart. He relays his anguish, his heartbreak, and his unwavering faith that his God would prevail. David did not shy away from asking God, "why?" but he knew, in time, he would understand.

When we take our disappointments and rejections to Him, we should work with Him to develop the *now what?*; but when we ask, we need to also be obedient to His response. Stay faithful to the task, maintain the right perspective while doing so, and understand that failures will arise. Be humble enough to step back, re-examine, apply a little patience . . . and remember that whether it's an exhilarating risk or it may be an obvious path, if it's His, your steps will be firm (or, in Michael Jordan's case, his jumps would catch air!).

No, life's not always fair—but our God is always just.

DAILY DIFFERENCE-MAKER
Ever had one of those nagging thoughts that won't leave you alone? They usually start with "I really should . . ." or " Someday, I hope to . . . " Finish that sentence today by acting on it!

Notes

What We Ought to Do

So likewise you, when you have done all those things which
you are commanded, say, "We are unprofitable servants.
We have done what was our duty to do."

–Luke 17:10

Sean was standing by quietly, watching Michael navigate the press line alongside the other All-Americans. Amid all the photos, hot lights, and tons of questions being directed at the players, Sean asked Michael if he would like some water and Michael said, "Yes, that would be great."

As Sean walked off to search for some water, another All-American (whose name I won't mention, but his initials are *Michael Crabtree!*) asked Sean for a water with lemon and if he would find out what time dinner would be served. Yes, he'd mistaken Sean as part of the wait staff, but Sean complied with his request—and my son looked at his fellow All-American and said, "Fool, that's my Dad." (I can only imagine what ensued from that point.) Maybe it didn't look cool to be so accommodating—but Sean knows how to manage his pride, and knew it was the right thing to do.

Now none of us are anyone's slave or servant—even if we work for someone—except the Lord's, and yet He chose to make us heirs. We are unworthy of His sacrifice, His grace, His mercy, and His provision. There is absolutely nothing we can do to pay Him back, and we cannot earn nor provide our souls' redemption. But since we are subject to Christ's rule, we should take note of His commands: To love. To serve. To practice humility. He came to earth long enough to demonstrate what that looks like in the day-to-day: Care for the sick. Feed and clothe the poor. Revere the elderly. Embrace the children . . . and yes, in Sean's case, provide some water and confirm the mealtime. As servants of the Lord, we aren't looking for pats on the back or recognition; nor do we get to pick and choose which commands to follow. To paraphrase today's verse, we do these things because they are things that ought to have been done.

DAILY DIFFERENCE-MAKER

Someone's going to bark an order at you today. It may not fit your job description; it may not be your responsibility; their bark may have quite a bit of attitude attached to it. Instead of letting your temper flare, be gracious. Accommodate the command, knowing that you're doing this as Christ's servant—not theirs.

Notes

Trained Warriors

You come to me with a sword, with a spear, and with a javelin.

But I come to you in the name of the LORD of hosts,

the God of the armies of Israel, whom you have defied. . . .

the LORD does not save with sword and spear;

for the battle is the LORD's, and He will give you into our hands.

—1 Samuel 17:45, 47

A friend asked me recently if I ever went "off-duty." I thought that was such an odd thing for her to say, but she had just spent twenty-four hours with me and witnessed a day in the life of the Tuohy family. She laughed about Michael Lewis's "warrior princess" description of me, and said I was more like a "trained warrior."

In many respects, she was right. Life is often like a battlefield! And a trained warrior has a much better chance of victory than an unprepared warrior. So I am constantly assessing, scanning, analyzing, planning, plotting . . . just ask anyone who knows me! But what good is any of that if it's not put to use?

No one in Israel's trained, experienced army was willing to step up and fight the Philistine Goliath. A young shepherd named David was on the battle outlines delivering supplies and he surveyed the scene. Now David's training was hands-on—he'd killed a lion and a bear that had threatened his flock, and now his country was under threat and his God was being mocked. He stepped up, refusing the armor that was offered—not because he was foolish but because he knew it could be a hindrance. David was trained to stay light on his feet—he wasn't used to heavy armor, nor did he need it. You know how the story ends . . . and you also know that's not the last we hear about David.

There are two things we can do in life: step up, or step down. Warriors step up, and fewer and fewer are accepting this challenge. Training isn't always a formal process; like David, sometimes our training is hands-on, to sharpen our instincts and skills for larger battles. We all need to be warriors in life—for family, for community, for country. You can make a difference—but only if you step up to the challenge!

DAILY DIFFERENCE-MAKER

Find potential locations for a community garden inside a food desert in your community. Appeal to the property owners to obtain whatever permissions, permits, and grants are necessary to break ground.

Notes

Two Common Denominators

Go and learn what *this* means:

"I desire mercy and not sacrifice."

For I did not come to call the righteous,

but sinners, to repentance.

—Matthew 9:13

The late Norman Vincent Peale said, "Change your thinking, and you change the world." I can tell you from personal experience that he was spot-on.

When we challenge our mind-set and realize that just because some event, process, or method is the way it has always been that it doesn't make it accurate, we also realize that maybe, just maybe, we *can* make a difference in this crazy world we live in. This is not open for discussion: Get out of your comfort zone! I can see a puzzled look on your face (no really, I can!). Stay with me here.

For just a minute, think about if your views on race, religion, socioeconomic standards, priorities, perceptions, values, and even your behavior were altered. We could only hope that people will look at us and think, "Something's different about this person."

Some of the most profound Bible heroes challenged the system, challenged leadership, risked associating with those deemed culturally inferior . . . even our Lord Jesus Christ was judged for cavorting with prostitutes, tax collectors, Samaritans, adulterers . . . as well as the wealthy, successful, respectable. What was His response? "Why yes, as a matter of fact, I do!" Actually, His response is found in today's verse. He wants compassion from us—not some gold-star checklist of niceties. He calls sinners, those who need a Savior, those whose gratitude for salvation will overflow into another person's life. Those who don't have time to worry with society's idea of who they are supposed to be because they are consumed with who God called them to be.

Are you a sinner? So am I. So are they. So are the others. So is everybody. Are you His child? So am I. So are they. So are the others. So is everybody. Those two common denominators are the only ones that truly matter; the rest is up to us to change.

....

DAILY DIFFERENCE-MAKER

If you want to see the melting pot in your city, go down to the DMV; all sorts of business takes place there, not just driver licenses. Take bottles of water, cookies, and a few camp chairs with you—as you know, people stand in line there for hours. Listen to their stories; ask questions about how they arrived there. Your smile may be the only one in the entire building.

Notes

WEEK
THIRTY
-THREE

Stay Gentle

A soft answer turns away wrath, but a harsh word

stirs up anger. . . . A wholesome tongue *is* a tree of life,

but perverseness in it breaks the spirit.

—Proverbs 15:1, 4

When we arrive at a point of bitterness, host of other emotions comes along with it; namely, anger, hostility, resentment. We dislike anyone else telling us to calm down or get a grip. While the person who is acting like a fool gets hurt more than everyone else, my experience in this arena is that when you fight fire with fire, someone usually gets burned.

Bitterness, anger, and hostility are destructive. They don't change any situation, are of no benefit to anyone, much less serve any beneficial purpose to those around you. And I'm not saying that Christians cannot get angry; quite frankly, it's easy to lose your composure. And while the expectation is that one would become defiant in the face of controversy, we need to set our standards higher; anything less is inadequate.

We are here to lead by example because we follow the One who led by example. Let's not lower ourselves to the level of others; raise others up to ours instead. As best we can, respond gently and soothingly when someone loses their temper; many times, a little humor and humility will silence even the most mean-spirited individual, so keep those two essentials in your back pocket. Most importantly, support and treat your team, your friends, family and those around you in a manner in which you would want to be treated!

....

DAILY DIFFERENCE-MAKER
See if you can go an entire day without raising your voice above a calm, soothing tone. Whether you're sitting in traffic, treated rudely by a fellow shopper who jumps in line ahead of you, or dealing with a child who hasn't done what he/she was asked to do.

....Notes...

Feed the Hungry, Feed Your Spirit

For you have the poor with you always, and whenever you wish

you may do them good; but Me you do not have always.

—Mark 14:7

This country was built on being a nation that worked; so I was feeling a broad range of emotions when I saw one news station report that the poverty level in our country had risen to sixteen percent. I felt shock, disbelief, fear . . . and guilt. How did we get here?

It's becoming harder and harder to get a leg up and get ahead. The ugly truth is our belief system seems to no longer go hand and hand with the facts; it's much easier to blame. Pointing fingers at financial institutions, the government, big business, gas companies . . . whatever you want to blame as to how we got here or change the situation, so we figure it's not our problem to fix—until or unless we become stricken by it, too. Yes, you. Yes, me. It could happen to any of us.

Poverty is not a part of anyone's American Dream. It is also glaringly apparent that there is no perfect solution . . . but we all have to be a part of some solution and not a part of the problem. Doing nothing is being part of the problem, and that is no longer one of your choices!

So we need to be an *active* part of the solution. The needs always seem to be greater around the holidays, but poverty is a year-round issue, so don't limit your involvement to a particular season. Poverty is powerful, it is ugly, and it is very difficult to escape. Let's face poverty head-on together; I know we can't prevent it, but we can certainly put a dent in it. Whether you deliver a nutritious meal, help with someone's utilities, purchase toys for a child, or contribute in some other way, it will have an impact on not only that individual, but also the community as a whole.

DAILY DIFFERENCE-MAKER

There are many local organizations that address hunger and always need volunteers for a variety of roles: to collect and organize donations, help prepare meals, deliver, or even drive participants to a group-dining location. Volunteer some time with one; serve and get to know some residents in your community who are hungry. Learn about any other needs you may be able to address individually, or ways to help them bridge the gap, like a small container garden or couponing.

Notes

Preserve, Strengthen, Build

As iron sharpens iron, so a man sharpens the countenance

of his friend. Whoever keeps the fig tree will eat its fruit;

so he who waits on his master will be honored.

—Proverbs 27:17–18

I often hear from people who say, "I want to make an impact, but I don't know where to begin!" This used to frustrate me but I think their point may be that it's overwhelming. And if you're trying to change the entire world all at once, it is—and you are setting yourself up for failure. So simplify your approach: preserve history, strengthen the vulnerable parts of the foundation, and build the future.

Preserve history by 'adopting' an elderly person. Too often, they are forgotten yet they possess amazing amounts of wisdom that could be passed on. Whether this person is a neighbor or someone you visit in a facility, they still count. They need to know they are still needed and useful.

When I think of strengthening the vulnerable parts of the foundation, I think primarily about those who are barely getting by and some months, falling short: families behind on their bills, individuals restricted by illness, those whose homes have fallen in disrepair . . . most are kind-hearted and hard-working. They need to know they matter. They need whatever shame they feel removed, because any one of us could be in their shoes.

There are any number of ways to build the future; but build carefully, because the day is quickly coming they will be caring for us! Resolve to meet a teenager and discuss the importance of education, the pitfalls of using drugs, the need to lower teen pregnancy, or just be a friend. If we care for them now, they will return that favor to us and others. They need to know they've been noticed. They need to be recognized. They need to understand the phrase "long-term effects" before they experience any.

This is not one-sided, however. God puts these individuals in our lives because we have something to learn, too. We may need conviction from a particular sin, we may learn a new skill, we may need to love a bit deeper. Be assured if we yield to His call to invest in others, it will change your life and theirs for the better.

DAILY DIFFERENCE-MAKER

Gather a group and introduce yourselves to a family who is in dire circumstances. Help them with minor repairs, yard work, or bringing groceries on an ongoing basis.

Notes

The Secure Phase

How fair and how pleasant you are, O love, with your delights!
–Song of Solomon 7:6

Oh, the fluttering butterflies, the singing birds, the sunshine in our hearts that come from the rush of a crush! We see it in the movies all the time, where the couple is destined to be together and nothing can prevent it . . . but for about ninety minutes, we're left on the edges of our seats wondering, just the same.

I'm certainly not perfect, but Sean treats me like I am—and that's what matters. So maybe we're not movie stars or airbrushed models from a magazine, but we all have endearing qualities that—when polished and honed—will hopefully put us in the "secure" phase of love. It's not the "movie-love" phase and too often, we want to settle there. No, the secure-love phase is a place we should all hope to be, but fewer and fewer of us get there. It's much deeper, more intimate, and much more satisfying because you've had time to grow together.

The romance is still very much a part of this phase, so get in the habit of celebrating February 14th, even if you've never made a big deal about it before. And don't wait until the next February 14th to keep celebrating what you've discovered and what you've built as a couple . . . cultivate the romance for the rest of the year, for the rest of your lives. Rediscover "how beautiful and how delightful" your significant other is; learn new "charms" to delight the person you've connected with! The gift doesn't always have to be something purchased, either. Make a habit of holding hands, opening the car door, asking an opinion, passing a compliment, or leaving a note in the briefcase or the car seat. Hopefully, this will keep the "wishing we had done it differently" to a minimum and ensure you of many years of happily-ever-afters!

DAILY DIFFERENCE-MAKER

Pick out a few verses from Song of Solomon—yes, even some of the naughty ones—and either handwrite them or print them from your computer. Periodically, leave one where your spouse will find it—in the coffee beans, in the freezer, in a shirt pocket . . . get creative with where they'll be hiding.

Notes

Your Day, Your Portion

Therefore do not worry about tomorrow, for tomorrow will worry about its own things. Sufficient for the day is its own trouble.

—Matthew 6:34

I like to take a walk each day, regardless of the weather, so I have outer gear for cold, wind, rain, etc.; coats, hats, shoes, gloves . . . I am prepared for whatever the elements throw my way. It won't surprise most of you that I have a method to my walk: I warm up, then walk briskly; then, I trot a little, sing a while, whistle and snap my fingers. If you drive by me, you might think I escaped my padded cell, but no matter—it's my method, my antics, and it keeps me taking in the present instead of letting my mind wander to the rest of the day's worries. In fact, we could all stand to be more in touch with the miracle of being alive and being present in the moment, and stop worrying about what is around the corner; each morning, we should remember to pray because God remembered to wake us up.

I am often times amazed at all these politicians and professional philanthropic do-gooders who go from one cause to another because they are always worried about the future of our children or the future of this or that . . . excuse me, but I am worried about our children today! Yes *today*, at this moment, in the present. If we don't get it right *right now,* who says they will even have this future they are all so worried about?

Most of us have known some amazing people who have left this world due to illness, and so many times I have heard people say that it's a shame that we have to have an experience like this to realize the wonder and gift of life's precious moments. Hear me: If you are reading this, you are alive today, right now, and you need to be *present* in your present. You will never live this moment again—go shelter someone who is shivering, go feed someone who is hungry, go visit someone who is lonely, do it now while they opportunity is right there in front of you . . . and make someone else aware of how, indeed, lovely it is to be alive!

DAILY DIFFERENCE-MAKER
Take a few rolls of quarters to a laundromat and fill the machines. Leave some detergent and dryer sheets.

Notes

WEEK
THIRTY
-FOUR

Heart Examination

Do not look at his appearance or at his physical stature,

because I have refused him. For *the LORD does* not *see*

as man sees; for man looks at the outward appearance,

but the LORD looks at the heart.

–1 Samuel 16:7

Who or what influences your thoughts, actions, and opinions? Are you one of those folks who stereotypes people? If your moral, ethical, and spiritual values are gauged by television talk shows, your spouse, cable news, or anyone/anything else, that needle is going to always be on the move. Now for some of you, that sounds ridiculous—who really gets their values from television, right?—but how many times have you let a cable news network or indignant talking head get you riled up? Yes, this stuff has influence.

On a God-directed trip to Bethlehem to anoint Israel's future king, Samuel the prophet was baffled; as each of Jesse's impressive sons passed by him, God kept rejecting them. Why? They looked fine to Samuel, but he was faithful to God's instruction. Only one remained, Jesse's youngest, and surely Samuel didn't intend to anoint him? When David came in from tending his sheep, God told Samuel immediately to get up—for David was, indeed, the one.

Now the Bible is quick to point out that David was a nice-looking boy (I find that part a bit amusing); but it still didn't make sense in a culture that put great value on first-born sons and mighty, battle-proven warriors. David didn't look the part—but his reign would change Israel's course and prosperity.

It would be a while before David took the throne, but thank goodness Samuel listened and remained obedient. God and God alone should set our values—we want to see as He sees, not as man sees. And certainly, God puts others in our path who can provide wise counsel on various issues; but we need to exercise caution against taking a poll among those who will agree with whatever we say or meekly going with whatever 'the crowd' tells us we are to think. The only way to be influential is to be mindful of your own influences.

....

DAILY DIFFERENCE-MAKER

Is there a church or place of worship in your town that is under scrutiny and suspicion for no apparent reason beyond prejudice? Look for opportunities for your congregation to join forces with theirs to do some good in your community—hold coat drives, clean up overgrowth, care for one another's cemeteries . . . common bonds create community.

.... Notes ....

Ode to Joy

Now may the God of hope fill you with all joy and peace

in believing, that you may abound in hope

by the power of the Holy Spirit.

—Romans 15:13

Research suggests that we are all chasing happiness . . . how sad.

You see, happiness usually depends on something external, like people or situations. This is why we continue to chase it and it continues to flee—we cannot control it. Joy, on the other hand, requires something much deeper, more internal, more intimate. It is true contentment that doesn't hinge on an invitation to the prom or whether or not you received a big promotion.

Now there is certainly nothing wrong with being happy and making ourselves happy, but we cannot stake our emotional well-being on it because, well . . . it will elude us at some point.

So what are we looking for when we chase happiness? When looking at the research of people who have won the lottery or are extremely wealthy, it seems all that money brought them nothing but misery. Many of us are the epitome of healthy and don't seem to be happy. And I can list pages full of folks who have jobs others would kill for, and they aren't happy. Given the divorce rate and infidelity stats, the perfect family does not keep us on the road to endless happiness, either. Then what is the answer to this question? Tragically, the foundation of many people's lives was built on chasing money, the fountain of youth, entertainment, and countless other things that they just knew would bring them an abundance of happiness. Does this sound familiar to you?

Joy is one of the many benefits of a believer's life; it comes to fruition by the power of God's Spirit, and sustains us when happiness eludes us. Peace and hope usually accompany joy—it's that "thing" that people sometimes can't define in others who are calm in a crisis or sincerely hopeful when their world appears to be crumbling. Joyful people rarely let anything fleeting infiltrate their spirit . . . not job loss, not a new boyfriend . . . and not even happiness. Will you seek authentic joy or just happiness today?

DAILY DIFFERENCE-MAKER
Hold a shoe drive for your local homeless shelter, particularly for new and gently used boots and sneakers. If the weather is turning cold, encourage donations of outer gear, too.

Notes

Hold On

Work out your own salvation with fear and trembling;

for it is God who works in you

both to will and to do for *His* good pleasure.

Do all things without complaining and disputing,

that you may become blameless and harmless.

—Philippians 2:12–15

When making a request, none of us likes to be told *no*. So many examples from the Bible demonstrate the good, the bad, and the ugly responses to *no*:

The Good

- David yielded to God's will and did not build His temple (2 Samuel 7)
- Paul did not enter Asia nor Bithynia the first time he'd wanted (Acts 16)
- Job was frustrated, but stayed faithful (Book of Job)

The Bad & The Ugly

- Lot's wife (Genesis 19)
- The Fall of Man (Genesis 3)

Don't hate being told *no*, especially by God. Sometimes, His *nos* are for the time being; other times, His *nos* should be regarded as permanent and as His protection.

Yes, we are to work fervently and to His glory; but we're not to do and ask for His permission later. We're not to do and, when it explodes in utter failure, ask Him to fix it.

Sometimes, the Holy Spirit's answers are clear and immediate, and we know exactly what we are to do. Other times, however, we think God's not listening when really, *we're the ones not listening, because we only want to hear what we want to hear.*

Don't run ahead just because God has told you no. Wait and anticipate without complaining. He has a plan and trust me, it's better than anything you and I could have concocted. When our impatience gets the best of us, then God doesn't.

DAILY DIFFERENCE-MAKER

Is there something you have been trying to strong-arm into submission? Even if it's for a good cause, now may not be the right time or perhaps you're not the right person. Help your cause by giving it some pause . . . and prayer.

Notes

Don't Tear Down—Build Up!

Whatever things are true, whatever things *are* noble,

whatever things *are* just, whatever things *are* pure,

whatever things *are* lovely,

whatever things *are* of good report,

if *there is* any virtue and if *there is* anything praiseworthy

—meditate on these things.

–Philippians 4:8

We are so quick to criticize; and too often, I'm the ring-leader. It's so easy, because all we have to do is pick apart instead of build up. Building up someone or some cause takes a lot more energy and time; so we take the lazy approach and the easiest route.

If you think about it, when we spend our time in the muck of criti-cizing, we don't have time to do God's work. The important stuff gets left undone because we're too preoccupied with the tearing-down business. Isn't that the best trick ever?

So look at what the verse says—we are to focus on truth, noble pursuits, justice, purity . . . because what comes from our mouths reveals what resides in our hearts. Let's promote what we love instead of bashing what we hate. You don't like the drug dealers hanging by the local schools? Then create an after-school program that focuses on physical health. If you don't like the salacious book your book club wants to read, suggest one that's more uplifting (and politely decline to participate if they decide to continue with the first option, but don't bash). If you don't like your son's taste in music, introduce him to Elvis, James Taylor, U2, Tim McGraw, The Temptations, or The Beatles (surely you like at least one of these?!).

We can make the same point and still change our delivery of it. Have you been battling, trash-talking, spewing venom over a particular person or issue? Which one? All righty, then—instead of taking that approach, what is your solution to that problem?

DAILY DIFFERENCE-MAKER

Drug dealers will move on if they can't get any business, and they love to attract student "reps" who can peddle their stuff in schools—public *and* private. An after-school program that focuses on health and nutrition might help counteract their intentions; take kids for a run on the track or on a trail, show them how to cook or assemble a simple, healthy snack, or maybe just play basketball with them.

Notes

Be a Refuge

I will both lie down in peace, and sleep;

for You alone, O LORD, make me dwell in safety.

–Psalm 4:8

Today, I'm going to get right to the point: Everyone should have a place where they feel absolutely safe. Yes, *everyone*. A shelter, a refuge, even another person can provide or reinforce that environment or attitude, but the Lord ultimately gives us our peace and security.

Children, in particular, need such a place. Insecure children usually become insecure adults—it becomes more and more difficult to correct that with each passing year. They are vulnerable and it's up to us to protect their innocence. Among developed countries, our nation has one of the worst records in terms of rescuing and caring for our children—each day, between four and seven children are lost to child abuse and neglect.*

That statistic sickens me. Today, a child will die not knowing what he or she did wrong. A child who probably knew nothing but hurt and pain, and thought this was how the world operated. A child who feared for his life and death. A child who—if they've lived to be a teenager—decides no one will care for him except himself; and since there aren't many career options for young teenagers, he makes himself even more vulnerable. It's not just irony—it's sickening, given the amount of resources we have.

We can do better—we must. Every man, woman, and child deserves a safe place where they are loved and feel loved. If the Lord provides this for us, how will we provide this for others today?

....

DAILY DIFFERENCE-MAKER
Buy some large teddy bears and donate them to the police department to give children involved in cases of abuse or neglect. Support an organization that deals with these same issues

.... *Notes* ....

*Source: Childhelp.org

WEEK
THIRTY
-FIVE

A Giving Lifestyle

By an equality, *that* now at this time your abundance

may supply their lack, that their abundance also

may *supply* your lack—that there may be equality.

—2 Corinthians 8:14

Not one of us is superior to another—but each of us has an abundance of something to give, whether it's money, time, or talent. And each one of us is lacking something, whether it's money, time, or talent.

So look at what Paul writes: our abundance can supply someone's lack, and someone else's abundance may supply ours. The young mother who is suddenly called up to her child's school cannot bring with her the little one that's still at home—but you may have time to watch her baby. The person ahead of you in line at the grocery may be digging for the last bit of change—but you have a five-dollar bill that will cover it. You may not have the skills, money, or time to address the noise in your car, but another neighbor does. How might you return the favor?

Listen, even the smallest gesture can make *all* the difference in someone else's life! If you've ever taken dance lessons, you know that you started off very aware of your steps and counting them. Eventually, the steps became easier . . . easy enough for you to *listen* to the music. At then at some point, you added a bit of style and flair, *feeling* the music . . . and the counting became almost nonexistent!

So look for small opportunities each day: Open doors, return grocery carts, plant flowers where there are none, feed children on a playground, offer cold bottles of water to those who work outside . . . when you incorporate small ways of giving into your lifestyle, they become second-nature; and you'll be looking for your next rumba because you've already mastered the basic box step.

....

DAILY DIFFERENCE-MAKER

Couponing can get competitive among those who do it—who saved the most? Who got the best price? But it can also result in a gluttony of products that a single family may never use—who needs sixty bottles of shampoo or aspirin? That stuff will expire at some point. Instead, work with an inner-city church or organization to find a space for all the excess you and your friends have from couponing, saving out only what you and your family will use within a reasonable amount of time. Allow residents to come and take as they need—no questions asked.

.... Notes ....

The Importance of Prayer

Seek the LORD and His strength; seek His face evermore!

–1 Chronicles 16: 11

Prayer is the most important conversation you'll have today; how often do you choose *not* to have it? Some of us would rather talk to our friends, coworkers, and even our television sets before we talk to God.

We also confuse support materials and groups with our time with God. Your Bible study group, your Sunday School lesson, even this book should never be used as a God substitute. Prayer was given to us as a way to reach Him; through prayer, we can share our hopes, dreams, disappointments, and fears in the most intimate ways. In fact, His Spirit intercedes on our behalf when we are at a loss for words (Romans 8:26). No one and no thing can do for us like God does—accept no substitutes.

Some of us rush through our prayers so quickly, we're already moving before *amen*. Meditation is one way God responds; in the still and quiet, His voice enters our minds and hearts, giving us things to ponder throughout the day or answers we have been seeking. God knew you before you even entered this world—He knows your wiring, your thoughts, your personality better than your own mother. Don't miss the blessings that come from quality time with Him.

Now if our prayers are not prompting us to eventually act, we're still not seeking His strength. If we're not moved to do something—change a behavior, give a second chance, fulfill a need, etc.—we don't have full confidence in His ability to transform us. You are not a lost cause; you are not too set in your ways to make a difference, unless you choose to be. Pray as if it's up to God; work as if it's up to you.

DAILY DIFFERENCE-MAKER

If someone crosses your mind, that may not be as random as it seems—say a prayer for them. If you are moved to pick up the phone and give them a call, please do not ignore this nudge!

Notes

The Way We Are

Glory, honor, and peace to everyone who works what is good

. . . For there is no partiality with God.

—Romans 2:10–11

When Collins was in high school, she participated in a week-long program called Bridge Builders. School children from practically opposite backgrounds live in college dorms to get to know each other and learn from each other.

During that week, one particular exercise made quite an impression on her. One of the program leaders lined twenty or so children single-file in a dark room; as she asked a series of questions, each student responded by taking a step either to the right or left. Questions like whether they'd get a car when they turn sixteen, did they live in a two-parent home, etc., etc. When they turned on the lights, they also turned on the light in Collins's heart and mind; just about all of the students were on opposite sides of the room. One step at a time, Collins could see the differences were based on family circumstances; it dawned on her, "So this is why we are the way we are."

Sean's background was humble, and he'll be the first to tell you he spent his childhood figuring out how to make a living in the land of the rich. He's known hunger, and often says the best part of his

Ole Miss scholarship was unlimited food. And while Michael's is the best-known story, we have taken in any number of children over the years for various periods of time, usually because their home lives are tumultuous or there are some financial challenges.

When we offer someone an opportunity to change their circumstances, none of us can predict the future; I am convinced, however, there are thousands of Sean Tuohys and Michael Ohers running around in cities and towns everywhere in the United States. The kid who knows the cure for cancer, or could be the best geography teacher or minister, could be walking the streets of inner-city Detroit, Memphis, Tampa, Dallas, Little Rock . . . you get my point.

Even if we change someone's circumstances for a short period, it may impact them for a lifetime. If circumstances are what separate us, it can also be the catalyst for bringing us together.

. . . .

DAILY DIFFERENCE-MAKER

Find a store (or school) that offers music lessons. Arrange to pay for a child who cannot afford them. Rent an instrument for a high school band student.

. . . . Notes . . . .

Relinquishing Control

You cannot serve God and mammon.

–Luke 16:13

Sean and I are perpetually modifying our giving philosophy. Like most, early on we wanted to make sure whatever we gave was managed properly. Over the years, we've been solicited by numerous organizations, causes, institutions, and individuals. Do we give a bit to everyone, or zero in on one and write a big check? Do we keep our help in the United States, or go global? Do we give cash to the guy with the sign on the street, almost certain he will drink away our donation (according to S.J.)? What is the right way to give? Are we giving or enabling?

If we weren't careful, we might have compared causes as though there was some sort of return on investment. Then, we'd start feeling guilty about the ones we declined, or decide we couldn't make much of a dent. There was so much indecisiveness, we were concerned about 'giving paralysis,' where our frustration overshadowed any sort of giving, cheerful or not.

We have arrived at the point we try not to confuse the *power* of giving with the *effectiveness* of giving. You see, giving is powerful unto itself; it doesn't require help from the recipient to be meaningful. It worked on the giver's heart—hopefully, making it bigger. What the recipient does with the gift—the effectiveness—is entirely up to him or her. They may change the world or buy whiskey. God judges each heart separately, including those of the giver and the recipient.

If we wait until we are fully informed about where our money is headed and that we are entirely comfortable with how it's used or managed, we will never give as much as we want to. We will miss the "Popcorn Theory" opportunities because we'll either ignore or over-analyze the situation. We simply cannot control everyone and every-thing—and don't need to try. We need to serve God by giving, and trusting Him with the rest.

I realize for some of you, this is a shaky step, but please take it with me—we're not asking you to give foolishly, only to give and not expect a result or return. Can you release that?

DAILY DIFFERENCE-MAKER
Loan money to someone in need without expectation that they will pay it back.

Notes

Give Them Security

Whoever receives one little child like this

in My name receives Me.

—Matthew 18:5

For most of us, a stable home is warm in the winter, cool in the summer, has an endless supply of food in the fridge. Really, a stable home is more of a mind-set and feeling that helps us overcome other hurdles in life because it provides a solid foundation to work from. So many children today have neither.

Sean and I knew there would be sacrifices when we decided to become parents, because you usually have to sacrifice to be a giver. We had no outline or book to follow, no contract to sign with the kids. Everything was used as a learning experience, because we had very specific values and qualities we wanted to instill in our kids. Yes, we had wonderful help along the way from family, friends, our church, and probably even a few strangers; collectively, they all helped us raise responsible, respectful children. We always worked as a team but there was never a question about Who was in charge!

You may live in an apartment, a grand mansion, a tiny house, or even on a sailboat, but the only way to build a stable home is with a strong spiritual foundation. Over two thousand years ago, in the original 'stable home,' a Savior entered the world to make our futures certain and secure. Think about it—as believers, we're taken care of . . . and we're free to share this reassurance with others. We can express our gratitude for God's grace by helping our most vulnerable feel safe and loved.

Our children, their children, those children, *all* children deserve a nurturing, safe environment in which to grow, reach, and yes, even fail sometimes; too many are entering our world without even a chance at having one. What are you doing to change the life of a child from uncertainty to stability?

DAILY DIFFERENCE-MAKER

Babies don't just grow beneath a woman's heart—they can grow in anyone's heart, so open yours. Find a children's home in your town that houses children who have been removed from their homes. Call in advance and arrange for you and some friends with you to go and hold those little ones. Read to them, rock them, hug on them, comb their hair, play with them. Be respectful of the rules in place, given the sensitivity of the situation—but please, please, go love on those children.

Notes

WEEK
THIRTY
-SIX

Say Yes

Blessed *is* she who believed, for there will be a fulfillment
of those things which were told her from the Lord.

–Luke 1:45

Will the world stop spinning if you aren't married by thirty, having a baby by thirty-five, achieve millionaire-status by forty, or retire at sixty? Of course not! Take a look at the lives of Elizabeth and Mary if you don't believe me.

Now Elizabeth was quite a bit older than Mary, and had more than likely accepted that she would not bear the child she'd longed for. And then there was Mary, a young teenager, who probably wasn't thinking about having a child in the immediate future, certainly not before marrying Joseph.

But God had other plans—big plans. Earth-shattering, foretold, save-the-world sorts of plans. And these two women were key. Which meant foregoing whatever their original plans were to follow God's crazy one . . . for a woman of advanced age to give birth to John the Baptist and a young, unmarried virgin to give birth to God Himself! Now that is some big 'happenins'!!

What if either woman had said *no?* What if Mary was unwilling to risk the social stigma, or Elizabeth decided she couldn't handle the task at her age? Aren't we grateful that both women stayed open and obedient to God's plan, even if it meant scrapping whatever plans they'd had? They believed. They obeyed. They persevered.

Don't lose your energy and enthusiasm just because your original plan didn't succeed. It's times like these that require good old fashion willpower and faith. Remind yourself that just because you had to shake the Etch-A-Sketch® doesn't mean there won't be a happy ending. God will turn your challenges into His opportunities; and when it's God's plan, I can assure you it will be the best ending possible—beyond anything we could imagine for ourselves.

DAILY DIFFERENCE-MAKER

Are you lingering over a past hurt that seems to be preventing you from moving forward? Do something today that's bigger than you or your pain—join Big Brother/Big Sister program, pick up trash in a public park, plan a trip to help an area affected by natural disaster. Be aware of anything God plants in your heart during that time.

Notes

Walk in Gratitude, Humility

Break off your sins by *being* righteous,

and your iniquities by showing mercy to *the* poor.

Perhaps there may be a lengthening of your prosperity.

–Daniel 4:27

We never need to get so full of ourselves that we lose sight of the fact that we are all on the same team in this journey called life. My hope for you is that you walk in humility and that you never think you are so important that helping others is beneath you. We can really make a difference if we are willing to put others' needs ahead of our own. People need to see value and integrity in our actions—and not just when we're sure we have an audience, because we have an audience more than we realize!

King Nebuchadnezzar of Babylon was enjoying life and saw no reason to change the course he was already on, in spite of Daniel's troubling interpretation of his latest dream. And if you're familiar with the story, you know that almost immediately, Nebuchadnezzar lost his mind. He was cast away from his kingdom, and lived among the cattle, even eating grass with them. His hair grew long and matted, his nails grew to be like claws. Nebuchadnezzar went from the very top to the lowest of the low in an instant; it can happen to any of us, too.

So be slow to judge the next person you see using food stamps or overhear explaining to the physician's receptionist that they have no health insurance; you've no idea the path they may have walked before they arrived. Your reference points might be inaccurate!

Instead, let's be fearless in the face of need; let's be generous and compassionate; and finally, let's not have our actions shaped by someone else's opinion—because we are all in this together. Our success as a society just might depend on it!

DAILY DIFFERENCE-MAKER

Pay someone's delinquent power or water bill. Most utility companies have a way of enabling this, or even to help on a regular basis. Regardless, request that you remain anonymous to the recipient.

Notes

Who Are Your People?

And a multitude was sitting around Him; and they said to Him,

"Look, Your mother and Your brothers are outside seeking You."

But He answered them, saying,

"Who is My mother, or My brothers?"

And He looked around in a circle at those who sat about Him,

and said, "Here are My mother and My brothers!"

—Mark 3:32–34

A common question in the South is, "Who are your people?" For those of you who don't know, that question is asking about someone's family tree—parents, grandparents, great-grandparents . . . as far back and as historically significant as possible. In recent times, most people don't respond beyond a generation or two unless they are pressed for more details. Obviously, my family could have some fun with that—with God's blessing, based on today's verse.

Well, what does a family look like? While we weren't intentional about it, I hope my own family has changed people's views on that snapshot. We might not look typical, but we feel and love as you imagine a family would.

So take another look at today's verse. We're not really sure why Jesus' biological family showed up that day—maybe they were trying again to convince Him to return to Nazareth; maybe His crazy antics were making them a laughingstock. Maybe they were encouraged and wanted to see Him in action. And at first glance, Jesus' response surely seems cold—had He disowned them? Of course not. Jesus loved His physical family, but His point was that our spiritual family was of greater significance and had eternal impact. 'Family,' then, need not consist of two parents, one girl with a bow in her hair, one boy with freckles, and a dog; now, that certainly makes a nice family photo, but there are other combinations that are just as wonderful, just as life-changing, and make equally beautiful portraits (and would definitely raise a few eyebrows for those on your Christmas card list!). Some families are not related by blood or marriage; some families are legally bound, while others are not.

Everyone deserves a family—a setting in which they are loved, have an opportunity to love, and feel secure—and to be connected to each member by something that goes far beyond our physical world. Given that—who are your people? And who needs to be?

....

DAILY DIFFERENCE-MAKER

Whether you're single, an empty-nester, or have a house full—invite someone to spend a holiday with you. Include them in your traditions; leave room for them to include theirs.

.... *Notes* ....

Be a "Bother"

Let not mercy and truth forsake you;

bind them around your neck,

write them on the tablet of your heart.

—Proverbs 3:3

Recently, I was driving down a very busy street in Memphis, Tennessee, and a middle-aged woman honked her horn and me, rolled down her window, and said, "Your gas cap is open." Since the gas station was several miles behind me, I'd probably passed hundreds of cars by that point; I wondered, how many people had seen this and just chose to ignore it. Out of hundreds of cars, one woman persisted . . . and succeeded.

Why do some people help perfect strangers, while others do not? Without question, our world is faster-paced so maybe it just feels like one more thing we don't have time to do. What gnaws at me, however, is that our accelerated world has embraced this, "it's not our problem, so let's not get involved" mantra. Not our worry. It's on them to figure it out, we have places to be and people to see.

I have no idea why this woman chose to help *me*. Was it her faith, her upbringing, her desire to better her community? Maybe she pictured herself, her daughter, or her mother in the same situation? She knew there was no reward for her effort, except maybe a thank-you (which she received!), yet she still decided to help a stranger. It took a matter of seconds for her, yet it meant the world to me.

Look at what today's scripture says about kindness: We are to bind it to us, embed it in our hearts. In other words, it should be visible, yet a part of us. Can you imagine a world where Christians bound and embedded their kindness in lieu of their judgment? A world where we 'bothered'? And each time we bothered, someone's day was made, and we'd start a 'bothering' epidemic?

We have all been on the receiving end of this sort of kindness at one time or another. It leaves one with a restored feeling in mankind, even from something as small as a flapping gas cap. Remember, the smallest acts of kindness may seem almost insignificant, but sometimes, they are heroic to those on the receiving end.

....

DAILY DIFFERENCE-MAKER

Let anyone and everyone in front of you in traffic. Some will be polite, casting a lingering blinker and hopeful look while others will cut you off aggressively; in either and all cases, wave them in with a smile and cheerful heart.

.... Notes ....

Put Away the Pressure Cooker

Be hospitable to one another without grumbling.

−1 Peter 4:9

It may have been the best Thanksgiving I've ever had . . . we were headed out-of-town because the NFL decided that Michael's team would play on Thanksgiving night. Since the airlines are pretty strict about bringing a turkey on board as your carry-on (who knew?), we would have to find food at the stadium. We would forego the traditional fare—seeing Michael do his thing and spending the holiday with him was much, much more important.

Now I was perfectly happy with this arrangement for other reasons, too. I didn't have to do the mad-dash to the grocery store, I didn't have to cook, and I was perfectly happy telling S.J., "You can either have a game dog or chicken tenders, and if you're really sweet, I'll throw in a funnel cake." Can it get any better than that???

Where is it written that it's not Thanksgiving, Easter, Christmas, or any other holiday unless we hit a specific mark? Unless we have a certain type of meal, set off fireworks, dye eggs, even put up a tree? Now I love certain traditions and customs . . . but guess what? That holiday is going to arrive whether you've hit your marks or not. And any perceived failures will be long forgotten before the next one rolls around—or become funny memories.

Sometime around one in the morning, after we'd cheered Michael's team to victory, we were happily munching on odds and ends found in the fridge. It occurred to me that for a few days, we managed not to stress ourselves out by chopping, dicing, and making three different trips to the grocery store because we forgot the pecans or ran out of brown sugar (grocery trips are usually my traditional contribution—for the my mother and cousins who actually cook!). Many more out there did not have it as good as we did that year, whether they were hungry or preoccupied assembling some massive meal. We could rest easy in what we were truly thankful for—eating hot dogs with happy hearts, and simply enjoyed spending quality time together as a family.

....

DAILY DIFFERENCE-MAKER
What is the next major holiday approaching? Invite someone who doesn't have plans—someone from your church, a coworker, a soldier, a child in foster care—to spend it with you and your family.

.... Notes ....

WEEK
THIRTY
-SEVEN

Blessings and Gifts

That their hearts may be encouraged,

being knit together in love,

and *attaining* to all riches of the full assurance of understanding,

to the knowledge of the mystery of God,

both of the Father and of Christ.

—Colossians 2:2

Listen to this—I recently read an article about the research of Francis Flynn at Stanford University. According to his findings, even with all our searching for that perfect gift, including the time and money invested, that—to use one of S.J.'s favorite phrases—it's a swing and a miss. *Thud*. Let me pick myself up from the floor, and then I'll help you do the same.

That's right—the gifts are not appreciated as much as we'd hoped. And according to *Consumer Reports*, fourteen million of us are still paying off those gifts a year later. Yep, those gifts that people didn't like.

This is definitely one of the few times I'll tell you to color tight inside those lines. There is no joy in unwrapping a credit card bill; we need to take one big step back, a deep breath, and just as Santa does, check that list twice. Create a plan for your gift-giving and don't stray from it. Envision January 10th (or any other month when that bill arrives). Was the gift that meaningful? Is it still bringing joy and ever lasting happiness to that person? Probably not. So we really are better off staying inside those lines and within our means.

Focus on the mission at hand and in all the chaos, look for an opportunity to make sure that we remember that these occasions are not about running up credit card bills, worrying about breaking the budget, or all the pressure created by the aforementioned. We have already received the gift of eternal life—there is *no* greater gift than that. When we wish others the gifts of blessings, love, health, success, peace on Earth, and goodwill toward all, those are gifts to enjoy for all of our years . . . and all that costs is a moment of our time. It's the most underrated, valuable, precious gift any of us can give.

DAILY DIFFERENCE-MAKER

Pick a yard that belongs to an elderly person. Offer to rake leaves in the fall, shovel their walk when it snows, and mow their lawn in the spring and summer.

Notes

Observing the "HOW"

Now Jesus sat opposite the treasury
and saw how the people put money into the treasury.

—Mark 12:41

Why is it exactly that we even give gifts during the holidays? For me, the idea of giving someone a gift is an act of kindness that acknowledges they are special, and that I appreciate them. It is a token of love and gratitude, because what they've brought to my life is invaluable.

Sometimes, we correlate one's value by the amount of money spent on a gift; the more we spend on the gift, the more that person on the receiving end is valued. That is absolutely inaccurate! Not all gift-giving has to be wrapped in beautiful paper or actually cost money—don't be fooled by this worldly perspective.

Today's verse comes from the well-known story of the widow's mite, told in the gospels of Mark 12 and Luke 21. In an odd twist, the gospel of Mark actually gives us a bit more detail than Luke; as the shortest gospel, Mark is generally known for brevity, so the added detail is kind of unusual. Mark's gospel tells us that Jesus observed *how* the wealthy were putting their gifts in the coffers; Luke leaves out the "how." Were they making a bunch of noise?

Were they pretending the sacks of money were heavier than they really were? Were they holding their heads high instead of bowing them in humility? I don't know. But I find it interesting that the Lord observed the *how*. The scriptures don't say whether the widow was elderly—she's always pictured that way—but her heart was so full of gratitude, her copper coins were far more valuable to the Kingdom. It's such a beautiful story about how we are to give.

Oh, and just to ensure I'm getting my point across: When you receive a gift, there is no need to rob their joy or steal their moment by sending a comparable gift or one-upping; at that point, it ceases to be about expressing love and gratitude and becomes a competition. Always, always give from the heart; you'll get much, much more in return.

DAILY DIFFERENCE-MAKER

The next time you're out to dinner, observe others in the restaurant; is there someone there who looks down? Looks stressed? Unhappy? Find the most miserable person in the whole place—yes, I realize we're judging, but body language and expression is fairly obvious—found them yet? Now buy them dessert or pay their bill anonymously.

Notes

183

Localized Impact

Why does the way of the wicked prosper?

Why are those happy who deal so treacherously? . . .

But You, O LORD, know me; You have seen me,

And You have tested my heart toward You.

—Jeremiah 12:1, 3

Have you ever paid much attention to what happens in your local government? Have you ever attended a city council meeting? So much gets approved in those meetings without residents even being aware until it's too late. Maybe it's not affecting your neighborhood right now . . . but it will.

So the next time you're watching or reading the local news and thinking, "that's someone else's problem," consider whether you're that "someone"? We need to hold our community officials more responsible, and we can't do that unless we take an active role in what's going on. (We the People have elected some doozies, to the point I'm not sure what We the People were thinking.)

We need to take a stand when there is a proposal to close the neighborhood library or YMCA. Neighborhoods should be included on any new building or development that directly impacts their properties. Advocate for a larger police presence in crime-ridden areas.

Explore those parts where sidewalks, playgrounds, and green space would be beneficial. Be the voice your community needs to hear, the voice that offers support in all the right places.

Real governing and real change takes place at the local level. We need to start in our own backyards and look out for each other. Become accountable, dependable, and available. Let the change begin with you and your choices. Don't relent until you see hope blossoming on the faces of those who haven't been as fortunate as you. We cannot let the bad guys continue to win—we gotta get moving.

I'll close with a familiar quote that has been attributed to many different sources, from theologians to Navy admirals: "A ship in the harbor is safe, but that's not what ships were built for."

DAILY DIFFERENCE-MAKER

While the vision of a large group locking arms and storming city hall is great, the most powerful storms build over time. Start by researching the bills currently active in your city council's docket or by driving around to see what your community needs. Pick an issue and give it your attention; get in touch with your representative for answers. Learn the process and respect it. Enlist an e-mail/letter-writing campaign or petition that asks for support or deferral. If your representatives are not responsive, remember this during the next election cycle.

Notes

All-weather Friends

A friend loves at all times, and a brother is born for adversity.

—Proverbs 17:17

Sean and I had an opportunity to speak in North Dakota a few years ago. We had been scheduled to speak earlier that year, and the event was cancelled due to the town flooding. Originally, we'd been asked to speak because of the sudden population explosion that had occurred; oil had been discovered in the area, and thousands of workers were brought in to do all the manual labor. Their housing conditions were inadequate, and they were being treated very poorly.

Then almost as suddenly, another type of flood arrived. This flash flood swept through the entire town, and amid its destruction, it suddenly no longer mattered who you were, where you were from, what you lived in or drove, or if you were educated. This disaster made everyone equal. It leveled the playing field.

Don't wait for disaster to be kind to people. As Christians, we should be polite to all people, especially the rude ones . . . not because we want to convert rude people into nice people, but because we ourselves are nice people and being nice is what nice people do. (Got that?)

Yes, it is possible to love people we don't necessarily like—not easy, but possible. And when we show love, we may be the one called on in their times of adversity. Romans 12:21 tells us to not let evil overwhelm us—instead, we overwhelm it with good. Rude people are often hurting or unwell; someone has spoiled them, either through indulgence or neglect, and bitterness has entered their heart. We can't let their bad behavior rub off on us, but we can find a way to reassure them that they can count on us—and sometimes, we can do this without saying a word.

Love at all times. When disaster or adversity strikes, we can be effective because we already know how to help that person best.

DAILY DIFFERENCE-MAKER

Think of someone who is not on your list of favorites. Do something nice for them today. Bring them a cupcake or cookie (I always recommend The Whimsy Cookie Company!), send a card, compliment their appearance, or just smile and greet them warmly if you haven't been in the habit of doing so. Ask them how they are doing and truly listen to their answer.

Notes

Honor the Aged

You shall rise before the gray headed and honor the presence

of an old man, and fear your God: I am the LORD.

−Leviticus 19:32

Recently, I read an article in the paper about an older American, an 86-year-old, World War II veteran in Detroit who had been car-jacked as he was pumping gas. Apparently, his leg was broken during the carjacking, and he was trying to crawl for help. The video surveillance cameras literally show people passing him by. That is unimaginable to me; how pathetic that no one—yes, no one—came to this man's aid.

And while I was reminded of Jesus' parable about The Good Samaritan from Luke 10—where so many passed by a man who had been left for dead—I chose a verse from Leviticus to remind us of God's command particularly for those who are elderly. This is not optional, nor is it a mere suggestion—we are to honor, respect, protect, and care for those who have spent the better part of their lives doing the same for us.

Americans, in particular, should be appalled at situations like what happened to this man in Detroit. We hear about these nightmare incidents far too often, and they involve those older Americans who have invested their lives in this nation. I just can't wrap my mind around it; this gentleman was part of the "greatest generation," the group that has taken the often-thankless job of serving as the backbone of our nation. He fought for the freedoms that we have today and when he needed help, people dismissed him. Surely he was groaning and asking—and he shouldn't have had to. Why must we wait for our national treasures to groan in pain? Why are we not caring for them all along, to relieve them of their pain?

You'll hear me say this often: Grow up, already. Caring for us is no longer that generation's role—it's our turn to rise up, and honor those who have spent far too long helping us have better lives than what they had. In gratitude and obedience, it's time they reaped their rewards.

....

DAILY DIFFERENCE-MAKER

Think of someone older you may have dismissed, maybe a neighbor who talks too much, or a relative who is unpleasant. Do something kind for that person today—bring them an easy-care plant, clean their kitchen, mow their lawn, or run an errand. But most importantly, visit with them; listen for clues as to how best to care for them.

.... Notes ....

WEEK
THIRTY
-EIGHT

Hurrah for the Underdogs!

For with God nothing will be impossible.

–Luke 1:37

America loves an underdog—probably because of its own humble beginnings.

Underdogs may be young, inexperienced, without a formal education, have physical limitations . . . they may have any number of attributes and hurdles that make them appear to be the last choice, worst choice even, for a particular task.

But when that underdog believes they can make a difference, has faith that God will fill whatever gaps necessary to fulfill His purpose, or simply takes that first step in recognizing they are not worthless . . . they have headed in the right direction.

Today's verse, spoken by the angel Gabriel, told a young teenage girl who had never known a man that she was pregnant. *What the what?!* What would her fiancé do? Would he dump her? Would her parents kick her out of the house? Would she be the talk of their little village? Who would believe her account? None of that mattered to Mary; the Lord chose her for a significant task, one that would ultimately change the course of the world. Like Mary, we never know how strong we are until being strong is the only option we have.

Now my family can tell you from personal experience that there is always an active little bugger-mosquito-gnat voice hissing in your head, "Walk away . . . fast! This is pointless. Don't waste your time. You've got a got a million things to do, and this is not on one of them." We need to gather the courage to tell that voice to *shut up*! Trust me, it's never pointless, worthless, or hopeless . . . it can, however, be life-changing for everyone involved—including you.

If you *believe* you make a difference in someone's—anyone's—life, then you can make an impact like none other. See it through!

....

DAILY DIFFERENCE-MAKER

Hold a mini-spa day for patients and staff at a crisis pregnancy center; hire a few professionals to massage their feet and shoulders or give manicures. Serve healthy foods that you would serve at any sort of ladies' gathering. Since some women may choose for their baby to be adopted, baby gifts may not be appropriate. Instead, focus on the ladies themselves.

....Notes..

Well, Shut My Mouth and Fill Me with Grace!

Let your speech always *be* with grace, seasoned with salt,

that you may know how you ought to answer each one.

–Colossians 4:6

I was on a plane returning from Los Angeles. Two gentlemen sat behind me discussing the pitfalls of having to go on a business trip to Memphis, Tennessee; their dialogue was so off-base that it was all I could do to contain myself from turning around and saying, "You two are idiots."(Yeah, there's a whole other way to "turn around.")

Now this was up-close and personal, human stupidity, right there within earshot. In their ever-so shallow minds, they categorized not just Memphians, but Southerners in general, as "hicks." Who even uses that word any more? I have traveled to the four corners of this country and beyond our borders, and let me tell you I have encountered every type of redneck, low-rent, and classless character imaginable—they're everywhere. Yes, Southerners might enjoy the outdoors a bit more, and we are usually very outgoing, polite, and well-mannered, but that doesn't mean we don't have indoor plumbing and can't hold our own with intelligent debate and discussion, funny sayings aside.

I was fuming, seething, probably could have powered the plane myself as these two prattled on . . . and I realized I was slowly taking the bait. All they had to do was reel me in, and I'd be right there, at their level.

Someone is always observing our behavior, and we represent more than ourselves when we're "out there." We represent our grandparents, our parents, our heritage, our spiritual family, our cities and regions . . . and we are ultimately made in God's image so that we can represent Him. So when our temperature rises, stop and ask yourself if you'd behave in the same manner if any of them were sitting with you. Those who have given so much of themselves to us—we owe it to them to represent well.

Speak your mind, defend yourself when necessary, then take a deep, deep breath, count to ten, and put your headphones on. Don't raise your voice or let things spiral out of control—remember, you are representing, and people are always watching.

. . . .

DAILY DIFFERENCE-MAKER

Spend an afternoon with a foster child in a local park, sharing ice cream cones and looking for figures in clouds. If you have children of your own, invite them along.

. . . . Notes . . . .

Other People Matter

Bearing with one another, and forgiving one another,

if anyone has a complaint against another;

even as Christ forgave you, so you also *must do.*

—Colossians 3:13

I once saw a t-shirt that read, "Other People Matter." Yep, it's true—other people matter a great deal! If we realize this and nothing more than this, the joy would overflow so beautifully.

My family has been on a very God-leading journey the past several years, and we have found that as opposed to putting self first, think of someone else. My, my, my, doesn't that sound rather biblical?

And sometimes, it's the little kindnesses that make the biggest impact. Instead of buying something for yourself, for example, get something for a friend. Next time you're pumping gas and the person next to you puts in five bucks, offer to fill up their tank, too. The unexpected kindness comes back to you in the form of unexpected joy!

Perhaps there's a cause that is extremely meaningful to you. Are you passionate about The American Heart Association because one of your parents died of a heart attack, or The American Cancer Society because your sibling died of cancer? Donate your time or your money to them. That will change the baseline of happiness in your life, and transition into the joy of serving others. You see, happiness is fleeting; but once you make your initial move and feel the joy, you will be apt to do it a second time, then a third, and then you're off to the races!

Other people matter. Always.

....

DAILY DIFFERENCE-MAKER

Research major holidays of other faiths to see if one is coming up. Call the given house of worship in your town to see if anyone needs a fill-in at their job, a babysitter, or help serving a traditional holiday meal (if that applies) so that these individuals can enjoy their day without stress. It is a peaceful way to show respect to those who are different.

.... Notes ....

189

He's Already There—Welcome Him

Can anyone hide himself in secret places,

so I shall not see him?" says the LORD;

"Do I not fill heaven and earth?" says the LORD.

—Jeremiah 23:24

Who is the godliest person you can think of? Maybe it's a grandparent, a pastor, a coach, a mentor . . . the sort of person we'd all 'be on our best' anytime they were around. They didn't demand our respect because they didn't have to . . . they just got it.

If they shadowed you 24/7, would you live any differently? Maybe you would have more patience. Perhaps you wouldn't walk past the panhandler as if they were invisible. Maybe you'd help a group of school children cross a busy intersection, or an elderly neighbor carry their groceries inside. Perhaps you wouldn't bark orders at the gentleman who comes to fix your faucet or insist that the repair on your window take no more than one hour, because that's all you're willing to pay for. If this person was standing in your presence, you would more than likely change your tune in any of these scenarios.

So if the godliest person you know could have that affect on you, have you considered that God Himself shadows you 24/7?

You cannot run from Him, nor hide; He knows your thoughts, your actions, your motives. Consciously carry Him with you today—to meetings, to the store, when you're dealing with your family or others. He is with you, whether you are aware or not—so make His presence known and welcome!

....

DAILY DIFFERENCE-MAKER

Wander an old cemetery; dust off/clear away any growth on unkempt graves. Have a few American flags with you—if any of the markers indicate they served in the military, leave a small flag nearby.

.... Notes ....

Reach Out, Reach Back

The wise in heart will receive commands,

but a prating fool will fall.

–Proverbs 10:8

When you were a teenager, how many times did you roll your eyes at something your parents told you (granted, most of us did it behind their backs!)? I can still hear my mother right now telling me what she was going to do to me for rolling my eyes! And then when you were older—perhaps with your own eye-rolling teenager—you realized they were right?

Now I'm a firm believer in wise counsel, and I think God places those messengers in our lives. So while we take our disappointments and rejections to Him, let's also not be too proud to reach out for help from those whose vantage point is better because they've traveled a bit further down the same road, enlisting their support and seeking their advice.

Seeking wise counsel is not the same thing as taking a poll. Sometimes, we aren't interested enough in sound advice as much as we are in simply finding someone to agree with our ideas—friends, acquaintances, flatterers. It's a bad plan. What if Noah had asked everyone whether or not he should build his boat? Or Moses took a poll on whether he should lead his people out of captivity? Can you even imagine? (That's like me asking Michael and S.J., "How do you like mom's new haircut?" Duh, now that's a poll.)

Seeking wise counsel is also not the same thing as seeking approval. This requires even more discernment and restraint. What if Paul had waited for the approval of his fellow Jewish leaders? Or even the approval of the other apostles? You're seeking wisdom—not approval.

When we seek wisdom from the wise, we are closer to becoming wise. And further down the road, you'll have the opportunity to reach back to help someone else who will be standing where you are today. Use your experiences to help others in their times of decision-making.

DAILY DIFFERENCE-MAKER

Visit an assisted living facility today. Bring flowers for the residents, and block time for those who don't receive many visitors; if weather permits, take them outside for some fresh air. You may be surprised at how much wisdom resides there if you'll close your mouth and open your ears!

Notes

WEEK
THIRTY
-NINE

The Heart Mirror

As in water face *reflects* face, so a man's heart *reveals* the man.

–Proverbs 27:19

When our economy tanked a few years ago, I observed a strange phenomena: Many 'haves' clung fiercely to their possessions while many 'have-nots' shared generously what little they had. What a missed opportunity for those haves to lift up others during a difficult time.

I get this. I have a favorite pair of earrings, handbag, pieces of furniture, etc., so I understand the impulse of, "No! It's my favorite! I worked hard to have it! I made sacrifices in order to purchase it!" But sometimes, we have to take a hard look at some of our possessions and resources and ask, "Do I really need this? Would someone else value this even more than I do? Will I really miss it?"

Folks, it's time to loosen our grip on some of our stuff. I'm not saying get rid of your great-great-grandmother's china that she brought over from Ireland or anything like that. I am saying our attics and basements are full of items that could help furnish a modest apartment; we throw out food each week, which means we have the capacity to feed a needy family from time to time. We have closets full of clothes that reflect our yo-yoing weight and our children's non-stop growth spurts. Our garages house old refrigerators because we're too lazy to walk back into the house for food and drink. We do not *need* these things—but someone out there sure does.

And once the excess is gone, do you know what happens? You'll breathe easier. Your heart is so full, it overflows with joy. You are content that you have made the right decision. You will already be thinking about a "next time." Between your head and your hands is your heart—let it dictate what they do!

....

DAILY DIFFERENCE-MAKER

Arrange to host a "Five and Under" yard sale in a low-income neighborhood where everything—including functional furniture and working electronics—is five dollars or less. Donate all money collected to the neighborhood's community center, shelter, or church, so residents will have given back to their own community!

.... Notes ....

Lather, Rinse, Repeat . . . ?

There is a way *that seems* right to a man,

but its end *is* the way of death.

—Proverbs 14:12

'm always amazed at those who do something the same way over and over again and still expect different results. Did they not pay attention in science class?

Listen, life is hard enough—but it's even harder if you do stupid things. Over and over. Still expecting that *this time*, there will be a different outcome. God gave you a brain and intended you to use it. If you're wondering why you can't seem to meet the right man or woman, take a step back and look for patterns in your own behavior. If you keep falling for get-rich-quick schemes, wake up and realize there's no real fast-track to material wealth. If your child is ill-behaved and demanding, is it because you always give in out of desperation? Don't think your child doesn't know that. After all, "lather, rinse, repeat" simply gives you more of the same lather to rinse out—right?

Things will not change unless you change them. If they seemed right at the time and produced dismal results, then it's time to change course. Maybe this path worked out for someone else—but it obviously doesn't work for you. Stop doing what you're doing. Shake things up.

No one ever lost weight by sitting around and complaining that they couldn't lose weight; no one ever cleaned up their house by complaining about how their house was always messy; no one ever launched a new career by staying in a job they hated. Hey, I'm not saying that we bring all of our troubles on ourselves—but when we're sitting around whining and complaining about how life *never* works out for us, a hard look in the mirror oughta be our starting point.

DAILY DIFFERENCE-MAKER

Change at least one thing in your routine today—take a different route to work, stay resolved if you tell someone no, fix your hair differently. I'm guessing the world will not fall apart with this change, so keep up this trend—don't leave breakfast dishes in the sink, assign your child the task of taking out the garbage, take a class . . .

Notes

We're Not Exempt

Therefore I exhort first of all that supplications, prayers,
intercessions, *and* giving of thanks be made for all men,
for kings and all who are in authority, that we may lead
a quiet and peaceable life in all godliness and reverence.
For this *is* good and acceptable in the sight of God our Savior.

−1 Timothy 2:1–3

et me ask you something—when's the last time you prayed for leaders, from the president down to your mayor? I don't care whether you voted for him or her, that's not what I'm asking—I'm asking do you pray for them regularly? We're not exempt from this.

We've become a nation that worships our politics. We no longer pay attention to what's truly in the Bible; we twist verses to fit political ideologies, instead of reading what the Bible actually says. We huff and puff about which "side" is Christian and make ripping apart our political opposition a national pastime.

So here you have it—we are to pray for "all who are in authority . . . this is good and acceptable in the sight of God." Every single leader. Every single elected official. Every single person who leads . . . a teacher, a home-group leader, a pastor, a state representative, a judge, a manager . . . they all need our prayers, whether they realize it or not.

For goodness sake, turn off the talking heads. Don't you know they make a living getting you stirred up with half-truths and distortions? (Okay, Shepard Smith aside—he's an Ole Miss guy, after all!). Learn what the Bible truly says, and you'll know that no matter who holds office, Jesus is always King, and we are all subject to His authority.

....

DAILY DIFFERENCE-MAKER
Sincerely pray for your leaders today, whether you voted them in or not. Spend time with someone whose politics differ from yours— you may have more in common than you think!

.... Notes ....

Watch Your Words

For every idle word men may speak,

they will give account of it in the day of judgment.

For by your words you will be justified,

and by your words you will be condemned.

—Matthew 12:36–37

There is a little-known congressional program that offers internships to young people who have aged out of the foster-care system. Since they are no longer eligible for state support and have no families, the program is designed to give them a leg-up in the working world.

We met a senator who employed one of these kids and he told us that one morning when he arrived at the office, the boy was already there and had reorganized the mailroom. It had never been so clean and so sensible. The senator complimented the young man, calling his work "amazing" and "great." A few minutes later, he saw the boy again, this time with tears streaming down his face. Thinking something was wrong or that he'd somehow offended him, he quizzed him until the boy finally said, "That's the first time in my life anyone's told me I did something good." While the compliment had been well-deserved and sincere, it made such an impact that it brought tears to this young man.

Words can harm or heal as much as hands. We need to be prolific with our compliments and stingy with our criticisms. I'm not talking about flattery, but I am talking about looking for the good, the positive, the hope, the potential in others instead of focusing on their flaws and shortcomings.

Had the senator not gone to retrieve a cup of coffee, he might not have known what his words meant to the young intern. We put words out there each day, never knowing where they might land or how. Choose them carefully, think about them before you let them escape; visualize whether they will harm or heal. Once they're out there, they cannot be retrieved.

DAILY DIFFERENCE-MAKER

Ask everyone you meet today—stranger or not—how they're doing. If you know the person, find a way to compliment them; their appearance, how they handled a particular situation, an admirable quality they possess.

Notes

Don't Parent Your Way Out of Your Marriage

Correct your son, and he will give you rest;

yes, he will give delight to your soul.

—Proverbs 29:17

Sean will tell you little-bitty babies make me nervous; it's true, I'd rather have them enter the world somewhere between ages ten and twelve so I can style their hair and make their clothes match.

While Sean and I consider our children to be the second great romance in our lives, we agreed early-on that they would not be the center of our lives. (I'll pause while some of you gasp and wag a finger at me. And I'll wag mine right back at you.) Certainly, our children were part of our family, but they were not going to be the nucleus and grow up thinking the world revolved around them. We are all pieces of a larger puzzle and if you're not teaching this to your children, you are doing them a great disservice. The marriage bed is *not* for children, and the marriage bedroom door is worthy of a courtesy knock and expressed permission before your child enters it. I did not 'child-proof' my home by taking up my breakable décor; through several days of constant supervision and an occasional swat of a curious hand, we taught our children to leave certain items alone.

I'm amazed by parents who hand off their techno gadgets and other valuables to toddlers and then are flabbergasted when they are broken or ruined. These are the same parents who see no problem with their children running around restaurants and disturbing other customers; if something is said, the excuse is that they are "just children." These are the same parents who, if and when the nest is finally emptied, realize their parenting cost them their marriage. Great children aren't born; they are built, loved, and taught so they can become great!

Are your children driving you crazy? Is your spouse distant and irritated that you pay him or her no attention? Stop and consider the last time you did something solely for yourself or the last time you spent more than ten minutes alone with your spouse; then ask yourself if the two of you have any interesting conversations beyond your children, headline news, and the weather. If you can't recall a time when either occurred, be concerned enough to change the direction you're headed.

DAILY DIFFERENCE-MAKER
Write your spouse a love note and schedule a date night, even if you just hire a sitter and picnic in the backyard.

Notes

WEEK
FORTY

No Sudden Moves

Do not believe every spirit, but test the spirits,

whether they are of God; because many false prophets

have gone out into the world.

—1 John 4:1

When the Holy Spirit transforms our hearts into cheerful giving, it's easy to go a little nutty. We may buy someone a gourmet espresso machine when they really would have been happy with the humble coffee-maker that retails for less than twenty dollars. We may buy an elderly person a laptop with all the bells and whistles when really, they just wanted an e-reader with retina display. When these items sit and collect dust or our gestures are met with a polite, "no thank-you," our feelings get bruised.

The point is to help people—not scare people. If our offers are over-the-top or sudden, some people get suspicious . . . and rightfully so. When you met your spouse or significant other, did you start lavishing them with fabulous gifts? Or have you yourself been treated like that—and instead of endearing the giver to you, it made you wonder about their intentions?

Generally speaking, those who practice discernment are those who value wisdom; don't get put out with them if your attempts to help are met with a caution light or even a flat *no*. These are the same people who will set appropriate boundaries and your relationship will develop gradually; their trust is *earned*, not given. Polish your ability to read body language and expressions; usually, theirs will indicate whether you've crossed a line or attempted to cross it too soon. In most cases, these people are deep thinkers and observe more than they speak; count yourself blessed, because they have a lot to teach you!

Sometimes, the guy on the street needs a bottle of water—not an air conditioner. After a while, you may be permitted further access into his world and can assess further, but for now, just meet the immediate need and get to know *him*. There are just those times when giving needs to be careful, discreet, and gradual; that doesn't make it any less cheerful, and in some respects, the joy will linger much longer.

DAILY DIFFERENCE-MAKER

Take pizzas to a firehouse or police station, or maybe some cookies (from Whimsy Cookie Company, of course) to a homeless shelter.

Notes

A Higher Purpose

And so we have the prophetic word confirmed, which you
do well to heed as a light that shines in a dark place, until
the day dawns and the morning star rises in your hearts.

—2 Peter 1:19

Michael's twenty-first birthday was rapidly approaching, and we told him we'd take him and a few friends anywhere he wanted to go—but it had to be somewhere he'd never been. We wanted to give him a brand-new experience, figuring he'd want to go to Las Vegas or Atlantis. *Wrong!* Michael wanted to ride rollercoasters. Simple enough. Deceptively simple, that is.

The day finally arrived, and we headed to Cedar Point amusement park, the "roller coaster capital of the world." Our first hurdle was getting a couple of his Ole Miss teammates on a small plane; they didn't trust it. None of them, except for Michael, had ever ridden in one. Okay, apparently we were giving more than just Michael a brand-new experience!

Off the collegiate field and not quite to the NFL field, these guys were fish out of water. Some found their 'rollercoaster legs' and made it just fine; others, not so much. Regardless, each one of them tried; these were decorated players who could have chosen to remain in their comfort zones but instead risked trying something different. They risked looking silly and not tough (you do know some of those rollercoasters take photos of your scared faces, don't you??). Some were humbled, watching scrawny twelve-year-olds ride rollercoasters they wouldn't dare; but everyone enjoyed themselves.

Stepping out of our comfort zones doesn't always guarantee a happy ending; sometimes, we have to create that for ourselves. The guys who decided amusement parks were not for them could have ruined everyone's good time, but instead they laughed, knowing they'd learned something about themselves. And what was more important, they were there to celebrate Michael and simply have a good time. They didn't have to be the best, or even the bravest, at everything.

Just like those guys, let's strive to not fear new experiences, or at least not give into the fear; let's relax and realize that new experiences don't always 'take'; and let's always, always look for the higher purpose that is beyond whatever it is we're attempting.

. . . .

DAILY DIFFERENCE-MAKER
Whether it's an amusement park, a county fair, or a pop-up parking lot carnival, take a group of kids and have some fun. Ride some of the rides with those who are a bit timid, even if you're screaming the whole time!

. . . . Notes . . . .

Be Patient with All

Now we exhort you, brethren,

warn those who are unruly, comfort the fainthearted,

uphold the weak, be patient with all.

−1 Thessalonians 5:14

you've ever taught kindergarten or attended an NFL game, you can identify with the above verse. In each of those scenarios—and okay, countless others—most of us know how to rally to the instructions outlined in today's verse . . . except maybe that last one. That last one is tricky.

- Be patient with all . . . when they cut in front of you in traffic.
- Be patient with all . . . when they call and tell you the same story, over and over again.
- Be patient with all . . . when they are in front of you in the check-out line at Wal-Mart, talking to the sales clerk, and you're late for an appointment.
- Be patient with all . . . when they want to make a bowl of cereal by themselves and leave a mess.
- Be patient with all . . . when, though house-broken, they have an accident.

- Be patient with all . . . when they sing a solo but can't carry a tune in a bucket.
- Be patient with all . . . when they can't find a record of your transaction.
- Be patient with all . . . when they call you to solicit, because it is their job.
- Be patient with all . . . when their old bones just don't move as fast as they once did.
- Be patient with all . . . when they don't understand what's being said.
- Be patient with all . . . when they haven't paid you back yet.
- Be patient with all . . . when they mess up at school, at work, or on the committee.

Be patient with all . . . ALL. Each one. Every one. Just because it's a tricky situation doesn't mean we can overlook it—meet it head-on and be patient!

....

DAILY DIFFERENCE-MAKER

Take your patience a step further—when you feel yourself losing it, that's when you ask the person what you can do to help them. Transform your impatience into something that's useful, positive, and productive.

....Notes...

Illusionary Weights

Give to him who asks you, and from him who
wants to borrow from you do not turn away.

—Matthew 5:42

Among the many blessings he brought, Michael opened our eyes and gave us the gift of realizing that yes, we could make a difference in someone's life. And in doing so, a difference would be made in ours.

Too often, we weigh ourselves down with implausible thoughts. We worry that if we do one thing, it will snowball into more requests, each one bigger than the last one. We tell ourselves that we can't possibly invite this person to do dinner, because then they'll expect and invitation every week and our grocery budget won't stretch that much. Or if we buy the football manager a necktie for the football banquet, he'll expect us to buy him a suit. We just don't know if we can help the lady on the street corner who holds up a sign; she's probably just some scammer and if she starts recognizing our car, she will expect us to give her money every time.

Oh my gosh, knock off the melodrama. Usually, it only takes a little to help fill the gaps people are experiencing. No one is suggesting you go into debt or give what you truly cannot give; but I maintain, each of us has *something* to give . . . and a person's life could actually hang in the balance of your decision (and I'm *not* being melodramatic about that!).

So you can't afford to purchase a new suit for the football manager . . . but maybe you could forego a dinner out to purchase a dress shirt? He's not expecting it; but can you imagine his face when you surprise him with it? And for that person who needs a square meal every now and then . . . I hear tell that pasta dishes stretch pretty far (remember, I don't cook, so this is just hearsay!). And it's perfectly okay that you don't know what the lady with the donation can does with the money she collects, what's important is that you're giving it!

Don't be weighted down by unnecessary worries—they are illusions. The need is what's real.

....

DAILY DIFFERENCE-MAKER
Find a venue and host an art show for those who might otherwise not have the opportunity—elderly, special needs, children. Alert local media, invite everyone you know, have a photographer on hand, and set up a box for a love offering that is either divided among the artists or used in a way they determine.

.... Notes ....

Give Love

Give, and it will be given to you: good measure,

pressed down, shaken together,

and running over will be put into your bosom.

—Luke 6:38

One of my favorite adoption stories is from a family who already had two teenagers when they adopted a six-year-old girl, and it resonates with our own experience.

It was Sunday morning, and the father went to rouse his children for church; both teenagers yawned, complained they were still sleepy, and told their father to go away. When he went to see about his young daughter, her bed was made perfectly and she was completely dressed, ready for church.

Now that's just a slice-of-life story, but my point is simply this: Give love, and you will always get it back. Maybe you never dreamed you'd adopt a child—but you might just get the child you always dreamed of. Not to discount this man's teenagers, but here was a girl who had an idea of how good she had it; in her own way, she was giving it back in a way she knew how.

If you glossed over today's scripture, let me highlight something that jumped out to me about Jesus' words: The phrase "good measure." Note here that He doesn't say, *equal measure* or *even measure.* No, what you give will be received, put through some sort of Divine processing, and returned . . . overflowing back into your heart. Each one of us has the capacity to give love, whether we're adopting a child or simply being dressed and ready on time. It doesn't cost a thing except a room in your heart.

What has been pulling at your heart lately? Does it frighten you? Do you think it's impossible, too expensive, or that you don't have enough information to act? Don't discount the yearnings in your heart, because the Holy Spirit may be responsible for putting them there. Take one step in faith, and He will illuminate the next. The more ridiculous, the more possible that God is responsible. He just may be up to something—don't you want to find out?

....

DAILY DIFFERENCE-MAKER

If you've been reluctant to consider adoption, many states' adoption requirements are not so much expensive as they are extensive—this is done to ensure they are finding loving homes for children who are in their system. Investigate what your state requires in order to adopt from their foster-care system; if you are not led to adopt, chances are you know someone who is and could use this information. Pass it on!

.... Notes ....

WEEK
FORTY
-ONE

When 'The Heavy' Needs Help

But Shem and Japheth took a garment,

laid *it* on both their shoulders, and went backward

and covered the nakedness of their father. . . .

they did not see their father's nakedness.

—Genesis 9:23

We are not meant to live as solitary creatures in our kingdoms of one. Nor can we always be 'the heavy' in a crisis, as illustrated in the story surrounding today's verse.

Through his obedience to God, Noah had saved His creation. Now he was drunk as a skunk and naked as a jaybird. I don't know if he was making a lot of noise, or if his sons just happened to pop by for an unannounced visit, but Noah needed help. While I imagine his elder sons were shocked at their father's indiscretion, they also wanted him to maintain his dignity. The one who had carried everyone now needed carrying.

Today's verse illustrates humility from all sides. By today's standards, the youngest son probably would have posted a cell-phone video of his father on social media—the same father who had saved his life. The elder sons chose not to look upon their father with disgrace and instead, help him. And finally, Noah—the man who saved God's creation—was in no position to help himself; he was humble enough to accept his sons' offer (that's tough for me to accept sometimes!).

None of us is perfect, and we're too quick to tear down high-profile people who are caught in bad situations. While I would never justify immoral or illegal behavior, I would caution everyone to slow down the stone-throwing; everyone makes mistakes. Unless the person caught in the scandal is a personal friend, you do not have the full story.

On the flip side, I always tell people to never turn down help. When someone offers help, take them up on it. Do not let your pride get in the way of something that could be God-ordained. You are missing out on receiving help and denying someone else an opportunity to help.

Let's resolve not to rip others to shreds when they are embarrassed or falter in their walk; let's help them, whenever possible. And if we're the ones in need, let's humble ourselves to admit it, then ask for and accept others' offers for help.

DAILY DIFFERENCE-MAKER

Have you shunned someone's offer to help? Retract your position and accept it. And the next time someone is caught in a scandal, whether they are famous or not—choose a higher path in response.

Notes

Space Invaders

You should know in your heart

that as a man chastens his son,

so the LORD your God chastens you.

–Deuteronomy 8:5

God made Michael easy for us to spot—he was bigger than most kids his age . . . okay, he's bigger than most people in general. So as His Spirit began to work in us, we became more and more intrusive of Michael's "personal space."

At first, Michael resisted—typical teenage behavior, even though his circumstances were atypical. Our tip-toe attempts to get to know him better, our attempts to help, and to provide him some much-needed nurturing . . . well, maybe he didn't *want* it —but he sure did *need* it. That night when I told Sean to turn around, I knew there would be no more tip-toeing—we were invading.

Sometimes we have to invade in order to impact. As someone who has been called "The General" on occasion by her own children (it was never as bad as they occasionally want you to think!), I can tell you that a parent reserves the right to know what their child is doing, with whom they are socializing (on- *and* offline), and that they can invade their personal space whenever necessary. This is what the Father does with us—His Spirit overtook me that night I uttered that two-word imperative to Sean—so it stands to reason we would follow His example with our children.

Your children are blessed to have a loving, caring family that has provided them with a home, love, and structure. That is not afforded to every child in this world. It was not and is not a right; it is a blessing and a gift. We need to teach them what adult strength is all about. Certainly, parenting is a road of understanding with different stations to stop and learn; where new things are learned and past wrongs can be righted. But your children do not become your friends until they are much, much older and your lessons have had time to cure in their minds and hearts. Until then, be a space-invader.

DAILY DIFFERENCE-MAKER

Whose space needs invading? They may be quiet, they may be obnoxious, but if you're looking, they will stand out. Each time you see them, call them by name and ask them how their day is going. Do *not* let them off the hook with an "okay" in response. Make eye contact, look for clues, listen for signals.

Notes

Ball in Play

The silver-haired head *is* a crown of glory,

if it is found in the way of righteousness.

−Proverbs 16:31

There stood a delivery man with the most breath-taking floral arrangement. I just knew he was at the wrong house, but much to my surprise he said, "Delivery for Mrs. Leigh Anne Tuohy." "Oh my, that's me!" I cried. The card read: *The first gift of birthday week. Love, Sean.*

Birthday week—I like the sound of that! And each day after that, the birthday fairy would come during the night and leave me a wonderful gift. These kind gestures by the big birthday fairy (who actually sleeps next to me each night) eased the pain of being another year older. Growing old is inevitable; how you face it is totally within your control. Basically, it boils down to this: We can moan and groan about being another year older or we can wear our "crown of glory"—gray or secretly gray—and be grateful that we're still here (the alternative is not good)!

Greatness is possible at any age; each day we're alive means we have purpose, we can be useful, we can learn, and *we're not done yet.*

When's the last time you read to a child? Strap on your bifocals and volunteer at an inner-city school or community program for kids who might not even own any books, much less have a parent who has time to read to them.

When's the last time you dried a teenager's tears? Spend some time in a crisis pregnancy center—perhaps even organize a diaper shower for some of the mothers-to-be.

Have you always wanted to learn how to play an instrument or tap-dance? Do you know how to Instagram®, "Tweet," or Skype®? I had a sweet young lady to teach me, and they're great—so ask some young people to instruct you.

Getting old doesn't mean getting out of the game. We're still in it; the ball is still in play. Today is another day to try, another day to risk, another day to learn, another day to love. Game on!

....

DAILY DIFFERENCE-MAKER

If you've ever wanted to see God's transformative power in action, get involved in a prison ministry or organization that works with prisoners and the formerly incarcerated. Your life skills and experience may bring a message of hope to someone who will never leave, or someone who never has visitors; you may teach skills to those who may be released; you may help formerly incarcerated parents reconnect with their children, find housing, or apply for a job.

.... Notes ....

Doing Nothing

The lazy *man* does not roast what he took in hunting,

but diligence *is* man's precious possession.

–Proverbs 12:27

It's so easy to do nothing. Doing nothing relieves us of any responsibility, takes zero initiative, lacks any conviction, and has no risk or rewards. Cowards do nothing. Yes, doing nothing is easy; anything that is worthwhile in life, however, is usually not.

We are losing the battle today as warriors because too many good folks are doing nothing! We need real men and women, regardless of their age, race, size, or color to prepare for battle. What are we doing to combat poverty? Disease? Trafficking? Illegal drugs? Illiteracy? Malnutrition and obesity? Crime? Racism? Gangs? I could go on and on naming the battles our communities face . . . but they're raging on because we are not stepping up to fight.

I'll say it again—age is *not* an excuse for ignorance, stupidity, or complacency. This little general can tell you what a difference we can make if we are firm yet gracious, exercise integrity and courage, and make a conscious decision to do the right thing. Why would we want our children and grandchildren to pay the price of our complacency?

Look at how the proverb refers to diligence—it is a precious possession. It is a treasure, it has lasting effects . . . sometimes, even heart-changing, eternal effects. A warrior isn't always harsh—in fact, God's best soldiers are often gentle, tender beings who love those who are not loved by anybody, protect the weak, are moved by social injustices, and stand in awe, not judgment, of those who are less fortunate than they are. Are you ready to join the ranks?

DAILY DIFFERENCE-MAKER

Make some brown-bag lunches that will keep a while without refrigeration—PB&J sandwiches, sealed pudding or fruit cups, bananas, chips, cookies. You may even want to include a small gift card for a cup of coffee or groceries. Hand them out to anyone who might be hungry—in bus stations, on playgrounds, on the street. Make a habit of this, even if you are rejected at first; it will take time to build trust and no longer be a stranger. Be diligent—be a do-er!

Notes

Setting the World on Spicy-hot Fire

So then, because you are lukewarm,

and neither cold nor hot, I will vomit you out of My mouth.

Because you say, "I am rich, have become wealthy,

and have need of nothing"—and do not know

that you are wretched, miserable, poor, blind, and naked.

—Revelation 3:16–17

We think comfort zones offer us protection, but more times than not they keep us in the same flight pattern; we start to believe we created our own comfort and peace because we no longer take those paths and detours that keep us on the lookout for God's miracles. They're too dangerous—they might require something that forces us to do or think differently.

Personally, I don't think we need as much protection from the world as we do changing our views and engaging in the world. Irish poet and priest John O'Donohue said it so well: "When you open your heart to discovery, you will be called to step outside of your comfort barriers; you will be called to risk old views and thoughts."

Look at what the Lord says He will do with those who are lukewarm—He will spit them out! Those who are so caught up in their own drama and hype are certain to never search Him out in the detours, forgetting His commands to love one another, and to go teach others about His love. This means love, teach, and nurture those who look different, who live differently, who are dirty, who have been shamed, whom no one else wants. He can be found in each faithful step you take outside your self-made security.

I don't know about you, but I'd rather not be spat out, vomited up, or cast away. Keeping with the hot and cold analogy, I'd rather be a spicy-hot and adding flavor in His eyes and to this world! The Lord has blessed each and every one of us with certain talents and resources that He never intended to be hidden away—they are to be put to use, to change this world. So what's it gonna be—ice-cold, bland, or spicy-hot? Your choice.

DAILY DIFFERENCE-MAKER

Once a month, take children from a local housing project to the local public library for story time or another children's program, and encourage children who are old enough to apply for a library card. You will have to establish a rapport with parents, grandparents, and guardians, but the benefits of exposing young children to the public library are immeasurable.

Notes

WEEK
FORTY
-TWO

What Are You Waiting For?

Therefore, as *the* elect of God,
holy and beloved, put on tender mercies,
kindness, humility, meekness, longsuffering.

—Colossians 3:12

I was leaving the store—arms full, mind preoccupied—and I was not paying attention to anything when I dropped my purse. Stuff went everywhere. I was looking under cars and trying to retrieve my things when this teenager with a nose ring and tattoos walks up and graciously helps me. While others walk by with stifled snickers, this young man, so different than me, stopped and got on with the task. Why?

I get it—we live in a very busy world. The years seem to accelerate past; as children, it seemed like forever before Christmas would roll around but as adults, it seems like we've just put the ornaments away and it's here again! But too often, we see someone struggling, and we can't be bothered to even hold a door open long enough for them to pass through.

Random acts of kindness are contagious and ultimately, affect us all! Our city, state, and this country would be so much better off if we all looked out for each other. It's the right thing to do and should be instinctive for Christians; and really, Christian or not, doesn't it just make sense? As the scripture says, God *chose* us. Let's trade our hurried, busy, preoccupied hearts for His—one that's overflowing with compassion, patience, gentleness, humility, and kindness. We could have such an impact if we helped the youngest child to the oldest senior citizen and everyone in between.

Some of you are reading this and may be within a stroke of a pen from losing your job or having the rug jerked right out from under you in some other way. If this happened, would it make you more empathetic toward others? Would you then be the one to help a stranger? When someone is stranded with a flat tire, would you pull over? None of us ever knows when we'll transition from giver to receiver of kindness. Don't wait for the rug to be jerked out from under you to wake up and realize that so, so many of us are slipping through the cracks and even the smallest gestures could provide the boost needed to get back to the surface. So what are you waiting for?

....

DAILY DIFFERENCE-MAKER

Next time you're in line at a drive-through, pay the tab for the person behind you. If you choose to go in to eat instead, bus all the tables—not just your own.

....Notes..

Don't Miss the Good Stuff

But one thing is needed, and Mary has chosen
that good part, which will not be taken away from her.

–Luke 10:42

With as many fires, floods, tornadoes, earthquakes, and a limping economy as our nation has experienced just in recent years, there are many who need assistance due to circumstances beyond their control. Not exactly the sort of subject matter Norman Rockwell is most famous for painting, yet we still think if our gatherings can't recreate the live-action version of many of his most famous paintings, we have somehow failed.

Enter the well-known story of Mary and Martha. Martha bustled about, making sure everything was perfect for their guest while Mary sat with Jesus. Martha appealed to Jesus about this, and today's verse is Jesus' response to her.

At times, I think Martha gets a bad rap in this story. I mean, you're telling me that if the Lord Jesus decided he wanted to hang out at your house, you wouldn't be in a clean-up tizzy? Oh my gosh! I would be in sheer panic! You would actually be willing to throw a bag of chips on the table, along with a container of dip, and call it done? Nooooo, not me—I'd be a mad, multitasking machine! But

Jesus wasn't necessarily calling out Martha for doing something *wrong*—only that she was distracted, and missing the good stuff!

Let's not miss the good stuff because we're so caught up in preparations. There are actions that are certainly less stressful and still very impactful:

- Call a friend who lives far away
- Help your parents with an easy activity
- Send a letter to a distant relative
- Give your time and money to a charitable organization

Embrace the unexpected. Perfect doesn't make it good. Erase the notion that it has to be a certain way because that is 'how we have always done it.' This could be the year to shake things up; try a more low-effort/high-impact approach so you don't miss the good stuff. I can tell you that if you do, you'll enjoy the occasion instead of enduring it.

DAILY DIFFERENCE-MAKER

Take some kids to the beach . . . or the mountains. Build a large structure in a common area of a housing project that will either hold sand or artificial snow, and fill the box according to the "opposite" season (if it's winter, fill with sand; summer, fill with snow). Stock up on plastic shovels and pails and just let the children play. Be sure to buy the kind of snow that can be formed into snowmen and snowballs.

Notes

Holiday Warriors

For all the law is fulfilled in one word, *even* in this:

"You shall love your neighbor as yourself."

—Galatians 5:14

Do you remember what Clarence the angel said to George Bailey in *It's a Wonderful Life*? "Strange, isn't it? Each man's life touches so many other lives. When he isn't around, he leaves an awful hole, doesn't he?"

I'm now going to separate the men from the women, because I have two different messages here. Men, you first: in my house, Sean's responsibility is to pay and carry. That's a big job. Huge, in fact. We love and thank you for it. Carry on.

Ladies, I'm going to focus squarely on you now. When it comes to certain holidays, what would happen if we removed ourselves from the equation? What would Clarence's "hole" look like? In my humble opinion, Santa is not the only one who delivers during the holidays. The ladies are expected to deliver with as much consistency as the big guy in the red suit.

I consider women the warriors of the holidays: Christmas, Thanksgiving, Easter, Independence Day, etc., because most of it falls squarely on us to make things happen. We are the ones who make the memory books, keep things moving, and pass down legacies (granted, I'm handing my daughter Collins the legacy of knowing the best places to call for food and the phone number of the aunt who makes the best caramel cake, but it's my legacy nonetheless!). We are expected to please, put up, place, plan, pick out, purchase, and then the guys have no idea why we're so worn out after each holiday! But have you ever heard someone remark, "This was my grandfather's special recipe," or "My uncle made Christmas cookies with us each year"? Yeah, me neither. Yes, they know to order the NFL channel on the appropriate days . . . but we know which box contains the fragile, breakable ornaments. We stick them with assembling the bicycles and dollhouses . . . but we know which child gets what.

Take another look at today's verse—yes, we are to love and care for others, but we are not to neglect ourselves in the process. Make today a day to celebrate, my fellow holiday warriors—just like Santa's elves, we are often overlooked!

DAILY DIFFERENCE-MAKER

Go do something to totally celebrate yourself—pedicure, hike, yoga, haircut, even just an hour to read a book in silence . . . whatever it is, make sure it truly celebrates *you*!

Notes

No Time for Ignorance

He who says he is in the light, and hates his brother,

is in darkness until now.

—1 John 2:9

During an interview sometime ago, Michael was asked what he thought about being adopted into a white family and I'll never forget his response. Looking straight at the interviewer, he said: "What does that matter?"

In our house, it absolutely doesn't; sadly, that is not the case everywhere. I can speak firsthand about the insensitive comments that have been made to my family over the years about having an African-American son. Our motives are questioned; our integrity and character put to the test. None of us has time nor inclination to stoop to that level to entertain them with a response. Once in a blue moon, however, I just want to stamp the word *STUPID* on some people's foreheads.

Our skin color, country of origin, or any other difference should not matter in a nation that was built by misfits, castaways, and run-aways (actually, it shouldn't matter anywhere else in the world, either). There is a lot of self-induced ignorance in this country. There are those who still don't get the fact that every individual should be treated with dignity and respect.

The late Maya Angelou said it so beautifully: "We must be warriors in the struggle against ignorance." Are you being a warrior? Are you fighting on the frontlines? If you are "in the Light," as the scripture says, do you welcome visitors to your church with open arms if they seem different? Do you ask the new coworker to lunch, even if his skin is darker or lighter than yours? Bigotry doesn't come in one shade or style—it's rudely present in many colors, shapes, forms, and fashions.

Hear me on this—hear me loud and clear: All people have inherent value and potential, and that value does not depend on social status, family background, or physical appearance. There is no excuse, ever, for prejudice. None. Learn to love those you were either taught or thought you never could. Step out of the darkness today!

....

DAILY DIFFERENCE-MAKER
Attend a festival, talk, or event that includes an ethnicity or culture you may have shunned out of fear; make every effort to meet a new friend who might be willing to teach you more. Please do not make this a "people-collecting" exercise; this is a genuine, sincere effort to learn the root of your fear and overcome it with godly love.

.... *Notes* ....

The "Those"

Do not cast me off in the time of old age;

do not forsake me when my strength fails. . . .

Now also when *I am* old and grayheaded,

O God, do not forsake me, until I declare

Your strength to *this* generation,

Your power to everyone *who* is to come.

—Psalm 71:9, 18

What does "older American" mean? When I flipped through some definitions of the words *old* and *older,* the answers I found amused me . . . *far advanced in years of life, made long ago, mature, belonging to a remote or former period of history, having become slower in flow, exhibiting the effects of time,* and let's not leave out that it "could suggest" *frailty or infirmity.*

You might as well just use the words *antique* or *relic.* They sound more like a piece of furniture than a human being.

Look at what the psalmist pleads to the Lord—not to be "cast off" or forsaken; he still wants time to declare what he as learned about God's character and strength to those, if they will only listen! Folks, we are the "those," and we are aging into the "cast-off" stage

. . . if we are not respecting our elders, doing what we can to help them maintain their personal dignity, then we haven't learned much at all about God's character. And if we haven't learned it, the new "those"—you know, the ones "who are to come"—won't know what they don't know, because our generation failed the previous generation in that regard.

At some point, you will look back and realize your mother, your aunt, your grandfather, or some other older person who tried to instruct you was right. Maybe they weren't up on the latest technologies or trends, but maybe that's because they were wise enough to know better than to chase those fleeting things. Sometimes, you don't get a second chance to learn those lessons, so block time to glean from those whose hair is graying, whose sight is dimming, and whose hearing isn't as crisp as it once was. The mind may slip from time to time, but the wisdom is ours for the taking.

DAILY DIFFERENCE-MAKER

Visit the oldest member of your family; take a list of questions to ask them. Maybe they are questions about your family tree, or questions about their own philosophies and experiences. Bring food, and make sure any leftovers will be easy enough for them to prepare.

Notes

WEEK
FORTY
-THREE

Life, by Definition

> Do not lay up for yourselves treasures on earth,
> where moth and rust destroy and where thieves
> break in and steal; but lay up for yourselves
> treasures in heaven, where neither moth nor rust destroys
> and where thieves do not break in and steal.
>
> —Matthew 6:19–20

What do you consider a life-defining moment? Now sometimes, a defining moment might not be our finest . . . like when I was pulled over in Florida for an expired tag on a rental car, and told the sheriff he suffered from short-man's syndrome (yes, I truly did) . . . but starting today, we have the power to change our definition.

When we engage in random acts of kindness, provide food to a family that has none, supply clean water to a town that was leveled by a F15 tornado, or help a child find his/her forever parents . . . those are moments that can also define you, and they're nothing short of awesome!

Life-defining moments are the ones that make that blueprint unique to you. So why chase after the same sort of home, same sort of lifestyle, same sort of trappings that others pursue? No matter how much money, power, or lusts a person accumulates, they will always run short. There is nothing fulfilling about any of it because none of it lasts. And certainly, none of it will have eternal impact.

Drink in life's miracles; know the Lord well enough to recognize them; and always, always be open to participating in them. You're not just defining a moment in that person's life—you're also defining your own.

DAILY DIFFERENCE-MAKER

Sometimes, it takes years to recover from natural disasters—if ever. Recall a hurricane, flood, earthquake, or some other disaster from a few years ago; find someone who is still trying to rebuild—maybe through a church, disaster relief organization or civic alliance in the area. Find out what they need and how you can help.

Notes

Inspiring Others

Nor as being lords over those entrusted to you,

but being examples to the flock.

—1 Peter 5:3

Have you ever read a story about someone who did something so inspiring it prompted you to act? Or maybe you witnessed something so simple and kind, it moved you to . . . well, *move?*

Time is something we don't get back, so we need to give it as often as we can. Unfortunately, it seems to me that we are a nation of people who like to draw lines in the sand. We want to say, "I've hit my mark, completed the minimum requirement, fulfilled my duty, someone else's trouble now. *Next!*" We like to have closure, a finishing point. It's like we want this imaginary finish line that says when you cross here, your mission is completed.

It just doesn't work that way with volunteering, or at least it shouldn't. There is always works to be done and precious ones who need to be helped. Once you become involved in the act of giving of yourself and your time, each day you'll want to do more and more. As you build relationships within the volunteer world, you will begin to think of endless possibilities that could change lives and move the needle. Your imagination runs wild with thoughts of potential. If you have dreamed of being a leader, here's your chance—volunteering is a great way to learn organizational and management skills. Good leadership inspires others; your family, friends, and associates will see a change in you, and may follow your example!

Get up and get going and don't make it seem like an impossible task. We can all do simple things each and every day that will have a positive impact on those around us; it's where the rubber meets the road . . . what we believe, what we think, and what we say will only be as effective as what we actually get up and do.

DAILY DIFFERENCE-MAKER

Research any children's homes or work through your city's foster system to start a birthday club for them—and find a way to celebrate each individual child's birthday, not a collective "monthly" birthday celebration. This may mean you yourself can accommodate one or two . . . but maybe a friend could accommodate two more . . . and so on . . .

Notes

213

It's Not About You

He must increase, but I *must* decrease.

He who comes from above is above all;

he who is of the earth is earthly and speaks of the earth.

He who comes from heaven is above all.

—John 3:30–31

ohn the Baptist was sitting in the catbird seat. His role was to announce the coming of Jesus Christ, his earthly cousin and promised Messiah. He was the head cheerleader. If you read much about John, he lived a fairly eccentric existence, even by biblical standards; he developed a bit of a following, however, and gained the trust of many.

So along comes Jesus, who was quite different from John but He was the One whom John promised. His followers weren't too keen on this idea, initially; they were in John's camp, liked his style, and were perfectly content to keep following him. If John's heart was not pure and his obedience not steadfast, John could have easily taken advantage of the situation. But he understood clearly a truth that the rest of us need to learn: *It's not always about you.*

We cannot always be the focal point, the center of attention, the nucleus of it all. This is imperative, particularly, if we're doing the Lord's work. *We* do not raise the funds; *we* do not increase the volunteers; *we* do not do anything, apart from God and His provision.

I like what John says; basically, 'more of Him, less of me.' Everything we do should point back to the One who equips us, provides for us, and sustains us. We should be gracious if someone acknowledges or even rewards us for a job well done—don't discredit or disregard your role—but always give credit to the One whose power enabled the accomplishment.

And when we serve, we serve others as if we are serving Him. We may be serving those who aren't as physically, financially, or developmentally capable, but they are not less valuable or less important. In fact, we are to treat them as if they are more important.

There is so much more joy when we share the spotlight or cast it on someone besides ourselves; be proactive about 'more of Him, less of me' and 'more about them, less about me.'

....

DAILY DIFFERENCE-MAKER

See if you can go the entire day without saying the word "I." Each time you slip, put a quarter in a jar. Tomorrow, take the quarters and put them in some parking meters.

.... Notes ....

Be You—Not Them

O LORD, You have searched me and known *me.*

You know my sitting down and my rising up;

You understand my thought afar off.

You comprehend my path and my lying down,

and are acquainted with all my ways

—Psalm 139:1–3

arents want what's best for their children . . . until the child embarks on a path of potential danger, adventure, or low wages. Then, we get a bit antsy. But look at what the psalmist writes: The Lord knows every move, every thought each one of us makes. The Lord *understands our path*—even if it's not clear to us or seems ridiculous to others. So some of the best advice a parent can give a child? Be you—not them.

- Not everyone gets married or has children. This does not mean something is "wrong" with that person—unless there was also something wrong with Jesus, who also remained single.
- Not everyone stays in the same job at the same company for forty years—there's been a cultural shift in recent decades and we are more transient than ever. Job security is almost non-existent, no matter where you work.

- Not everyone gets their food from a large grocery store. Many people grow their own or trade/barter with others.
- Not every family looks the same.
- Not everyone attends worship on Sunday mornings, or attends a church with a steeple, robed choir, and pipe organ. At the same time, those who do are not necessarily just "going through the motions" of worship.
- Not everyone lives in a single-family home as a single-family unit. Many people live communally and it does not mean they are in a cult.

Once upon a time, centuries ago, a group decided that not everyone worships the same way . . . and risked everything to start a new life where people were free to do so. Eventually, this crazy idea became known as the United States. The Lord knew what they were thinking and what they were up to . . . see what He thinks of *your* plans. Be a trailblazer. Be a pilgrim. Be you—not them.

DAILY DIFFERENCE-MAKER

Do you have prejudices against those who live differently than you? Have you harbored a secret dream to live your life differently, outside of society's expectations? Explore this. Don't go into this with walls up—stay open and see what you might learn.

Notes

215

Protect Your Name

A *good* name is to be chosen rather than great riches . . .

Thorns *and* snares *are* in the way of the perverse;

he who guards his soul will be far from them.

–Proverbs 22:1, 5

When you have an African-American child, you are used to being open game for people's opinions, judgments, and ridiculous comments. Most of the time my motto is, "in order for you to insult me, I must first value your opinion." Society operates without a filter sometimes, and we're more than happy to spew opinion about things we know nothing about—saying things that are hurtful and insensitive.

It will happen to you, too, if it hasn't already. The older woman who is asked, "Why aren't you married?" An infertile couple who politely sits through another child's birthday party and an exasperated mother says, "See? Aren't you glad you don't have kids?" Or the older, adopted child who is asked, "Do you remember anything about your *real* mother?"

Mark Twain is credited with the quote: "It is better to keep your mouth closed and let people think you are a fool than to open it and remove all doubt." I learned years ago to take several deep, cleansing breaths and move on when I encounter ignorance that is beyond my game-changing capabilities; but admittedly, I still have some near-misses. People who practically relish their ignorance are not worth wasting our time and energy on, and when it happens to us, we would be better served channeling that same urge on something that was productive and uplifting.

It's up to you to make a good choice; and I get it, the whole turn-the-other-cheek rah-rah can be difficult, especially when you'd prefer to offer someone a punch in the nose. So while you cannot control someone's ignorance, you are solely responsible, solely accountable for your response. It takes years and years and years to develop good character and one irresponsible outburst can ruin it in a split-second. Don't let someone who is unrepentantly ignorant ruin your good name.

....

DAILY DIFFERENCE-MAKER
The next time someone says something rude or insensitive to you, smile as widely as you can and say, "Have a nice day." Then, walk away. Do not answer or react to their ignorance; simply cut them off with nice words that have nothing to do with your conversation—then leave. As you're walking away, pray for forgiveness to come quickly.

.... Notes ....

WEEK
FORTY
-FOUR

216

Intellect Ain't Wisdom

For I will give you a mouth and wisdom which all your

adversaries will not be able to contradict or resist.

–Luke 21:15

The Bible warns of false prophets, skeptics, and mockers. And the world certainly gives attention to those who either pervert the gospel or laugh at how ignorant we Christians are. That's why I have so much respect and admiration for a number of Christian apologists; while the Lord doesn't need anyone to "make a case" for Himself, the really gifted individuals can educate, clarify, and reinforce our faith—not to serve as a substitute, but rather as a means of support.

Now, some of the false prophets and skeptics certainly make a good case; some are very intelligent and very astute in their positions. But if you think about it, if there was no God, there would be no atheists. And if God's just a great-big Santa Claus, He is indulging some very selfish people while denying many of His own children the most basic needs. Who wants to worship a god like that?

Think about this though: Their existence and ideas actually underscore what the Bible already tells us to expect. And we can never tell when or if the Lord may use one of us to touch their hearts (so stay calm!!).

You see, there is a difference between intelligence and wisdom; God gives us the opportunity to build both into our lives, but wisdom is far more valuable. Wisdom takes intelligence and filters it through life experience, humility, and compassion . . . and finds thoughtful, practical applications.

It's up to us to partake of the Lord's wisdom. And when we encounter those whose 'truth' is not *the* Truth, He will equip us with words and wisdom to respond. Notice the verse doesn't add . . . "so you can get into a screaming match or hurl personal insults freely in My Name" (ahem, need to study this more in-depth myself, so please pray for me and my mouth!).

Remember, Jesus responded to naysayers and false prophets on a case-by-case basis; armed with godly wisdom, we are equipped by Him with the same discernment.

....

DAILY DIFFERENCE-MAKER

Do you know someone who either scoffs at your beliefs or tries to reduce Christianity into an economic or political argument? Maybe they are a coworker, neighbor, or someone you are trying to help. Whether they are trying to get a rise out of you or simply so hopeless they can't see, how will you respond to them today?

.... Notes ....

217

Break the Habit

Those who have believed in God

should be careful to maintain good works.

These things are good and profitable to men.

—Titus 3:8

Many times we give gifts that embarrass others. Now stay with me on this, I'm not talking about *those* kinds of gifts, I'm talking about the large gestures that don't fit the situation or the gifts given that seem to be habitual instead of heartfelt.

Prior to our father's passing, my brother and I pooled our funds and purchased him a new television for him. He just kept telling us we shouldn't have done this, and at one point, I really felt a little uncomfortable that we had given him a gift he felt he had to compete with; neither my brother nor I felt that way, but I have often wondered if we struck a nerve that day. That wasn't our intention, and we were thrilled to give him the television . . . but maybe for him, it was a bit over-the-top.

Other times, I think we give gifts out of habit. My neighbor and I had exchanged gifts for years. I had received candles of every fragrance you can imagine and picture frames of every size. Finally, one year we decided to join forces and buy a gift for our postman. Now we take great joy in changing the recipient of our joint gift each year and we look forward to this new tradition we have created. Don't buy a gift just so you won't show up empty-handed—that's like trying to pay off self-induced guilt. It's so much more fun finding interesting ways to celebrate another person beyond the obligatory trinket or bauble—and trust me, it's far more meaningful!

DAILY DIFFERENCE-MAKER

If you have neighbors or coworkers with whom you're in the habit of exchanging gifts, consider pooling resources to purchase something really nice and/or useful for some of the people in the background: waste management, local police precinct, postal service, fire hall, cleaning service, maintenance crew, landscapers . . . anyone who works in the background to ensure your neighborhood or office running!

Notes

Shaky Steps of Faith

The steps of a *good* man are ordered by the LORD,

and He delights in his way.

Though he fall, he shall not be utterly cast down;

For the LORD upholds *him with* His hand.

—Psalm 37:23–24

f you've ever taken a walk on a foggy day, then you know that you can't see your surroundings clearly until you've taken a step. And then another. And then another. The fog is still in the distance, but each step you've taken makes the path a bit clearer.

The same holds true when we're asked to step out in faith. There are just those times when we haven't a clue where we're headed—but we know we're being told to go. Look at what today's verse says: If you're headed in the right direction, God will make things clear. You might stumble a time or two, but God's got your back!

John Wayne (one of my favorites!) once said, "Courage is being scared to death, but saddling up anyway." Sometimes, we can't wait for the fog to clear; we must go right then and there, stepping out in faith that He is there to make our steps firm.

What fog is in your life currently? A career change? A life change? A child deemed "unadoptable"? A former convict who needs a chance? A community center that needs to be built? A food bank that needs to be established? A senior who needs assistance? When things look foggy, consider whether He is leading you to accomplish something, while He is accomplishing something in your heart: *trust*.

....

DAILY DIFFERENCE-MAKER

Arrange advance payment with a taxicab company, or enlist an army of friends, to help you pick up homeless people and take them to a shelter on a cold or hot night. Buy them a meal along the way.

....Notes...

Crossing the Bridge

What then shall we say to these things?

If God *is* for us, who *can be* against us?

—Romans 8:31

We're often asked if we weighed the risks of taking Michael into our home. Well, guess what? You take a bigger risk driving your car across a bridge. You don't know whether you'll blow a tire, if a drunk driver is headed directly toward you, or even if the bridge will support you. In fact, you don't take the necessary precautions to ensure this, do you? You don't kick your tires before crossing it, get a read on incoming traffic, or ask an engineer to provide a report on the bridge's structure. You just get in your car and drive across.

We loved Michael the same way—we just crossed over and didn't think twice. And you know what? We think all of us should approach other risks in the same way. Have you heard the old saying, 'it's risky out on the limb, but that's where the good fruit is'? Nothing is truer, and that fruit is much sweeter!

Yes, we've had our share of problems and awkward moments along the way, but tell me one family who doesn't. We believe. We honor. We forgive. We keep the faith. That is what families do. If God is for us, no one and no circumstance is any match.

What have you been holding back, trying to calculate the risk? It's time to get in the car and cross over the bridge. Fearless. Unafraid. Confident in the One Who is ultimately driving.

....

DAILY DIFFERENCE-MAKER

Get up early one morning, armed with hand-warmers and pastries (and maybe fruit and hot chocolate, if you're really on top of things!), and drive to a school bus stop where children will be waiting. Hand out the treats and remain there until the last child is picked up.

....Notes...

Three-dimensional children

A child left *to himself* brings shame to his mother.

—Proverbs 29:15

I n our house, church is a non-negotiable. If you're too tired to get up for Sunday School, then you're too tired to participate in all voluntary and extracurricular activities—so you'll sit out of those for a while. Yes, this means cheerleading, basketball, football, or even the school dance.

We also put a time limit on toys and gadgets, including cell phones (which were promptly confiscated every evening for the night). This went hand-in-hand with them not coming home from school and jumping on the computer or playing video games—they needed a broader, three-dimensional world. So we didn't mind lessons of all sorts, team sports, writing for the school paper, after-school jobs, and certainly volunteer work; we hoped these endeavors would instill discipline and dedication, two very important values. Over the years, I can't say they loved everything they attempted; and yes, there were times we insisted they stick with some of the activities they didn't enjoy; however S.J. refused to do swim team due to the swim trunks (speedos) that had to be worn! I did allow him this one time to change sports in mid stride—it was a wardrobe malfunction in my eyes. He was not being a quitter! And obviously, as they got older, we gave them more independence—because during those years, they'd learned how to be somewhere on time, practice, get along with others, take direction, receive constructive criticism, have a conversation, and follow-through . . . all foundational skills that would help them be productive, no matter where life took them.

Sure, it would have been much easier to stick a gadget in their hands and let them sit in a corner—and become adults who could not deal responsibly with the real world. Adults who wouldn't know how to listen, how to look you in the eye, would expect unlimited chances to get something right, and quit when something became difficult.

Parents, I know you're tired; I know your house is a mess; I know the surrogate sitters are out there, ready to entertain our children and keep them occupied for hours. But most of the time, the right thing to do isn't the easiest thing to do—make sure you're raising well-rounded, three-dimensional children.

....

DAILY DIFFERENCE-MAKER
What rules are in place in your home? Have they been made clear to your children? Are they more about control or are they in place to teach values that will make them productive contributors now, and in the future? If you don't have any, it's time to create some.

.... *Notes* ....

WEEK
FORTY
-FIVE

Get One, Give One

In all things showing yourself *to be* a pattern

of good works; in doctrine *showing* integrity, reverence,

incorruptibility, sound speech that cannot be condemned.

–Titus 2:7–8

Sean and I realized that our kids were growing up in a very different world from the one we knew. They had different expectations, stronger peer pressure, many more channels of temptations made possible through media (social, movies, television, Internet, etc.), bigger choices, and far greater dangers. We realized that we needed to introduce giving and being generous to combat these others things infiltrating their lives.

By the late 1990s, Sean and I were both enjoying great success in our respective businesses and we had a better understanding of wealth's trappings. So wealth didn't just present us with a moral dilemma, it now presented us with a parenting dilemma: How could we give our children all the advantages possible without spoiling them rotten?

And admittedly, we liked our stuff; we didn't exactly deprive ourselves, and didn't pretend we didn't enjoy spending money (look,

I'm being fully transparent here!). So Sean and I came up with a family philosophy we call "Get One, Give One." Essentially, if we got something, we gave something—and this philosophy extended to our children. If they hadn't worn something in a year's time, it needed to be given to someone else who would wear it. We subjected our kids to lifestyles that were completely different than theirs. Your kids need to realize most of the world doesn't live like they do. For every privilege they had, we wanted our children to give something in exchange for it.

This idea, this philosophy, simplifies generous giving. It embodies the biblical directive to love your neighbor as yourself, to do unto others as you would hope would be done unto you . . . and it dismisses the notion that giving is always about grand gestures. Giving is a lifestyle; what are you getting today—and what will you give in exchange?

DAILY DIFFERENCE-MAKER

If you see someone eating alone, buy them desert, and give them a smile. Give the Sunday paper vendor or deliverer a few extra bucks because you can.

Notes

Health Care, Spirit Care

Pure and undefiled religion before God and the Father

is this: to visit orphans and widows in their trouble,

and to keep oneself unspotted from the world.

—James 1:27

When it was clear that Michael would come to live with us permanently, it dawned on me that he had been denied even the most basic child healthcare . . . sixteen years of missed vaccinations, dental appointments, and the like.

Granted, Michael didn't speak to me for three days following his first vaccinations, and he probably wasn't thrilled about going to the dentist any more than the rest of us are, but it was a miracle that his health had not suffered much beyond slight neglect. At any point, he could have broken a bone, suffered a disease, or contracted something minor that would have developed into something major. How many other Michaels are out there who are not as fortunate? How many colds and sniffles develop into pneumonia, how many broken bones are never set in order to heal properly? How many teeth are decaying into rotten, painful infections? How many feet are ruined from wearing shoes that don't fit properly?

Regardless of the strides made by government agencies and organizations, we still have too many people who neglect their health. Maybe they don't have "time" or cannot afford to pay; maybe they're too young; maybe they are afraid of what they might hear. If you look at Jesus' ministry, very often he met physical needs before addressing the spiritual and emotional ones. His intentions were purposeful, connecting the immediate to the eternal.

Maybe you are led to help others learn about nutrition; maybe you want to purchase toothbrushes, floss, and toothpaste to hand out. Maybe you want to start an inner-city soccer league, organize a health fair, or take kids for a jog in the afternoons. Maybe you are a licensed physician or a nurse practitioner willing to go into low-income communities and provide check-ups. Be as proactive about someone else's health as you are about your own—don't make them pay for it later.

....

DAILY DIFFERENCE-MAKER

The phrase "free clinic" is a bit misleading—it's costing somebody something, and some services are not free. Research low- or no-cost clinics in your town; ask if you can pay someone's bill, anonymously, and overpay it so they have a credit on their next visit. Take someone to get a flu shot or provide vitamins to a child in need.

....Notes...

Wants vs. Needs

Therefore if you have not been faithful in the unrighteous

mammon, who will commit to your trust the true *riches*?

—Luke 16:11

A very typical comment we hear periodically from our three kids goes something like this: "I really need this for _____." We always respond, "You might want it, but you certainly don't need it." There is a difference.

So many of us don't really need anything, and it's very tricky to avoid splurging on the stuff that you think your loved ones can't live without . . . until next time, when the cycle continues.

So when I talk about the "needy," I'm talking about those whose needs are inadequately supplied, if at all. We can be 'starving' for a pizza, but first of all, we're not starving and secondly, we can afford to fill that craving, even if we can only afford one slice; there are some people in your town who consider a slice of pizza a luxury, a rare treat. When we walk in from the cold and exclaim, "I'm freezing," we have a warmer place to walk into and we can add to our warmth with blankets and jackets. There are some in your town who don't have a blanket, jacket, or even a door to walk through to get in out of the cold.

For most of us, any wealth accumulated has been done with honest work and careful planning—not 'unrighteous' gain—but the question remains true: If we are not faithful in how we use our wealth, we cannot be entrusted with the true riches—God's grace and the eternal treasures of heaven.

To be clear, there's nothing wrong with improving our own circumstances, but there is always going to be a nicer home. A nicer car. A better television and stereo system. Better furniture and clothes. Even better food! Get off the merry-go-round! We can spend a lifetime wanting these things so badly that we focus squarely on acquiring them . . . meanwhile, somewhere not far from your front door, someone just needs a room, transportation, a chair or a bed, and food. You will never truly satisfy your *want* until you help someone meet a *need*.

....

DAILY DIFFERENCE-MAKER

Give your coat to someone today. Not the coat you were going to donate. Nope, not even the coat that's collected dust in your closet for three winters. Give someone a coat that you still wear. There will always be a better coat out there for you to buy—always.

.... Notes ....

Everyone's Out of Their Comfort Zones

After you were illuminated, you endured a great struggle
with sufferings: partly while you were made a spectacle
both by reproaches and tribulations, and partly while you
became companions of those who were so treated . . .
do not cast away your confidence, which has great reward.
—Hebrews 10:32–33, 35

When we help someone, we're often required to step out of our comfort zones; remember that the person we're helping will be stepping out, too.

When Michael joined our crazy life, we wondered if he was truly okay moving at the pace we did, or if he just didn't want to hurt our feelings. At first, he didn't talk much about his former life but every now and then, a few bits and pieces would escape.

What was particularly interesting was the give-and-take impact he made on all of us. Whereas, S.J. would help Michael with math skills, he also longed for Michael's promptness; Collins taught Michael the proper swimming strokes, but Michael introduced her to his favorite music. We may have helped Michael adjust to certain cultural situations, but he helped us in ways we never imagined; we learned to be more compassionate and open-minded.

Nothing exciting ever happens inside comfort zones. As we moved out of ours and into inclusion, there were a few bumps along the way. His backpack, for example, eventually tore beyond repair; so I bought him a very nice one. Some of his buddies teased him about it, probably envious; survival instincts still intact, Michael went digging through the garbage looking for his old one. That wasn't gonna happen, not on my watch—so I sat him down and explained that he *was* rich, his life *had* changed. Did I advise him to ignore his past? No—you know me well enough by now to know that I told him to tackle it, head-on, telling those idiots the same thing I'd just told him.

Whether we are the ones helping or the ones in need, *everyone* is taken out of their comfort zones when it would be easier just to remain in them. But this is not what God commanded, for buried treasure is hidden in there, and no one is intended to stay the same.

....

DAILY DIFFERENCE-MAKER

Here's a great way to revisit the past: Research a few historical sites in your area, maybe within a thirty-mile radius. One Saturday a month, take a group of children (preferably those who have never been outside of their own neighborhood) to visit one or two.

.... Notes ....

Thank a Teacher

So Philip ran to him . . . and said,

"Do you understand what you are reading?" And he said,

"How can I, unless someone guides me?"

–Acts 8:30–31

Have you ever considered that elementary school teachers, in particular, probably spend more time with your child during the school year than you do? Our educators are heroes. That's all there is to it. And I'm talking about every educator—faculty, administration, staff—who play a direct role in keeping our children safe and cared for in our schools. Many of them are the only 'parents' some children have.

Many of them left other careers and turned down other opportunities to do what they do. Today's verse serves as an example of that; Philip was one of those dynamic preachers who attracted large crowds. Yet when God asked him to go immediately to the desert and wait on a chariot, Philip obeyed. The encounter with the Ethiopian official introduced the gospel to Africa, where it would spread. Philip had no way of knowing that—he simply educated the one.

Our educators guide, direct, coach, inspire, never knowing exactly which kids will take what they've learned and apply it. Yet every gadget we hold, every miracle drug that has appeared on the market, every bridge or building that was designed, started with a teacher igniting a spark. Think about your own experience—that one teacher who motivated you. (We all have at least one!) Our future, in many respects, is held by those who give the next generation a reason to hope . . . to me, those are today's teachers! We see all these bumper stickers that say, "Thank a Teacher"—please take time to do just that today!

DAILY DIFFERENCE-MAKER

Go door-to-door and deliver coffee and a warm bagel to every person at the school—teacher, office staff, maintenance crew—and thank them. Do not plop a tray in the teacher's lounge where these items will get cold and left untouched for someone to throw away; these heroes deserve to be served individually! If you have children, make sure you are raising them to respect these wonderful individuals.

Notes

WEEK FORTY -SIX

Nuts and Bolts

You are the salt of the earth; but if the salt loses its flavor,

how shall it be seasoned? It is then good for nothing

but to be thrown out and trampled underfoot by men.

—Matthew 5:13

Why was *The Blind Side* successful? Our family is fairly ordinary. We earn a living, go to school, go to games, do our thing . . . but why was our thing a box-office draw? Obviously, God had a major role from start to finish. His hand remained on each point in the process because He had a message. And the reason the message resonated is because we *are* ordinary people—and people identified with us, or another character in the film, who invested in one person's life. The film clearly shows that we can all change lives by investing time in individuals—and it didn't have to always be something grand or parade-worthy.

So when Jesus calls us "salt," He is reminding us of its many functions. Salt makes all the difference in a dish; it gives flavor, locks in tenderness, preserves. Some salt melts away cold, hardened surfaces and other salt can kill weeds. If we are not serving in these capacities to help others, we will lose them to the world. Our paths crossing theirs will be meaningless.

Let's not lose out to those whose flavor is artificial; let's seek to tenderize and preserve those who are teetering on the edge. Let's melt those whose hearts have grown cold, and get rid of the weeds that entangle and ensnare those who are without hope. If each one of us took the time and effort to help another—just one other person—each day, think of the shift that would occur worldwide. If we were to base our help on absolutely nothing except the Holy Spirit's nudge—not regarding the person's appearance, background, religion, politics, lifestyle, etc.—we would have to grab hold of something bolted to the ground, because we'd be in for a heckuva shift. Let's grab a few bolts and make some waves!

DAILY DIFFERENCE-MAKER

Do you already volunteer at a soup kitchen? Check into your state/county requirements for obtaining a food handler's license, and see if any of the recipients would be interested in learning. Offer to pay the fee, if applicable (in many states, the fee ranges from five to fifteen dollars).

Notes

Don't Grasp the Wind

Then I looked on all the works that my hands had done
and on the labor in which I had toiled;
and indeed all *was* vanity and grasping for the wind.
There was no profit under the sun.

–Ecclesiastes 2:11

The Book of Ecclesiastes is often referred to as Solomon's book on reality; whereas, Proverbs was the book of his ideals and aspirations, Ecclesiastes was the rest of the story. Later in life, having been sucked into a lot of philosophies, pleasures, and misguided objectives, Solomon realizes that none of it mattered. It was as productive as "grasping for the wind." Generations of us have been trying to grasp the wind ever since—we haven't applied the lessons learned from Solomon's mistakes.

Because we can glean lessons from the wisest man who ever lived, his life was meaningful—but I wonder if Solomon felt that way when he wrote this. His is a definite message of "do as I say, not as I do"—man, that has "Leigh Anne Tuohy" written all over it—but I like to think it's said with the best of intentions. Solomon wanted us to learn from the error of his ways so that our energy is focused on meeting immediate needs to fulfill eternal purposes.

Cheerful giving has amazing power. Even the smallest token can have significant effects, and concern for others is a self-renewable energy that produces a kind of chain reaction. When we give to someone, we pass along not just cash or an object, but the kind intention behind the gift. This is passed along in turn, triggering a cascading effect of successive giving.

Altruism (concern for others) is not really as much a phenomenon as it is something to be replicated and multiplied simultaneously; we see "real" people doing things we've thought about doing and realizing that it can be done. We want to do it, be a part of it; we're jumping around, waiting for the wand to be passed to us, knowing it will multiply and be handed off multiple times over at each leg. It has amazing power that, when shared, becomes even more powerful. How will you strengthen this power today?

....

DAILY DIFFERENCE-MAKER
Call your parents (or someone else who has cared for you) today—do not text, do not email—call them. Schedule a visit and offer to bring something that will help them—a meal, a gardening tool, a packet of batteries . . . doesn't matter, as long as it helps them!

.... *Notes* ....

Working Together

Then they took the body of Jesus, and bound it in strips of linen with the spices, as the custom of the Jews is to bury.

—John 19:39–40

While none of us knows for certain, there appears to have been no confusion nor conflict among those who placed the body of Jesus into the tomb. Each one gave a portion, no one tried to do it all by themselves; no one lay claim to the entire burial, each person just did their part.

Joseph of Arimathea was wealthy; he certainly could have afforded to do the whole she-bang, but he stepped aside to allow others to contribute—namely, Nicodemus, who brought the expensive spices that were customary to burial in those days. Several women went with them, as they would visit the tomb after the Sabbath to anoint Him, so they needed to know the tomb's location. Men and women, working together, to accomplish a goal. Each person simply used the talent and resources they had to meet the need, with little or no regard to status, gender, age, or wealth.

Maybe you're the sort of person who just wants everyone to do it your way (yes, I'm talking about myself right now); or maybe you're the sort of person who's okay with letting someone else do it. If either describes you, you're missing out on some huge blessings. A unified group—a class study group, a book club, an alumni association, or even a volunteer team—catapults the chances for success. Each person brings something to the table, and each person must be willing to try something different.

If you think about it, group dynamics only get complicated by egos and apathy; when we can get over everything *not* being done our way and when we can decide that yes, we will proactively contribute, group efforts run much, much smoother . . . and the results are worth it.

....

DAILY DIFFERENCE-MAKER

Think about the different groups you participate in—Bible study, support, athletic teams, civic clubs, etc.—and get honest about your role. Next time the group needs volunteers—whether your participation leans more toward ego or apathy—sign up for a role that no one else wants, and resolve to not complain about it.

.... Notes ....

Calling Them Out

So he began to speak boldly in the synagogue.
When Aquila and Priscilla heard him, they took him aside
and explained to him the way of God more accurately.

—Acts 18:26

Apollos was a cheerleader for God and The Messiah, for lack of a better way of putting it; however, his knowledge was incomplete. He didn't know, or wasn't fully educated, about Jesus' death and resurrection. He had the energy, the eloquence, the talent to get people's attention—again, the whole cheerleader thing—he just didn't have the full story.

Priscilla and Aquila could have called him out. Had they been mean-spirited, they would have gotten a kick out of knocking him down a few pegs in front of everyone. Instead, they saw his sincerity and talent—so they took him aside to explain the Good News. No doubt Apollos had questions; but using the Scriptures, Apollos came to believe and subsequently preach, the Gospel of Jesus Christ.

How do we handle those who speak boldly, those who have the gift of captivating an audience, when they're sending the wrong message? Maybe it's a dynamic personality at your school or office;

maybe it's a person in your social circle. Do we envy their magnetism, wishing we had the attention instead? Do we hang on their words, not to learn, but in wait, hoping they'll stumble?

Or, perhaps *we* are the ones to whom everyone listens. How do we respond when someone kindly takes us aside to set our facts straight? Do we brush their admonishments aside? I can tell you, I don't like being corrected but good grief, I get things wrong all the time—and need a loving correction when that happens.

We need bold speakers—and they need to speak the facts. When we take up a cause, let's make sure we have filtered information through credible sources—and not just listened to what someone tells us. And if we're in the 'Priscilla and Aquila' position, we need to carry out our correction respectfully—the point is not to demean or embarrass, but rather to make sure they are using their God-given abilities for good, so to speak.

We should humbly give, and humbly receive correction. When handled with grace and humility, correction is one of the most loving gifts available.

....

DAILY DIFFERENCE-MAKER

When someone posts false information online or in an e-mail forward, don't hit 'reply all' or call that person out publicly; message them privately, and document your claims with facts, keeping your language kind and informative. If you have been called out for sending or posting something that's false, take responsibility for your actions and issue a retraction—simply deleting it does *not* count!

.... Notes ....

Good Intentions Are Not Enough

Now you also must complete the doing *of it* . . . .

For if there is first a willing mind,

it is accepted according to what one has,

and not according to what he does not have.

–2 Corinthians 8:11–12

Many rookie runners don't know how to pace and don't understand when they lose steam after a few yards; they decide, then, that they are no longer interested in running. Today's verses should speak volumes into our own personal giving, particularly in terms of the pacing and following through long-term. It's not enough to look upon those in need and shake our heads in pity. Nor is it fruitful to commit ourselves and our resources, then bolt when the cause no longer holds our interest, or the task is more difficult than we thought.

Let me be clear—I'm not talking about those times when we seize the moment and give right there on the spot; those are marvelous ways to give, and we should always be on the lookout for those opportunities. What I'm talking about here are the long-term commitments—pledges, regular volunteer hours, etc.—where we exit the gate strong and never finish the race. Sometimes, we're so caught up in the emotion, we don't consider the sustainability of what we've promised. Paul is simply asking all of us to consider carefully what is realistically manageable, so that we're not inclined to walk away. We need to be the sort of givers people can count on.

Believe me, I know what it's like to have a multitude of causes asking for help. And I understand the gnawing feeling that you want to do it all, help them all, and fix it all; but realistically, we can't. And it's not God's intention that the burden fall on one person, but a person of character will honor his/her commitments, in part by choosing them wisely.

....

DAILY DIFFERENCE-MAKER

If you're unsure what you can commit, start conservatively. Maybe your budget can comfortably give five dollars a month; if that's what your budget can realistically sustain, you are giving them five dollars they can count on. If you know for certain you can devote a specific hour each week to volunteering, don't commit to more just yet; staff will spend more time filling the timeslots you miss than finding someone else who could be there regularly.

.... Notes ....

WEEK
FORTY
-SEVEN

Sometimes, Timing Is Everything

Yet who knows whether you have come

to the kingdom for *such* a time as this?

–Esther 4:14

Are you facing a difficult change or confrontation? Are you dreading it, even though you know in your heart it is the right thing to do?

Queen Esther is a shining example of someone who was in the right place at the right time, but her task would put her life in jeopardy. Now when she arrived at the palace, she had no idea that her people would be threatened; but once the threat was real, she did not act impulsively. She knew the timing was delicate and she needed a strategy.

Had Esther approached the throne prematurely, she might have lost her life; if she'd waited any longer, the Jews would have been destroyed. While God is never directly mentioned, it's clear God was at work and Esther was paying attention; she considered her options, calculated the costs, and knew the king well enough to know the best way to reach him.

Sometimes, abrupt change—a relocation, job loss, confrontation, etc.—doesn't feel very affirming, but could very well be God placing you in a situation or position to help. Instead of fighting it, we should consider it an adventure and opportunity; we should explore and build new relationships that result from the change; and we should keep our eyes and ears open for the *why* behind the change, but remain certain that it is purposeful and will be used for His glory (see Romans 8:28).

....

DAILY DIFFERENCE-MAKER

What have you been putting off because you dread dealing with it? Today's the day to put it in motion—a bully at school or work, an unpaid bill, a resignation, a difficult friend, a new neighborhood— today, take at least one step to confront it.

.... Notes ....

Your Management Style

But who *am* I, and who *are* my people,

that we should be able to offer so willingly as this?

For all things *come* from You,

and of Your own we have given You.

−1 Chronicles 29:14

Percentage-wise, individuals making between $200,000–$2 million annually give less than individuals making less than $200,000 per year. It bears mentioning that the highest percentage of giving from this entire sample comes from those making $45,000–50,000*.

Make no mistake—everything belongs to the Lord, and all things are subject to Him. We are managers, plain and simple.

If you have ever worked under a manager, you know something about management style. Some have no mercy, managing all the fun, spontaneity, and compassion right out the door; others have no leadership, and let everything (including employees) walk all over them. Others micromanage, demanding an accounting for every last detail instead of trusting that wise decisions, along with some mistakes, will be made; other managers have no clue about what's going on, nor do they care—they're too puffed up with their self-importance. Too often, our giving reflects these same sorts of management styles.

Good managers allow enough freedom for people to grow and develop, while ensuring they protect, and not neglect, their responsibilities; they listen to ideas, discerning and supporting the best ones. They do not allow others to abuse their subordinates, and treat their charges with respect. Good managers sometimes have to make unpopular decisions, if the overall vision truly benefits those affected by the decision.

Whether we have a little or a lot, God has entrusted us with a portion of His possessions. Are we grumbling about giving, like the manager with no compassion? Do we think it belongs solely to us, and no one else? Or do we give willingly, balancing our support with responsibility? Do we give, and still manage our household expenses?

God gave, so we could give back in gratitude. I don't know why some of us have more than others, because wealth is not an accurate measurement of intelligence, beauty, education, success, or even someone's Christian walk. Let's not become so proud that we think that what we have is actually ours. To paraphrase the chronicler, why us? Our response should be, "why not?"

....

DAILY DIFFERENCE-MAKER
Take a stack of bills (any denomination) to the public library or college campus library. Insert the bills into random books, trusting the bill will be found by the right person at the right time.

....Notes...

*Source: National Center for Charitable Statistics http://nccs.urban.org/nccs/statistics/Charitable-Giving-in-America-Some-Facts-and-Figures.cfm

233

Ruling Over It

So the LORD said to Cain, "Why are you angry?
And why has your countenance fallen? If you do well,
will you not be accepted? And if you do not do well,
sin lies at the door. And its desire *is* for you,
but you should rule over it."

–Genesis 4:6–7

Look carefully at God's warning to Cain—sin is at the door of our desires, but in fact it's ready to devour us; God gives us the power and choice, however, to rule over it. In Cain's case, his anger opened the door and jealousy swept its way into his heart. Jealousy fueled Cain's actions, and prompted him to kill Abel.

We don't know exactly why Cain's offering was rejected, but God was willing to give him another chance, making it very clear that Cain get to the source of his anger, and quickly; otherwise, it would interfere, intercede, and overtake. Cain needed to manage his anger; it was tainting his actions.

Do we give something that's substandard, deciding the recipient should just be grateful for anything? Do we shirk on our promises and pledges occasionally, thinking it won't matter or no one will notice, or give out of obligation and guilt? How do we feel when someone else's work or contribution is recognized, and ours isn't?

Each one of us has a weak spot—I myself have many!—and sin can find each one. In Cain's case, it was his temper, but for others it could be pride, selfishness, flattery . . . and sin knows these are the entry points into our hearts and minds. Whether we're volunteering our time, writing a check, donating items, or throwing cash in someone's cup, our hearts are not full of love and gratitude when sin is taking up space. Don't let sin distort your perspective and taint what you have to offer—God has given each one of us the strength to rule over it.

....

DAILY DIFFERENCE-MAKER

Get honest: Charities are not junk-haulers to assist you in spring-cleaning. Any used item you donate should be in good condition and, when applicable, in good working order. Establish this as a new rule and dispose of the rest responsibly.

.... Notes ....

Cough It Up!

Give to everyone who asks of you.

And from him who takes away your goods

do not ask *them* back.

And just as you want men to do to you,

you also do to them likewise.

—Luke 6:30-31

At some point, we adopted an elementary school. I didn't set out to adopt a school, and we didn't adopt it legally; it was just more Popcorn Theory in action.

This elementary school is located in one of the poorest zip codes in Memphis, but the community is rich with civic pride. You may find this hard to believe, but I attended first grade at Evans—it's a dinosaur, just like me!

Not every student at this school will grow up to be a Michael Oher, Michael Jordan, or the President of the United States . . . but I believe some of them will, given the right opportunity and inspiration. In fact, this scenario is true at a lot of our schools across the nation. They're teeming with children who will have to fight their way toward a future of their own, with very little help beyond the education they absorb. Franklin D. Roosevelt said, "We can't always build the future for our youth but we can build our youth for the future." Children can't learn properly if they're hungry or sleepy; they won't explore every opportunity without guidance and yes, I'll say it, *financial assistance*.

So cough it up—whether you're buying a kid lunch, paying his college application fees, or outfitting the entire football team. Give that kid the opportunity to *focus on learning* and be proud of what they're accomplishing; if they have to worry about their most basic needs, they just might give up—and then, we've possibly relinquished the cure for cancer, a solution to world hunger, or the next technological breakthrough. Those discoveries may be hidden deep in your city's schools—are you willing to risk them never being found?

DAILY DIFFERENCE-MAKER
Connect with a student who wishes to be college-bound and offer to pay their application fees. Help a student with some basic life skills, like writing a check, learning what FICA is, or help them prioritize their school selections.

Notes

235

Caring for Ministers

Freely you have received, freely give . . .

for a worker is worthy of his food.

—Matthew 10:8, 10

Who ministers to you? How do you care for them? Today's verse is actually part of Jesus' instructions as He sends His disciples into ministry. The disciples were instructed to work, but trust in His provision instead of pay. There would be others who would care for their needs.

If there is a relationship in your life where you feel as though you're always receiving, it's time to give to that person. Maybe they are your "rock," your "confidante," the one you always turn to . . . maybe they're a relative, a friend, a pastor, a teacher, a Bible study leader . . . they have needs. They need care. They need to know they have your support—and should not have to wait for that to be tested. Affirm them, encourage them, and find ways to demonstrate the impact they've made in your life. Take them to lunch, remember their birthday, give them a gift card that would cover a family outing, build them a bookshelf, mow their lawn, baby-sit their children, invite their entire family to dinner at your home . . . there are any number of ways to use your special talents and gifts to care for those who care for you.

One final thought on serving those who serve: They need to be served in ways that don't tax their ministerial gifts; so when you give, remember this is not about you—do not do something, then shift gears back to your current problem. Just serve, and let it be nothing but you, caring for them as they have done for you.

....

DAILY DIFFERENCE-MAKER

Identify three people who have ministered to you within the past month. Send each of them a card, thanking them and recognizing their influence in your life. Then, think of one way you can minister to each of them specifically—consider their needs, not just your gifts, in the process. It doesn't have to be over-the-top—you can spread this out over time.

.... Notes ....

WEEK
FORTY
-EIGHT

Indestructible, Infallible Treasure

Provide yourselves money bags which do not grow old,

a treasure in the heavens that does not fail,

where no thief approaches nor moth destroys.

–Luke 12:33

When we spend money, *poof!* it's gone. Eventually, it circulates itself out of circulation. We use money to buy food, which is consumed. Money to buy clothes, which we grow out of, become less stylish, or just wear out. Some of our money goes toward something that may last our lifetime—maybe a home or jewelry, for example—but it won't last forever. Nothing on this side of heaven will. Except our souls.

When we give our life to Christ, we are sealed with Him for eternity. We live for Him, and do our best to live as Him; we see the world and its contents as finite, and our focus shifts to the eternal. If you look at today's verse in context, Jesus is trying to right our perspective and attitudes about money; in fact, he instructs us to sell whatever we have until our goals include generous, cheerful giving.

Money doesn't last, but it is the means by which most of us get through this world. Do we use a generous portion of it to help others?

To invest in our churches and ministries? To feed, clothe, and shelter those who cannot make those ends meet? This is how our treasure can last forever—investing our time and resources in others, giving them relief, assistance, and maybe even opportunities they never thought they'd have. With each paycheck, get in the habit of asking yourself, and asking God: *How can I make this last forever? How can I make this matter to someone without a paycheck?* It's the possibility of changing someone's life that should make your days interesting and your life rewarding. So make it matter!

DAILY DIFFERENCE-MAKER

Before you have another yard sale or sell another item online, just donate it. Unless you need the money to pay an expense, you do not need the money and obviously no longer need the item—but someone else does. Donate it.

Notes

Fouling Up Satan's Plans

Do not fear them. . . . there is nothing covered that will not

be revealed, and hidden that will not be known.

—Matthew 10:26

There is a lot of irony in Christianity . . . the Messiah entered the world as a lowly servant, not a bejeweled king; salvation is free, yet costs us everything; and sometimes, good is called evil. In Jesus' case, He was called evil by the Pharisees because He could drive out demons and heal.

As Christ-followers, we will receive our share of criticism and scrutiny—but in this country, please don't call it persecution. We are mocked, made fun of, criticized, called evil—but we are not imprisoned nor put to death for our beliefs and behaviors. And I'm not saying that our critics can't be scary, but look at what Jesus says—we are not to fear them. They will be revealed, in time, and they cannot hide from their wrongdoing.

So what do we do in the meantime? We stay strong. We keep on keepin' on, in His name. We disregard those who will put us down for giving money to the guy with the sign; we smile when someone calls us a wimp for forgiving someone; and in fact, we will choose to love the very person who is criticizing us. And I'll admit, that last one just may be the toughest!

I am one of many, many others who adopted a child of a different race; you'd be shocked, or maybe you wouldn't, by the amount of criticism our family has received. How I've tried to exploit my son, deny his heritage, push him into this or that . . . and troops, that's just the tip of the iceberg. Some of it gets downright ugly; some of the language used makes me feel nauseated. As a family, we've learned to look past this, claiming Christ's promise that's featured in today's verse. I personally love fouling up Satan's plans, and their criticism is evidence that we're right on target!

Rest easy—your critics *will be revealed*, so you have nothing to worry about. Claim His promise, and channel your energies on what's hopeful, what's uplifting, and what's eternal.

....

DAILY DIFFERENCE-MAKER
Are you in the crosshairs of someone based on how you're giving, or why? Be polite to your critic, and steadfast in your giving—you are agitating the Enemy!

....Notes...

238

Cleaning Up

If I then, *your* Lord and Teacher, have washed your feet,

you also ought to wash one another's feet.

For I have given you an example,

that you should do as I have done to you.

—John 13:14–15

If you've ever sent a young child to school, you know something about the spreading of germs—every bug, sniffle, virus, and fever gets passed through classrooms. So today's passage kind of puts this action in reverse. Peter was mortified. His Lord, His King, His Christ performed a lowly act of washing his feet. Now, this was not a nice little pedicure that some of us enjoy periodically; this was cleaning caked mud, dust, stench, and anything else Peter had picked up during his travels with Jesus. Nothing glamorous about it. And not only was Jesus washing his feet—He was suggesting that Peter and the others wash *other people's feet*!

The example Jesus gave is multi-faceted, however; first and foremost, He was a king performing a servant's job. Secondly, He was making them clean, empowering them to go into the world and share their cleansing with others, making them clean, too.

Too often, we just want to cleanse those who are already clean; people we know very well, people who are just like us, people who will not necessarily challenge or stretch us . . . in the South, we call it "preaching to the choir." In contrast, Jesus had pulled together a somewhat rag-tag group, but they didn't stay that way. After having walked with the Twelve, lived with them, and formed authentic relationships with each one, Jesus determined it was time to wash them clean.

It's really easy to be with people who are just like us—but from an eternal perspective, what are we really changing? Somewhere in your city, there's an addict who would rather be on the streets than in a shelter . . . a young teenage mother who has never known anything but tough breaks . . . a frightened gang member who wants to get out . . . God loves the ones society has cast away, and desires their cleansing; are you willing to help?

DAILY DIFFERENCE-MAKER

Arrange a ride-along with your local police department or meet with leaders at a church located in a less-desirable neighborhood. Learn about the residents, meet a few of them, brainstorm ways you might join forces.

Notes

Tuning In

Your ears shall hear a word behind you, saying,

"This is the way, walk in it," whenever you

turn to the right hand or whenever you turn to the left.

—Isaiah 30:21

In ancient times, we had these things called radios. They were most interesting and provided entertainment and enjoyment to many! In order to listen to our favorite songs or news, we had to manually twist and turn the dial, often suffering from static interference, in order to find just the right frequency. Sometimes, the song would be heard clearly; other times, it could be a bit fuzzy. When nothing else worked, we'd stand in a particular spot, turn the dial delicately, stand on one foot—whatever it took to listen. Each person "knew" their radio and therefore, knew what was necessary to get a clear sound. The one I had required aluminum foil on the antenna—but hey, it worked!

We need to be in the same habit with God. Too often, we wait until a critical moment of decision or crisis before we attempt to tune in; not being familiar with His voice, we risk listening to anybody and thinking it's Him. This is where prejudices, fears, and distrust creep in; this is where we make idols like celebrity, politics, and technology our gods.

Let's spend some time preparing our hearts and getting familiar with God's voice. Be sure to spend quality time with him in good times and personal triumphs; don't just wait for a crisis or a crossroads to occur so that when they do come, you'll know how to cut through the static and interference.

DAILY DIFFERENCE-MAKER
Read all of Isaiah 30 in one sitting. Invite the Lord to tear down any barriers that prevent you from preparing your heart for His voice.

Notes

Open Them Wide

For the poor will never cease from the land;

therefore I command you, saying,

'You shall open your hand wide to your brother,

to your poor and your needy, in your land.'

–Deuteronomy 15:11

Well, today's verse could have been written by me, right? I certainly spend a lot of time conveying its message.

We will always have the poor . . . those who are lacking in food, clothing, shelter, and hope. Yes, some of the world's wealthiest people are very poor in spirit—they seek fulfillment by accumulating possessions, confused over the quick high/crash they experience instead.

So regardless of the type of poverty we witness, we know it will never go away—but that doesn't mean we just leave it alone and do nothing about it. We are commanded, not just to open our hands but to open them *wide*. And look at the last part of God's command: *in your land.*

I do not want to take anything away from global efforts to help the poor, but poverty is *right here*, in our backyards. We become very mission-minded when, safely in our homes, we view the videos of poverty-stricken people in faraway lands; but when is the last time you offered a cold drink to someone working in your home, or on your street? When is the last time you bought a meal for a street person? Or comforted a coworker who is struggling? Do you open your hand *wide*, or do you keep a bit of grasp on whatever you're offering, making it conditional?

"But they're in their situation because of _____!" you protest. It's not our job to point fingers at whomever or whatever may be responsible for that person's condition. Our role is to simply meet the need in response, without expectations or conditions. That—not the amount—is giving generously. Until we arrive at that point, we will never know what it means to open our hands *wide* to the poor. Remember, it is much easier to send money in an envelope to a foreign country than it is to open our front doors to those in need.

....

DAILY DIFFERENCE-MAKER

Buy a sack of groceries that include fresh vegetables, a few canned goods, bread, crackers, cookies, and some milk—buy the brands that you would buy for yourself. Drive to a government housing project and hand it off to someone willing to take it, no questions asked (unless you want to exchange names).

.... *Notes* ....

WEEK
FORTY
-NINE

The Jiggly Arms

But Moses' hands *became* heavy; so they took a stone
and put *it* under him, and he sat on it. And Aaron and Hur
supported his hands, one on one side,
and the other on the other side; and his hands
were steady until the going down of the sun.
So Joshua defeated Amalek and his people
with the edge of the sword.

—Exodus 17:12–13

f you've ever worked out with weights, you know what it's like to get the jiggly arms after a hard workout—where you think you can't even lift your water bottle? Try holding them up all day, knowing that lives are depending on it. This is the position Moses was in.

Try to envision it: Israel's army squaring off with Amalek's, and Moses who stood above it all, robe and hair flowing (I always picture it that way, maybe because of Charlton Heston . . . yeah, I love old movies!). When Moses raised his hands, the Israelites prevailed but if he lowered them, the Amalekites gained on them.

Enter Aaron and Hur. Here was their leader/brother, the one who led them from captivity, the one who received the Ten Commandments, spoke with the Lord directly and delivered His messages . . . needing a boost. Moses had the jiggly arms. Aaron and Hur stood on either side of him, holding up his arms for the remainder of the day until Israel defeated their foe. It's such a beautiful picture of how to support a leader, friend, and relative.

Those who lead or mentor us are not super-human; they are mere mortals, like the rest of us. They have a gift that they share with us, but they have problems, too. They have vulnerabilities. They are not gods, and too often, we expect them to be.

Moses knew that as long as his hands and rod were raised, Israel would be victorious; but Moses could not sustain that position without support. He was only human, after all. The parting of the Red Sea? The plagues? That wasn't Moses—that was God. No matter what the Egyptians, or even the Israelites, might have thought.

Do you recognize the humanity of your leaders enough to know when they're getting the jiggly arms? They're not weak—just weakened. They need your strength and support.

....

DAILY DIFFERENCE-MAKER
Reach out to someone who leads—a committee leader, a volunteer organizer, an instructor, anyone in a leadership role—and reassure them of your support. Ask them what you can do to help.

.... Notes ....

When Separation Is Necessary

Then the contention became so sharp

that they parted from one another.

—Acts 15:39

Where others saw Saul, Barnabas saw Paul. He took Paul under his wing, and the two men worked together in ministry; in fact, they were part of the team sent to settle the whole debate about whether one must be Jewish in order to be Christian. A short time later, the two parted ways in a huff—and both men went on to do even greater things for the kingdom.

Now here's what I find interesting; Paul and Barnabas had a disagreement, but we know that Paul did not hold a grudge. In fact, he speaks respectfully about Barnabas later, and even about John-Mark (the point of their contention). Whatever occurred was settled and forgiven; they may have agreed to disagree on some finer points, but they placed these at the foot of the Cross, a point where they both could strongly agree.

How do you handle disagreements among the various groups you participate in? Do you consider the greater good? If the point of disagreement can't be resolved—not because anyone is stubborn or selfish—it may be time to part ways. In Paul's and Barnabas's case, there was no right or wrong answer—simply a disagreement. It was time to part ways, for the greater good.

As we go about doing God's work, He intends to grow and challenge us. We can get too comfortable serving in a certain way and disregard His nudging us in a different direction. As tension builds, we might get angry; we might say things that hurt, things we don't really mean; we might attempt power-plays, sabotage, or a gossipy tear-down. What's godly about this? If there's no resolution, and no right or wrong answer—when it's truly a mere difference of opinion, it's just time to separate. No one said it's forever, no one's finding fault—God may have put different instructions in each heart and we have to trust that.

So when it's time to separate, let's not resent those involved; let's show respect for what was accomplished, and thank God for what's next.

....

DAILY DIFFERENCE-MAKER
Have you abandoned a group in a huff, thinking, "I'll show them"? Or has someone left a group in this manner, leaving you confused? It doesn't matter. Stuff happens. Today is the day you will reach out and make amends, for the greater good.

.... Notes ....

Just Because

Entreat me not to leave you, or *to* turn back
from following after you; for wherever you go, I will go;
and wherever you lodge, I will lodge;
your people *shall be* my people, and your God, my God.

—Ruth 1:16

Some comedians and television shows have made entire careers out of in-law jokes. Even if we're in pleasant in-law relationships, most of us can appreciate the humor.

Naomi was no laughing matter; in fact, she changed her name to Mara, which means "bitter," after losing her husband and sons. The woman was understandably grieve-stricken and pushed away the little family she had left—her daughters-in-law. She complained non-stop, insisting the Lord had turned against her, and she didn't have anything nice to say (clearly, Naomi was *not* from the South!). Naomi was a bit of a pill.

Ruth saw through it, though—and refused to leave her. If Ruth had done nothing else, I would consider her a saint based on that one action alone. But not only did Ruth remain with her mother-in-law, she worked to support them both. Honestly, I'm not sure I could have done this. And even though, legally speaking, Ruth had no obligation to Naomi, she did everything Naomi asked of her; Ruth could see Naomi's need when Naomi didn't see it herself.

Do we extend the same sort of care to the difficult personalities we encounter? Or, when they push us away, do we shrug and say, "okie-doke," then walk away? Sometimes, the very ones who insist they don't need our help are the ones in most need of it. They fear a loss of independence, they fear we will have expectations and conditions . . . and they fear we will abandon them.

Our broken world has become a world that is distrustful of the "just-because" kindnesses. (Believe me, I know—some people think every time I do something kind, there has to be some sort of motive or agenda. Seriously?!) Many are so jaded, so cynical, they don't understand someone simply helping or extending kindness to them because it's the right thing to do; their knee-jerk response is often, "yeah, well, what's in it for you?"

Like Ruth, be the person who sticks to their guns. Don't be swayed or turned off by a cynical attitude—be an example of unconditional love and care. Demonstrate kindness, regardless of their response. Be a presence, be trustworthy, be consistent, and be patient—gaining someone's trust does not happen overnight.

. . . .

DAILY DIFFERENCE-MAKER

Reach out to someone in your community whose heart has been hardening . . . just because. Show them how tenderness can break down even the toughest walls. Write their name on paper and in your heart—remember to pray for them.

. . . . Notes . . . .

Investigate Further

Valuable as fine gold, how they are regarded as clay pots,

the work of the hands of the potter!

—Lamentations 4:2

didn't win the Oscar. Surely you are already aware of that (I didn't even get a duplicate statue!). But you know what? Oscar or not, I still have value. Everyone has value. We are all created equal.

Sandy's Oscar did, however, give me a platform to take my message to a much broader audience—so I took God up on this offer and got busy. It didn't make me any more or less valuable, just more recognizable.

Here's the deal: It shouldn't take a fancy suit, expensive tie, nice dress, or Oscar-winning film for us to recognize value in others and therefore, treat them with respect. I don't know how many cars passed by my big, shivering guy on that cold, wet, Memphis day, but I do wonder how many 'fear alarms' went off inside people's heads and subsequently, how many doors were locked as they drove past my future son. Did they look at him with pity, fear . . . or did they even see him at all? Regardless—they didn't look hard enough.

And admittedly, my alarm went off, too—my maternal alarm. I had no idea what his deal was, I just knew something wasn't right about what I'd just seen. Sometimes, circumstances are just odd; maybe Michael hadn't seen a weather report, or didn't realize the school was closed. But sometimes, we uncover something that needs attention or needs to change, and that, in fact, was Michael's case. One thing's for certain—if we don't stop to investigate, nothing will be made clear and nothing will change. Someone out there today doesn't think they're valuable—you have probably walked or driven past them dozens of times. Are your antennas up, ready to respond to a '911 look'? What message will you send them today?

....

DAILY DIFFERENCE-MAKER

Think about some of the people who seem to linger in the margins of your day. Do you ever wonder about them? Does something seem out of place? Today is the day you will stop and investigate further. They need to know they've been noticed and accounted for; but they may have needs beyond that. It's up to you to clarify why your paths cross as often as they do. Don't worry if you can't do it all—you can connect them with the person or organization who can!

.... Notes ....

In the Know

Judge not, that you be not judged.

—Matthew 7:1

I was interviewed on a talk show once and the host, a generally benevolent person, admitted to me when he saw panhandlers, his immediate thought was that they were on drugs. Oh, don't gasp and recoil in self-righteousness—appreciate that this man made an honest admission. It's the first step to overcoming any sort of prejudice.

And the reality is, most giving people still have certain prejudices. We judge the person rolling up in a luxury SUV who uses food stamps; never mind that person may be a nanny driving her employer's vehicle, or someone buying groceries for a SNAP recipient who is a shut-in. We glare at the unkempt person stranded at the train station because they're just looking for their next fix, or to pick our pockets; we look disdainfully at the person who is trying to understand the bank teller, but doesn't speak English, thinking they're probably a terrorist. We even watch the teen wearing a hoodie, because they're probably trying to steal something or hurt someone. It's not that we know any of them personally, we just *think* we know them. We know their kind. We know what they do. Without any sort of truth attached to it—*we just know*.

Well, guess what? If this is how we roll, then we don't know diddly-squat. Prejudice is taught, and prejudice is learned. And prejudice has no basis in truth. When we make a blanket decision about someone or a group of someones having never even spoken one word to them, we are flying our prejudicial flag. Bottom line: If you have it, it's your responsibility to give it. Yes, money to the panhandler. A ticket to the person at the bus station. Patience and maybe even assistance to the person at the bank. A bottle of water or a hot meal to the teen (you could at least give your name and get his/hers).

Each time we choose *not* to do, we are opening the door to someone else's prejudices. Give without trying to control that person's actions; you are freeing yourself from judgment and working through your prejudices.

Today's verse is an oldie, but a goodie. It pretty much says it all—let's admit our prejudices so we can step out of them to make a difference. Humanity is so much stronger when it's united!

DAILY DIFFERENCE-MAKER
Buy a hot breakfast to-go; slip in a $20 bill and hand it to a panhandler today, along with a sincere smile.

Notes

WEEK
FIFTY

246

A Word on Bullying

For we do not wrestle against flesh and blood,

but against principalities, against powers,

against the rulers of the darkness of this age.

—Ephesians 6:12

Bullying is a huge problem in our country. It's a huge problem in our schools, but it's fine-tuned and polished into adulthood. Bullies pressure others in the workplace, using office politics to destroy anyone who is a perceived threat. You find them in churches and organizations, silencing anyone who comes with a concern or idea. They prey on the elderly, the young, and the vulnerable.

Here's what I also know: Bullies are cowards. They're insecure. And they're working for the Enemy. They're not hopeless cases—but they are mean.

Now that may seem laughable (particularly to any of you church bullies out there), but when you're exercising your power to diminish another person's dignity, that's exactly what you're doing. And it's cruel. What did this person do to you, and even if you have some alleged 'reason,' it doesn't give you the right. And for those of you not speaking up and rushing to that person's defense? *You're just as guilty. And so are your friends, family members, coworkers, and anyone else who chooses to do nothing.*

Who's getting picked on at school? At the office? In your church? Who's made fun of, made to feel unwelcome, or downright threatened?

And finally, *Who are you working for?*

....

DAILY DIFFERENCE-MAKER

You're probably expecting me to say find someone to defend today. I would hope you'd already be doing that, so instead I want you to ask the meanest person you know to lunch today. Yes, actually try to be friendly and find out why they are so insecure they choose to take it out on others.

.... Notes ....

Stand Up, Be Loud, Be Proud

Do not be overcome by evil, but overcome evil with good.

—Romans 12:21

Good guys, we're letting the bad guys win. It's time we stand up—and be loud and proud.

Most anyone who has met me personally, or even heard me talk will tell you I'm outspoken. And they're absolutely right—but there is a heart behind it. I want to be the voice for those who have none, I want justice served, and I champion right over wrong always.

There are too many loudmouths out there who hurt, belittle, and marginalize others; whether they are picking on someone on the school playground, denying care to a certain group of people, or killing others based on their faith or skin color, they need to be stopped. They seek division in order to feed their own interests and insecurities. While I agree they're a sad and pathetic bunch, they are also evil. And I think they're outnumbered.

I believe in my heart there are more good people out there than bad people, but I also think, fellow good-people, that we're wimping out. I'm not asking you to become the town crier, but I am saying we need to stare down injustice, evil, and wrongdoing until it whimpers. Through our words, our deeds, and our Lord, we have the power to whittle evil down to the nothing that it is.

But don't miss the point made in today's verse—if our words are just as mean and our actions just as cruel, then we're not working with or unto the Lord, either. I don't care how cliché it sounds, we are to do the right thing, always. I'm just saying we need to make a lot more noise while we're doing it.

Have you been quietly grieving some injustice or cruelty? Draw a very public line in the sand and take a stand. Take action, make some noise within earshot of people who need to join you and right this wrong. Embed the wisdom of Romans 12:21 into your heart, both as a reminder to not let your temper overtake you and to be vigilant about finding "good" ways to triumph over evil. It's time to get bold and be bold!

....

DAILY DIFFERENCE-MAKER

You will witness an act of cruelty within the next week, and it's probably one you've witnessed before—a kid picked on at school, a coworker being berated, an elderly person being belittled, or even an animal being taunted—commit yourself now to step up and say something.

.... Notes ....

248

Not-so Extreme Makeover

But we all, with unveiled face, beholding as in a mirror

the glory of the Lord, are being transformed

into the same image from glory to glory,

just as by the Spirit of the Lord.

–2 Corinthians 3:18

"Makeover"—that just sounds like a magical word! It holds the promise of transformation, creativity, freshness . . . a metamorphosis of what once was.

Some makeovers are relatively minor: *prest-o, change-o, done-zo!* Unfortunately, most are much more complex and require a great deal of time and effort. With interior design, I can tell you that makeovers include mounds of research and development; depending on the job, we might glean insight and opinions from those who are educated on the subject, and clients usually have already spoken to those who have conquered a similar challenge. More than likely, we would have a camera on-hand for before, during, and after photos. There is a definitive start and finish.

Our spiritual transformation, however, is a life-long process, marked with any number of light-bulb moments that can only come from God: Some of us give up certain habits, certain schools of thought, even certain possessions or relationships . . . and we develop new interests and deeper insights that keep our hearts pliable.

I can tell you firsthand that as I walk with the Lord, part of the joy and fun is how I continue to "morph" into a giver. And this is where I want my message to sink in, loud and clear.

As the Spirit leads us into a closer walk, perhaps we already give to our church or favorite charity, and think we're 'good' on the giving front . . . but when we're intentional about seeing where God takes our giving, new and exciting opportunities start popping up everywhere—and some of them don't cost a dime! We might start holding doors for everyone, walking the dogs at the shelter, mentoring a child . . . or we may be led to pick up an extra item of some sort when we shop . . . for no real reason, except to give it away. Others may think we're just being considerate and kind, but we're really being transformed into givers—taking make-over to a whole, new level. It's a glorious, never-ending process that changes the internal *and* the external in a positive way—guaranteed!

....

DAILY DIFFERENCE-MAKER

Start a new habit: Pick up an extra package of diapers, baby formula, or canned good each time you're at the store. Donate to a crisis pregnancy center or shelter.

.... Notes ....

249

A Word About "Giving Tuesday"

Be kindly affectionate to one another with brotherly love,

in honor giving preference to one another.

—Romans 12:10

This is one time I'm going tell you to give in to the marketing hype of Giving Tuesday, which appears in the aftermath of Black Friday and Cyber Monday.

I have found time is one of the most valuable assets I possess. You may not be able to write a big check with tons of zeros on it, but you can give of yourself. So give of your time—that's a great beginning. Keep it simple and entry-level: Give your kids a day at the zoo, the neighbor a slice of cake, or repair something for someone, share a talent you have with someone, fix dinner for the teacher, baby-sit, give someone a hand unloading groceries . . . you get the idea. Now in the spirit of Giving Tuesday, this entry-level giving will allow you not only to endure this stressful season called the holidays, but you might find yourself actually *enjoying* this time of year.

Mother Teresa said, "If you can't feed a hundred people, feed just one." In the literal sense, that leaves one less-hungry person in the world—and demonstrates a much bigger point. Many people think giving is a daunting task; but it certainly doesn't (and shouldn't!) be done in big, broad strokes—certainly, small acts of kindness can add up to big, sweeping change . . . in your life, on your street, in your community. And if each of us cultivate this new-found tradition of Giving Tuesday together, our entire nation would feel the effects. Ask others what they will be doing, or did, on this day—make it a topic of conversation. Highlight it on your calendar, set the alert on your smart phone. (Oh, and be sure to tweet me what you did, or let me know on Instagram. I'd love to hear about it!)

Now for all I know, you may be reading this in July—so why wait until Christmas? In fact, why wait until Tuesday? You may work a few Make a Difference Mondays and Thank-you Thursdays into your Giving Tuesday tradition!

....

DAILY DIFFERENCE-MAKER

Donate a book to either a public or school library, or visit LeighAnneTuohy.com to join us in improving the inventory of several school libraries.

.... Notes ....

Candor and Class

Render therefore to Caesar the things that are Caesar's,

and to God the things that are God's.

—Matthew 22:21

Our nation has the privilege of actually voting for our president. Instead of being thankful for the fact that we are free to watch two candidates debate on our television, learn about their positions on issues that are important to us, and decide for ourselves who is the best fit to lead our nation, we complain about the number of ads on television and if the candidate we wanted to win did not. Then we spend the next four years ripping this person to shreds, posting half-truths and disrespecting them at any and every turn.

I bet people in China and North Korea sure would enjoy their voices being heard, or having the freedom to criticize their leadership. But I really want to zero in on the disrespect. If you have no more interest beyond finding any half-truth article or reading tacky posts on social media and not checking its sources because it tears down the guy you didn't want, then you may be worshipping your politics and not God. If you think it's funny to post photos of a dog defecating on a former or current president, or it's funny to hear your young children repeat whatever disrespectful thing you've said about the president, you're not "on God's side," regardless. There's nothing godly about this sort of behavior.

And if someone is kind enough to point this out to you, particularly if you're posting an article that isn't true, what is your response? Anger? Accusations? Or do you take responsibility for your actions and post that the article was in error? Regardless of whether you voted him in, our President is our commander-in-chief; we need to respect him and the Office itself.

Freedom isn't free and ours has been hard-fought. Let's not pollute ours with irresponsibility and tackiness. We can exercise our political differences with candor *and* class, honoring the Leader who is King of all kings and Lord over all lords.

....

DAILY DIFFERENCE-MAKER

Pray for our president today. Pray for his leadership, his family, his safety, and for his advisers. Remember, God placed that person in office at this appointed time (Romans 13:1).

.... Notes ....

WEEK
FIFTY
-ONE

251

To the Lukewarm Giver

Be troubled, you complacent ones.

—Isaiah 32:11

Maybe you're a nice enough person, but not one to pursue much more beyond being nice. So let me be frank: Nice ain't cutting it. Too many of us do nothing to change our world because we think we don't have the money or other resources to accomplish anything worthwhile. Permit me to question that for a moment:

- **Do you own a computer, even an old clunker?** It is estimated that less than one percent of the world's population owns a computer†.
- **You're obviously alive today,** but about 151,600 people die every day, which equates to about two people per second†; today is a gift.
- **How many times do you open the fridge and mumble about seeing nothing in there that you want?** An estimated 805 million people in the world do not have enough food (that's one in nine people who are hungry). Hunger kills more people each year than AIDS, tuberculosis, and malaria combined*.

- **Now, let's take that one step further**—how many people are not afforded the luxury of even owning a refrigerator?

I know this message is very cliché, but we truly do have so much that we are blessed with, particularly in this country. We are so focused on the things we don't have that we fail to see, and therefore make use, of what we do have. When we squander or selfishly cling to our resources, we are missing the point of why we've been blessed with them in the first place.

Theodore Roosevelt said, "In any moment of decision, the best thing you can do is the right thing, the next best thing is the wrong thing, and the worst thing you can do is nothing." Today is a day for action—you have the ability to change something today in His name. If it's a misstep, He will surely right your path (Isaiah 30:21).

DAILY DIFFERENCE-MAKER
Take advantage of any stores that offer a 'round-up for the hungry' that rounds your bill up to the next whole dollar and donates the difference, or pick up an extra item or two at the grocery to give away.

Notes

*Source: World Food Programme
†Source: Ecology Global Network, http://www.ecology.com/birth-death-rates/

Game Day Style

Let another man praise you, and not your own mouth;

a stranger, and not your own lips.

—Proverbs 27:2

Collins and I were once featured as part of a "game-day style" sort of piece, where we were asked about tailgating and game-day fashions. Whereas, tailgating is an option at any SEC school, it is an absolute must in "The Grove"; from linens to food to fashion, Ole Miss fans make sure it's done correctly and with style. We don't flaunt, we don't compete—we are just the leaders of the pack when it comes to tailgating. We teach our children the traditions and train them to respect, love, and be gracious to everyone in The Grove. It's worked that way for generations, and it's something worth experiencing at least once. (You are always welcome at the Tuohy tent!)

So when it's time for game-on giving, what is your game-day style? Do you do the bare minimum and move on? Are you posturing for others to see? Do you give so you can tell everyone you're doing so? Are you trying to compete with someone else? Or do you give it your best, add a few extra touches and details, stay focused on the cause, and find the most fulfilling reward is in helping others?

Do you stay flexible, realizing that your giving style doesn't have to be the same each time?

So many want their pictures in the paper, their name in lights, bragging rights, or to attend lavish parties, particularly the higher-profile fundraisers—but they couldn't care less about the causes. And sadly, many participate in these hoity-toity gala fundraisers just to be seen and hear their name publicly announced when they win a live auction item; I sure hope these organizations got their money upfront, because many 'winners' never pay up. They are exploiting those in need for their personal ego trip. We all enjoy the occasional pat on the back—I get that. I'm guilty. But if that's why we're giving, or if we want to do the bare minimum just to cross it off our to-do list, we're not giving from the heart. And people, that's just not acceptable.

Don't seek praise. That way, when it comes, you'll know it is coming from someone's heart. Keep your game-day giving style simple and humble, letting the gift shine for itself.

....

DAILY DIFFERENCE-MAKER

If you receive a fundraiser invitation, go ahead and purchase a ticket—and give your ticket to someone who has never attended the event or could not afford the ticket. Let them borrow a dress, suit, and throw in a manicure!

.... Notes ....

Fiercely, Fervently, Fearlessly . . . and Fully

He said to them, "*All too* well you reject the
commandment of God, that you may keep your tradition."

—Mark 7:9

As a Southerner, I can vouch for loving certain traditions, like sweet tea, fried chicken, best china, good manners always, and best manners on Sunday. As a Christian, however, I worship a Savior who granted me freedom to color outside the lines. People, we need to take Him up on it or we miss a very big part of Who He is.

If you study His earthly ministry, Jesus pursued others . . . sometimes, very specific unsightly, unholy others: Prostitutes, cheats, adulterers, non-Jews, working-class, poor, lepers, mentally and physically ill, revelers . . . and yes, even the very rich. Even the ones who would betray or reject Him. And He often met physical needs before He addressed the spiritual; healing the blind, the lepers, the deaf . . . giving them sight, cleanliness, and hearing that went beyond the physical and into the very soul. Some of them took Him up on this cleansing and healing of their souls—others, not so much.

Listen, we can't sit in our Sunday pews and "reject the commandment of God" to love by demanding others come to us. We need to pursue the ones the world has deemed dirty, unsightly, or unworthy, rejecting the premise that we don't want to be seen with 'those types.' Without Christ, we are 'those types.' If Jesus is our Source of joy, how we are received by 'those types' and perceived by onlookers should not matter.

Enter the relationship authentically, trusting the Holy Spirit will guide the rest. You may be planting a seed or harvesting the crop— but nothing can be done outside of His power. And nothing will be done if we're not willing to break a few rules, get outside our comfort zones, and color outside the lines. Fear comes from the Enemy; *God is Love*. Put on the armor of God to love fiercely, fervently, fearlessly . . . and fully. (Ephesians 6:11)!

DAILY DIFFERENCE-MAKER

Who in your school, your workplace, or even on the street, is shunned? Maybe they were "caught" in a scandal, or have a wild reputation. Maybe they do not practice good hygiene or wear ill-fitting clothes . . . maybe their home life (assuming they have a home) is very different from yours or they practice a different faith that's in the minority for your community. Befriend that person, just as Jesus would.

Notes

254

Hit the Reset Button

Let us run with endurance the race that is set before us,

looking unto Jesus, the author and finisher of *our* faith.

—Hebrews 12:1–2

What's the last risk you took? Was it some sort of feat, like zip-lining or skydiving? Was it facing a fear, like a new relationship or cause?

Where are you with that risk now? Are you still working through it? Are you comfortable with your decision, having settled into it? Or do you laugh and now wonder why that was such a big deal? When we get to a place of comfort, it may be time to hit the reset button.

"You've got to be kidding me, Leigh Anne!" you're probably saying. "Do you know how long it took me to arrive here? What I had to overcome?"

Maybe I haven't experienced the same risk—but I can understand where you're coming from. I took a risk having all three of my children, not just Michael. In fact, part of the reason there's such an age difference between Collins and S.J. was due to fear—I'd gone through a lot, particularly during labor, with Collins. And yes, adopting Michael was another risk; different circumstances, but a risk nonetheless. At some point, however, it was no longer risky; my children are now adults, productive citizens, and no longer need me in the same manner. As a family, we are comfortable and don't worry about the kids as we did when they were younger. But by no means does that mean my work is done—only that particular chapter is done. So, I hit the reset button—and found other risks, other needs, other ways to invest.

If you're at a place where you took a risk and now, it's no longer risky—no doubt you've grown. But don't rest too long—there's still work to be done. Hit the reset button, and move forward.

You remember how, don't you? Maybe start in small, baby steps; be consistent, be diligent, because doing small things well can also be a game-changer for someone. In fact, you build momentum that way. What risk will you take today?

....

DAILY DIFFERENCE-MAKER
Talk to strangers. See how many you can engage in actual conversation; for starters, tell them your name and ask them for theirs.

.... Notes ....

Have Ministered . . . Do Minister

For God *is* not unjust to forget your work and labor of love
which you have shown toward His name, *in that* you
have ministered to the saints, and do minister.

–Hebrews 6:10

I love this quote: "To make a difference in someone's life you don't have to be brilliant, rich, beautiful or perfect. You just have to care." There is absolutely something each one of us can do to make a difference, whether we change that person's life for an hour, a day, or a lifetime.

Don't miss some of what's key here in today's verse—that we "have ministered . . . and do minister." Whatever we do in His name, whatever our "labor of love" involves, we are to keep doing it. With diligence, persistence, and a lot of patience, even the seemingly small acts of kindness can manifest into something much, much larger. You may smile and greet someone each day—someone who had been wondering if anyone ever noticed them. Or you may have 'paid it forward' in a fast-food or coffee drive-through, encouraging the recipient to do the same. Perhaps you helped someone struggling with groceries, unaware that the person you were helping was recovering from shoulder surgery. Maybe you purchased a basketball for a needy child, who will escape the lure of gangs and focus instead on perfecting his game. Maybe you drive a van of kids to an after-school program that keeps them off the streets.

They just added parking meters to the parking spaces around the square in Oxford. I recently was putting change in my meter and realized the next meter had expired so I dropped a few coins in it. That was easy and took 10 seconds, but those 10 seconds were right when the meter maid approached. A small act of kindness . . . it makes a difference.

While I will always encourage people to expand their giving opportunities, don't underestimate the multitude of seemingly small actions that bridge, connect, and support; they're very important to the person on the receiving end, and they are counting on these small kindnesses. This is an essential part of the "have ministered . . . do minister" Paul is talking about. When small acts of kindness are done consistently, persistently, and diligently, we are making a difference!

....

DAILY DIFFERENCE-MAKER
Is there a neighborhood in your town where children walk to school, or wait for the school bus? Appoint yourself the 'weather-change' person: Hand out small pocket warmers and gloves when it's cold; hand out inexpensive umbrellas when it's raining; bottles of water when it's hot; etc. You don't have to do this every day—just when the weather shifts and kids aren't prepared for it. In fact, they will look forward to rainy, snowy, or steamy days because they know you'll be there. (And do something celebratory on the first and last days of school!)

.... Notes ....

WEEK
FIFTY
-TWO

Adopt a Senior

He said to His mother, "Woman, behold your son!"

Then He said to the disciple, "Behold your mother!"

And from that hour that disciple took her to his own *home.*

–John 19:26–27

Do you know of an older person whose family lives far away, or has already passed? Maybe they never married or had any children. Maybe their children are too caught up in other things to visit or care for them properly. I spend a lot of time speaking about adoption, particularly adopting older children—but we may have occasion to "adopt" an older adult. (Our family has adopted Ms. Sue; well, not really, but in my mind, she's ours!)

Jesus was dying on the cross, yet He had concerns about his mother's care. We know that Jesus' ministry often caused some uncomfortable and somewhat embarrassing moments for Mary (see John 7, Mark 3), but clearly Jesus didn't neglect His mother—and sought to ensure her care even after His death. What's interesting is that He entrusted her care with (most believe) John. Not Jude, nor James, nor any of his biological siblings—Mary was to be cared for by one of Jesus' disciples. Jesus' directive is clear—families are not defined by DNA, and we need to show tenderness to those who do not share ours!!

Whether they are blood relatives or not, our elderly need us to check on them, visit with them, and maybe help them from time to time. By the same token, we need to learn from their wisdom and experience. One of the most heartbreaking ways a person dies is from neglect and feeling as though they are more burdensome than useful—ladies and gentlemen, that is one-hundred percent preventable. Many seniors fear their loss of independence, and some of them enter facilities when they don't need full-time care; in fact, they just need an occasional meal cooked, a ride to appointments or the grocery, or to have someone mow their lawn. Like the rest of us, they need a warm smile and a little attention.

All it takes is your time—adopt a senior and let them know they matter.

....

DAILY DIFFERENCE-MAKER

Reach out to a senior today—bring them an extra dessert you've baked; ask them to walk their dog while you walk yours; see if they'd be interested in attending a football game, or having coffee and conversation. Whatever your interest or theirs, find a connecting point.

.... Notes ....

257

keep Your Word

And as for the matter which you and I have spoken of,

indeed the LORD *be* between you and me forever.

–1 Samuel 20:23

Jonathan took quite a risk for his best friend, David. He knew that David would someday be king, and knew that his father Saul, who was the current king, was troubled by David.

Yes, he was in a quandary, even with just two of the Ten Commandments: how would he honor his father, and how could he spare David's life? To add to this, by sparing David, Jonathan would give up his right to the throne—that's quite a sacrifice.

If you read the passage, Jonathan never actually disrespects Saul—he merely asks him what David did wrong. And if you read 2 Samuel 9, you'll read how David continued to honor his covenant with Jonathan, even though Jonathan, at that point, was dead.

When most of us read the story of David and Jonathan, it's easy to see the right choice because it's spelled out for us; but try living in Jonathan's shoes for a moment. He is giving up a kingdom. He is, on the surface, betraying his father. He is making a covenant with the very man his father considers his enemy. When reading the story of Jonathan and David it's also significant to understand the difference between covenant and promise; generally speaking, a promise can be one-sided while a covenant requires both parties' active participation. David kept his covenant with Jonathan for the rest of his life—not Jonathan's.

Listen, life is some messy business at times; it's not always fair and certainly not always fun. We want to do right by everyone, but sometimes, the right choice won't be popular and certainly won't make everyone happy. When we are certain of the right thing, we need to keep our word to right the wrong—respectfully. No matter if it topples a kingdom, institution, law, or relationship, keep your word to make things right. People who keep their word are people of character; like David, they understand there is no "statute of limitations" on keeping a confidence, a promise, or a vow. These are the friends we want, and these are the friends we need to be. How will you accomplish this today?

DAILY DIFFERENCE-MAKER

This is simple—you have been promising to have lunch or dinner with someone and have yet to follow through. Today's the day you do so—get it scheduled, keep your promise.

Notes

What Is Acceptable?

And certain women . . .

helped support Jesus and the apostles.

—Luke 8:2–3

I f I've said it once, I've said it a thousand times—I was raised in the South where there are so many unwritten rules, someone needs to write them down . . . so I can then point to them and tell you to break them (or at least, encourage you to bend them to the point they scream for mercy).

I'm not talking about good manners, being respectful, and wearing pearls on Sunday—I'm talking about these little rules we either make for ourselves or pass down to others about what is socially acceptable. Well, doesn't today's verse blow all of that out of the water?

Gender roles, in particular, tend to fall into this category. One reason I think women responded to Jesus is because He treated them as fellow human beings, not property. And it states right here that they helped support His ministry—no doubt financially, but also by showing them hospitality. Women supporting these men—sharing meals with them, giving them money . . . and these men *received their help gladly and with gratitude* . . . this flies in the face of many cultural rules!

Do you avoid certain areas of town because it's not "fitting" to enter? Do you avoid certain relationships, especially those who need your help, because it might look "inappropriate"? Yet you claim to follow a Savior who defied man-made rules because they were . . . well, man-made, not God-made (Matthew 12, Mark 7).

Sometimes, we are the biggest hurdle to making a difference; our insecurities and fear of what others might think hinder us from helping another human being. If this is where you are today, look to the Lord's example. Break down the rules and protocols that are building walls around you; they're not as safe as you think. Truly follow the One who challenged man-made rules about class, race, and salvation to accomplish a much higher goal. Seek what is acceptable to *Him*—not some other human being who is no better than you.

DAILY DIFFERENCE-MAKER

Who is considered unacceptable in your community? Someone with a past? Someone of a different race? Someone of a different faith? Someone of a different socio-economic status? Someone of a different lifestyle? Well, guess what? They're not unacceptable to God, so it's time to break down whatever barriers have stopped you so that you can reach out to them.

Notes

Using Our Social Status

When Joseph had taken the body,
he wrapped it in a clean linen cloth,
and laid it in his new tomb
which he had hewn out of the rock.

—Matthew 27:59–60

Joseph of Arimathea was a wealthy man; he was a member of the Sanhedrin, so he would have been a contemporary of Nicodemus and Paul (who was still Saul at the time of Jesus' death). He is only mentioned in the gospel accounts of Jesus' burial, but his role is significant.

For starters, Joseph had achieved financial and societal status. Some of the gospel accounts state that Joseph was a disciple "in secret," while others state that Joseph disagreed with the Jews. But thanks to his status, he could request and receive the body of their supposed enemy, a criminal who was guilty of no crime. Jesus died a criminal's death and more than likely, would have been buried in a nearby criminal graveyard (according to some sources, less than six hundred yards away from the site of His crucifixion).

Joseph, among others, saw to it that his Lord received a proper burial instead—his contribution included claiming the body, providing a new tomb, and wrapping Him in fresh linens. Where the world saw a pauper and crazy man, Joseph of Arimathea saw his Messiah.

It would have been so, so easy for Joseph to forego his role; surely Pilate wondered what Joseph would do with the corpse. Maybe he figured, given Joseph's status, that he might subject it to even more abuse—but he probably didn't count on Joseph giving Jesus a dignified burial.

Do we appreciate those who are decidedly different than us? Those who are shunned and mocked by our peers and contemporaries? Or do we decide they have value and can teach us something? If you are a person of prominence in your community, do you walk humbly in your status to give a voice to those who have none? Let Joseph of Arimathea symbolize the sort of giver we want to be; let's use whatever status we have to serve others.

....

DAILY DIFFERENCE-MAKER

Research how the homeless (or elderly without family) are buried in your community. Consider that each person was someone's daughter or son; how can you remember one of them? With a marker? With flowers? By contributing to the expenses? Moving forward, how will you help a homeless person who is still alive?

.... Notes ....

Love the Stranger

He administers justice for the fatherless and the widow,

and loves the stranger, giving him food and clothing.

Therefore love the stranger.

–Deuteronomy 10:18–19

I am no master storyteller; really, I'm not. I do know from personal experience, however, that there are some books, newspaper articles, blogs, e-mails, etc., that can really change a person. Now I'm not sure what you expected when you purchased this book; I really believe expectations should encourage us to be the best we can be, but I also realize that expectations should be fair and reasonable. My prayer is that as you read each page, you took away something that will inspire and motivate you to make a difference—not just in your own life, but also in the life of another individual. Perhaps something you found within these pages inspired you to find other creative ways to make a difference. Whatever you gleaned—I really like that word—my hope is that you are prompted to action—and that you become a difference-maker.

While there's a lot of conflicting information about just how far Jesus traveled during his three-year ministry, one thing we do know:

He addressed the immediate community, regardless of His location. He loved the stranger—and sometimes, He *was* the stranger. But He met needs on-the-spot, and lives were forever transformed . . . two thousand years later, we're still talking about it. Let's pray for Christ-like eyes that see need, a heart that loves, and a resolve to never lose faith in anyone.

While I do not want to take away the beauty and value of serving others halfway across the country or halfway across the world, I do think we can also help those in our immediate communities. If each one of us made this sort of effort, we *would* usher global change. The sort of difference that would impact many generations long after we're gone. I'm not saying you have to become the Welcome Wagon, but we all need to get in the game. If we could learn to spread love and encouragement quicker than we spread hate and negativity, what an amazing world we'd live in. I challenge you: Turn around. What are you waiting for?

....

DAILY DIFFERENCE-MAKER
Drive somewhere within ten miles of your front door, in any direction—preferably, a direction you've never driven before. Stop your car and introduce yourself to a stranger; find out if they live in the area, explain that you were curious. Remember, in order to love a stranger the way the Bible instructs, we've got to talk to them first.

.... Notes ....